The Half-Way Covenant

The Half-Way Covenant

CHURCH MEMBERSHIP IN PURITAN NEW ENGLAND

by Robert G. Pope

Wipf and Stock Publishers
150 West Broadway • Eugene OR 97401

Wipf and Stock Publishers
150 West Broadway
Eugene, Oregon 97401

The Half-Way Covenant
Church Membership in Puritan New England
By Pope, Robert G.

ISBN: 1-57910-955-1
Publication date: May, 2002
Previously published by Princeton University Press, 1969.

FOR

Norman Holmes Pearson

PREFACE

IT IS no longer necessary to rescue the Puritans from the depths to which they were once consigned or to apologize for studying the society they created. Two generations of scholars have resurrected and cleansed them. If they have not been restored to the pristine state in which Cotton Mather saw them, they are now human and comprehensible in their own terms. To all those who labored before me—and in particular to the late Perry Miller, whose vast erudition in the labyrinth he called the New England Mind is a constant source of wonder and humility—my debt is immeasurable. Again and again he anticipated the scholarship of his successors; the more we learn, the more we discover how much he already knew. If we occasionally revise, it is only a further acknowledgment of our debt to him.

As this study has grown from seminar paper to dissertation to monograph, I have received so much help from so many people that the end result is as much theirs as it is mine. The Graduate Research Council of the University of Massachusetts and the Faculty of Social Science and Administration at the State University of New York at Buffalo both provided financial support for this volume. The staffs of the Essex Institute, the Massachusetts Historical Society, the Massachusetts State Archives, and the Connecticut State Library were courteous and generous in making materials available to me. The resources of the Yale

University Library and the help of its staff were invaluable in every stage of research.

David Hall of Yale University, George Williams of Harvard Divinity School, and David Flaherty of the University of Virginia kindly read the manuscript, and I have profited from their advice. To Robert Doherty of the University of Pittsburgh and C. C. Goen of Wesley Theological Seminary I am especially indebted for giving me new insights and understanding drawn from their own scholarship. This study was begun and nurtured under Edmund S. Morgan and Sidney E. Ahlstrom, who never failed to listen and to challenge; to them I owe a special debt. For my wife Dorothy, who typed incessantly, listened untiringly, and kept the faith when others doubted, I am tempted to repeat the dedication of another scholar: she was the "power behind the drone."

ROBERT G. POPE
Buffalo, New York
September 20, 1968

CONTENTS

List of Graphs and Tables

GRAPHS

LIST OF GRAPHS AND TABLES

TABLES

The Half-Way Covenant

INTRODUCTION

New England's Crisis

This is my covenant, which ye shall keep,
between me and you and thy seed after thee;
Every man child among you shall be circumcised.
[Genesis 17:10]

THUS GOD sealed the covenant with Abraham. But in the New Testament Christ recast the injunction to the Jewish nation and took away Abraham's easy formula for identifying the covenant seed. Three millennia after God appeared to Abraham the New England Puritans wrestled anew with the question, "Who are the seed in whom the covenant should be sealed?" On their answer hung the "New England Way."

The Puritans never anticipated the dilemma which baptism would pose for them in the middle of the seventeenth century. They came to Massachusetts confident that their congregational polity answered all the basic questions and preserved the essential characteristics of truly reformed churches: congregational autonomy, limited membership, and religious uniformity. Although the Puritans refused to separate from the Anglican Church, because schism from a true church violated the principle of uniformity and dishonored God, they discarded the hierarchical structure of Anglicanism and erected in its place independent churches free from the compulsion of bishops or synods. The power of the churches was vested in the congregation. Unlike comprehensive Anglican parishes, congregational churches restricted church membership to those who gave reasonable evidence that they were among the "elect." Only these visible saints qualified for the sacraments and were subject to church discipline. Although after 1646 Massachusetts Puritans required all inhabitants, saints and sinners alike, to attend church, visible saints alone could participate fully.

Before coming to New England few Puritans had had the opportunity to erect congregational churches, and therefore few had faced the problem of determining who was a visible saint, fit for church membership, and who was not. Only the Separatists, those Congregationalists who openly separated from the Church of England, had had experience in founding and running congregational churches. Of potential members the Separatists demanded three things: renunciation of the Church of England, acceptance of true (Reformed) Christianity, and a moral life. Except for the renunciation of Anglicanism, the first churches, established after the "Great Migration" of Puritans to New England began in 1630, followed the Separatist example. But before many years had passed the Puritan zeal for a pure church brought a tightening of the requirements and the imposition of new burdens. Good behavior and acceptance of Calvinist Christianity no longer sufficed. By 1640 most of the churches expected candidates for membership to relate the process of their conversion to the assembled congregation.

The "morphology of conversion," initially developed by English Puritan divines as a guide for individual souls, was transformed into a yardstick for measuring the faithful.[1] Saving faith, as distinguished from historical faith—an intellectual assent to the doctrines of Christianity—and from a simple belief in Christ, was the achievement of man. No matter how well intentioned or how respectable, those who desired entry into the churches of New England had to wait for the Lord's quickening of the spirit. The new test put beyond the grasp of many what had once been within the reach of most men of good will. Thus New England Puritans excluded not only the notorious sinners who had plagued English parishes, but also many civil, professed Christians. The Puritans readily admitted that testified regenerate membership was not an infallible test: dissemblers and hypocrites could and did breach the portals of the church, despite the probing questions of elders and members; and perhaps even some of the elect were left outside. But within human limits Congregationalists had done their best to separate the wheat from

[1] The introduction of testified regenerate membership by the Nonseparating Congregationalists of New England and the problems this new test created for Congregational polity and doctrine have been convincingly argued by Edmund S. Morgan in *Visible Saints: The History of a Puritan Idea*, New York, 1963, particularly pp. 36-47, 77-93. My debt to Morgan's scholarship is immense and throughout this volume I have relied heavily on his work; without *Visible Saints* this volume would have been impossible.

the chaff and narrow the gap between the visible and the invisible church.

New England Puritans, however, failed to adjust their baptismal practices to the new test. Still, only communicants and their children qualified for baptism, and this became the source of Congregationalism's quandary; for the continuing life of the church was predicated on hereditary growth of faith. The children, as heirs to the covenant through the membership of their parents, would be baptized, learn their catechism, observe the faith of their fathers, benefit from church discipline and the preaching of the word, and ultimately qualify for communion. But the regenerative experience now required placed a new barrier between the baptized children and the realization of full church membership. If these children were members in their infancy, albeit incomplete, what happened to their church status if conversion failed to materialize? Were they still members? If not, when had their membership ceased? More important, what was the status of their own children: could the next generation receive baptism even though its parents were not communicants; did apparently unregenerate parents terminate the covenant relation?

In the years immediately following the introduction of the new test most churches restricted baptism to those children who had at least one parent in full communion. In other words, they continued a practice which antedated testified regenerate membership. But the problems that this practice raised, both theological and practical, forced a reassessment. In 1662, after fifteen years of debate among the clergy, the Massachusetts General Court called a synod to resolve the question, "Who are the subjects of baptism?" Eighty lay and clerical messengers, representing virtually every church in the colony, answered unequivocally: "Members of the Visible Church . . . Confederate visible Believers, in particular Churches, and their infant-seed."

But the synod's decision met strong resistance; a small outspoken segment of the clergy labelled it apostasy and unwarranted innovation. The heart of the controversy lay in the synod's fifth proposition which called for the enlargement of baptism:

> Church-members who were admitted in minority, understanding the Doctrine of Faith, and publickly professing their assent thereto; not scandalous in life and solemnly owning the Covenant before the Church, wherein they give up themselves and their children to the Lord, and subject themselves to the Government of Christ in the Church, their children are to be Baptised.

Churches adopting the synod's recommendation created a class of half-way members, persons capable of transmitting baptism, recognized as members and subject to church discipline, but barred from the Lord's Supper and from voting in church affairs. To qualify for this partial membership an individual was not required to give evidence that he had attained saving grace; he had only to renew or "own" the baptismal covenant made for him by his parents. Owning the covenant enabled parents as yet unqualified for communion to present for baptism children who would formerly have been excluded. Eighteenth-century critics derisively labelled the synod's innovation the "half-way covenant," a term which has retained its currency to the present.[2]

The Half-Way Synod of 1662 answered the questions which had vexed the churches. The membership of the children of the church did not cease in maturity even if they failed to experience saving grace, and these children of the church could have their offspring baptized provided they personally owned the covenant. This adjustment of polity by the synod provoked controversy because many New England Puritans held tenaciously to the idea of a pure church in which all adult members had given evidence of saving grace.

The half-way covenant occupies a central place in the transformation of New England from the isolated, sectarian community of John Winthrop to the prosperous, more "secular" society of Cotton Mather's later years. The crisis the half-way covenant created occupied the attention of ministers and laymen for a decade and a half and forced them to redefine the covenant relation. When external pressures threatened New England after 1675, the half-way covenant offered the congregational churches a way to signifi-

[2] The term "half-way covenant" probably originated in the 1760's when the followers of Jonathan Edwards renewed the debate over the extension of baptism to the children of non-regenerate parents. I have found the term used for the first time in Joseph Bellamy's *The Half-Way Covenant: A Dialogue*, New Haven, 1769. The term never appeared in the controversy which followed the so-called Half-Way Synod.

cantly alter their traditional role within the society and to respond to new demands.

For generations historians of seventeenth-century New England have recognized the centrality of the innovation, but they have perpetuated misconceptions that have little basis in fact. They have accepted at face value contemporary judgments of New England's religious condition. Swayed by rhetoric, historians have lost track of reality. The Puritans themselves, perplexed by the changing world around them, started the myth of declension. In countless jeremiads, ministers bemoaned the irreligion, apostasy, and worldliness of the rising generation. The Reforming Synod of 1679 and the covenants of reformation adopted by a score of churches add credence to the myth. Once the historian has absorbed the contemporary literature, he can find obvious examples of institutional change which reinforce the impression of decline. The half-way covenant, the mass covenant renewals, and the admission of "strangers" into the covenant become signs of a weakened religious life. Thus the half-way covenant is normally interpreted as an attempt to make church membership more easily attainable to a generation that had lost personal piety.

The misconceptions about New England Puritanism have resulted primarily from the attempt to extrapolate church and social history from intellectual sources. The history of the New England mind is not the history of New England; the latter must rest on more concrete local and institutional data. The confusion that surrounds the half-way covenant is apparent. One historian sees it as symptomatic of the loss of religiosity: "any commentary on the half-way covenant should place it in the context of this decline and institutionalization."[3] Another argues: "the very fact that the half-way covenant was needed may be testimony, not to the decline of religion, but to the rise of an extraordinary religious scrupulosity. . . ."[4] Although full measure has been taken of the theological ramifications,[5] no one has adequately assessed the impact of the half-way covenant on the churches of New England. The result has been the perpetuation of misconceptions and the failure to recognize the relationship between social realities and church polity.

The fundamental question about the half-way covenant has too long remained unanswered: how did the churches of New England respond to this innovation? This book attempts to answer that question and others raised by it in several different ways. The major part of this study is a descriptive survey of the ways in which the churches confronted and solved the problems of baptism and church membership in the second half of the seventeenth century. An attempt has been

[3] Darrett Rutman, "God's Bridge Falling Down," *William and Mary Quarterly*, *19*, 1962, p. 421.

[4] Edmund Morgan, "New England Puritanism: Another Approach," *William and Mary Quarterly*, *18*, 1961, p. 241.

[5] Perry Miller, "The Half-Way Covenant," *New England Quarterly*, *6*, 1933, pp. 676-715; also Miller's *The New England Mind: From Colony to Province*, Boston, 1953, chaps. 4-7; Morgan, *Visible Saints*, chaps. 3-4; Norman Pettit, *The Heart Prepared: Grace and Conversion in Puritan Spiritual Life*, New Haven, 1966, chap. 6. Pettit has carefully distinguished the differing attitudes of the Puritan clergy regarding the efficacy of baptism and suggested the relationship of this to the half-way covenant.

made here to discover and interpret the practices of all the churches for which data still exist either in church records or in parish and town histories. Only by studying the churches in their breadth can one demonstrate the range of solutions, both in time and form, that the churches devised. The churches of Connecticut are treated separately because the problems they faced were distinct from those of the other colonies and led to different solutions.

In addition to the comprehensive survey, four churches were selected for extensive internal analysis of their membership. In this section the relationship of individuals to their churches was followed over several decades in an effort to understand the effects of changes in polity over extended periods of time. It is not suggested that these churches were representative of Massachusetts churches; they were chosen because of the depth of material available for each. The statistical data that these computations produced are summarized in the tables and graphs which appear in the appendix.

Because this is primarily the study of an institution operating within its social context, the focus is on the individual churches. The diversity created by local circumstances and congregational autonomy, which is apparent in this book, reinforces the emphasis on the particular. Generalizations have been made only after the reader has seen the spectrum of response. But New England churches also functioned within the larger society and interacted with it, and after 1675 the rapidly changing patterns of New England had a measurable impact on the churches. In the later chapters an attempt has been made to interpret the new standards of church membership that emerged in the last quarter of the century in response to pressing external realities. The picture which emerges from this study sharply contrasts with the traditional portrait of religious life in New England and suggests that historians need to reread the literature of Puritanism in a new light.

ONE

Hesitant Answers: 1646-1661

NEW ENGLAND started moving toward the half-way covenant the moment the churches introduced regenerate membership. If parents, though themselves baptized, could not give satisfactory evidence of saving faith, their children faced exclusion from baptism and loss of the nurturing influence of "Christ's nursery." Had access to the sacraments been easier, had knowledge of the faith and a moral life remained the bases for church membership, baptism would never have troubled New England. But the churches rapidly accepted the test of conversion, and by 1640 this had become an integral part of the New England Way.[1] How severely it restricted admissions to full communion, and as a secondary effect limited the number of children subject to baptism, depended in large measure on the minister. He could, like Thomas Hooker, recognize grace when it was still a mere bud, or like John Davenport, demand that it appear in full flower.[2] The number of communicants in any parish tended to be inversely proportional to the minister's rigor in measuring saving faith.

With few reservations orthodox Congregationalist

[1] Morgan, *Visible Saints*, p. 93.

[2] Pettit, *The Heart Prepared*, pp. 87, 105, 123, 168-170.

ministers accepted the principle of regenerate membership as a significant advance in church reformation and found clear precedents in the New Testament. But even at the outset several ministers realized the profound effects this policy might have on the life of the churches and the meaning of the covenant. They feared that church membership would shrink markedly in relation to the total population and that excluding the children of so many godly, but not visibly regenerate, persons from the churches would betray their "errand into the wilderness."[3] These ministers advocated, not the elimination of regenerate membership, but new ways to extend church discipline. In 1645 Richard Mather proposed the baptism of the children of all church members, even the children of those who had not yet reached the stage of experiential religion which would qualify them for the Lord's Supper.[4] Peter Bulkeley of Concord and George Phillips of Watertown shared his view. Both conceived of the covenant as continuing unto a thousand generations; cutting it off at the third was unthinkable.[5] The revisionist ministers, if we may so designate them, thought they had found an escape from Congregationalism's dilemma. As the effects of

[3] Perry Miller, *Errand Into the Wilderness*, Cambridge, 1956, pp. 1-15.

[4] *A Plea for the Churches of Christ in New England*, quoted in Increase Mather, *First Principles of New England*, Cambridge, 1675, p. 10.

[5] Peter Bulkeley, *The Gospel-Covenant*, London, 1646; and George Phillips, *A Reply to a Confutation*, London, 1645; quoted in Jonathan Mitchel, "Preface," *Propositions Concerning Baptism*, Cambridge, 1662; reprinted in Williston Walker, *Creeds and Platforms of Congregationalism*, Boston, 1960, p. 307.

regenerate membership became more obvious, other ministers joined with them and increased the pressure to broaden the scope of baptism.

But many ministers found it impossible to justify an enlargement of baptism. For some the decision was made with obvious reluctance. Thomas Hooker confessed, "if I should have given way to my affection . . . the scale might have been cast upon the affirmative. . . . But after all the stones I have turned . . . there be some reasons which yet arrest my understanding."[6] Others rejected the revisionists' arguments on the ground that they threatened to corrupt the church by polluting it with strangers; "the Sacredness of the ordinance of Baptism is of such weight with us, as that we Dare not Doe otherwise, then profess that wee are for Strictnes in the Administration of that Seale."[7] So strict Congregationalists baptized only children of visible saints. They refused to consider the viability or the necessity of any other course, and they exerted their influence everywhere to keep others from enlarging baptism. At John Davenport's instigation, the Commissioners of the United Colonies warned each General Court in September 1646 to take care that only "such as hold forth effectual callinge" be admitted to church membership and that baptism "be administered onely to such members & their immediate seed."[8]

[6] *Survey of the Summe of Church Discipline*, London, 1648, Bk. 3, p. 12.

[7] Charles Chauncy, et al., "Preface to Two Essays," transcript of MS, Yale University Library, p. 57.

[8] Nathaniel Shurtleff, ed., *Records of the Colony of New Plymouth: Acts of the Commissioners of the United Colonies of New*

Congregationalists, although the majority in New England, were not the sole occupants. There were laymen and ministers in the country who thought the New England Way reeked of hypocrisy and demanded wholesale revision of the polity. Thomas Parker and James Noyes were among the most successful advocates of this dissent. At Newbury they constructed a reformed English parish system where they admitted to baptism and the Lord's Supper all but notorious sinners.[9] The *Remonstrance* of the English Presbyterian Dr. Robert Child, which caused such consternation in Massachusetts in the summer of 1646, appealed for the admission of all godly men to the sacraments. Child's reward for challenging the civil and religious order was imprisonment and a heavy fine. Rev. Richard Denton of Stamford led the majority of his congregation to the Dutch jurisdiction on Long Island rather than submit to the restriction of baptism which prevailed in New Haven Colony.[10] The Presbyterian faction that these men represented asserted that only God knew the elect; any attempt to identify saving grace in individuals was pretentious and hypocritical. Churches should extend the sacraments to all but the obviously unregenerate.

New England's Baptists stood at the other end of the spectrum. They held that in a true church com-

---

England, Boston, 1857, *I*, p. 81; Isabel Calder, *New Haven Colony*, New Haven, 1934, p. 102.

[9] James Noyes, *The Temple Measured*, London, 1647, pp. 63-66.

[10] Calder, *New Haven Colony*, p. 101.

munion and baptism belonged only to the saints. Since no one could determine whether a child had grace, children had no place in the covenant. Their solution to the quandary of Congregationalism was simple: eliminate infant baptism, which had no scriptural warrant anyway. Although concentrated in Rhode Island, the Baptists had a congregation in Plymouth Colony; and individual Baptists kept appearing in Massachusetts, sometimes in such embarrassing places as the presidency of Harvard College.

The Massachusetts General Court recognized that a problem existed and warned that the variety of opinion and practice regarding baptism "must needs, if not timely p[re]vented, begett differences as will be displeasing to the Lord, offensive to others, & daingerous to ourselves."[11] But the Cambridge Synod (1646-1648), called by the Court to consider this issue and work out a uniform polity for the churches of New England, spent very little time debating baptism. The synod appointed Ralph Partridge of Duxbury and Richard Mather of Dorchester to prepare models of church government for its consideration, and both ministers explicitly recommended an extension of baptism. Mather's draft, which provided the basis for most of the *Cambridge Platform* stated: "Such as are borne in the ch[urch] as members, though they be not found fitt for the Lords Supper, yet if they be not culpable of such scandalls in Conversation . . . it seemeth to us, when they are marryed &

[11] Nathaniel Shurtleff, ed., *Records of the Governor and Company of the Massachusetts Bay*, Boston, 1853-1854, 3, p. 70.

have children, those their children may be rec[eive]d to Baptisme."[12]

Although a majority of the messengers apparently favored Mather's suggestion, the synod deleted it from the Platform "because some few dissented, and there was not the like urgency . . . for present practise."[13] John Norton, among others, had argued for its inclusion, but "the fierce opposition of one eminent person, caused him . . . to forbear urging [the proposal] any further."[14] The "eminent person" was probably John Davenport, who, together with Charles Chauncy of Scituate, led the obstructionist faction which ultimately prevailed in the Cambridge Synod. The cry "innovation" and the general unwillingness to risk open division doomed the recommendations of Partridge and Mather. *The Cambridge Platform*, the standard of "orthodox" polity and doctrine for New England, testified to the will of these strict Congregationalists.[15]

Several factors contributed to this lack of "urgency" that defeated Mather's suggestion. First, the threat of English intervention in the political and ecclesiastical affairs of New England had declined markedly after 1647, and this may have lessened the external pressure for liberalization. Second, the general task

[12] Quoted in Walker, *Creeds and Platforms*, p. 224; the pertinent section of Partridge's draft is in Mather, *First Principles*, p. 23.

[13] Mitchel, "Preface," p. 309.

[14] Cotton Mather, *Magnalia Christi Americana*, Hartford, 1820, *1*, Bk. 3, p. 265.

[15] Walker, *Creeds and Platforms*, pp. 222-225.

of preparing a platform of church discipline diverted the attention of the elders from the specific question of baptism. Finally, and perhaps most important, the number of children excluded from baptism because their parents could not gain admission to communion probably remained too small to exert significant pressure on the synod.

Failure to confront the question of baptism realistically did not eliminate the problem. As more of the second generation married and began their own abundant families, the simple fact of procreation added daily to the number of children excluded from baptism. The shortsightedness of the synod compounded the difficulty. But ministers who had refrained from extending baptism prior to 1646 "for avoydence of offence" and yet sincerely desired "more liberty & latitude" gained some encouragement from the synod. Before 1646 they had hesitated to extend baptism on their own initiative; now they realized that the majority of the ministers sympathized with this liberalization.

Richard Mather continued to work toward the fulfillment of his ideas. In 1645 his plea for broader baptism had been ignored; in 1648 the synod omitted this recommendation from the "Model of Church Government." In the decade after the Cambridge Synod, Mather provided the leadership and the rallying point for the revisionist ministers. He corresponded with many of the ministers, soliciting their views and offering his own sentiments. As early as 1647 ministers wrote to him seeking direction in the matter of baptism.[16] He frequently preached to his Dorchester congregation about the enlargement of baptism; and his catechism of 1650, which interpreted saving grace very broadly, gave additional weight to his arguments for the membership of the children of the church.[17]

In 1651 Mather described the situation in his own church: "we have not yet thus practiced, but are now considering of the matter, and of sending to other churches for advice."[18] Apparently this discussion had no immediate result, but in 1655 the Dorchester church tentatively accepted the half-way covenant: children of the church "Haveing children they should have them baptized if themselves did take hold of their fathers covenant (but wt that takeing hold of their fathers covenant is was not clerely agreed upon) albeit themselves beinge examinyed were found neither fit for the Lords table nor voteinge in the Church." Enough members regarded the doctrine as "strange and unsaffe" to force the elders to dispatch letters to neighboring congregations informing them of Dorchester's plans and notifying them that unless they, the elders, received reasons to the contrary, their church would initiate the practice.

Answers came quickly and reassured those members who feared innovation. "Boston desires Rather our forbearance & declares ther 2 votes upon what we had done[.] Dedham sees not Light to goe so farre as we & Roxbury though divers of them feare it

[16] Henry Smith to Richard Mather, August 23, 1647, *First Principles*, p. 24.

[17] *ibid.*, pp. 11, 14.

[18] *ibid.*, p. 11.

might make the [. . .] & bring in time the Corruptions of Old England wch we fled from yet have voted that they see noe cause to diswade us." The obvious reluctance of all three acted as a brake on the congregation. A month after the answers came, Elder Edward Brecke asked the members "why after so much waiting they did not put into practice their arg[u]m[en]t about Baptizinge church members children." When Mather answered that the disapproval of other churches had discouraged many, Brecke replied that he thought it better to offend than to neglect. Several weeks later another elder requested the congregation to affirm its vote and give the pastor authority to "Baptize whom he would." The members deferred their decision for a month so that Mather might preach a sermon on the relevant portions of Genesis, but then the debate lapsed for eighteen months and Dorchester's polity remained unchanged.[19] This deferment marked only the first of many rebuffs which Dorchester dealt Richard Mather, and it suggests a dimension of the controversy that was to become more common. Not only did ministers disagree with each other, congregations frequently demonstrated extraordinary reluctance to follow the leadership of the clergy.

Nevertheless Mather found some encouragement in the reports he received from ministers in Connecticut and Massachusetts, many of whom broached the topic of baptism in their churches and recommended

[19] *Records of the First Church at Dorchester in New England; 1636-1734*, Boston, 1891, pp. 164-165.

liberalization. Samuel Stone of Hartford wrote Mather:

> There have been a sinful neglect of such children in New England. I spake with Mr. Warham [Rev. John Warham of Windsor], and we question not the right of children, but we conceive it would be comfortable to have some concurrence, which that we have waited for a long time. And I think unless there be some conference of Elders this year, in the Bay, that we may see some reason to the contrary, our churches will adventure to practice according to their judgment, i.e., take in all such children as members.[20]

Thus in 1650 the ministers of the two largest congregations in Connecticut recognized the need to extend baptism and threatened to proceed on their own. Despite Stone's bold talk, a half-dozen years elapsed before either Hartford or Windsor practiced what their ministers advocated. Real fear existed of "walking alone." Only synodical endorsement could surmount the apprehensions of many churches, and Stone's plea for a meeting to settle the issue followed the Cambridge Synod too closely to have any real impact.

Even from New Haven Colony, where Davenport and Eaton had established the strictest Bible commonwealth, came murmurs of dissent. Peter Prudden of Milford admitted, "touching the desire of such members Children as desire to have their Children baptized, it is a thing I do not hear practiced, but for my

[20] June 6, 1650, *First Principles*, p. 38.

own part I am inclined to think, that it cannot justly be denyed."[21] At Salem in 1652 Edward Norris proposed that the church permit baptized adults not as yet admitted to the Lord's Supper to have their children baptized and placed under the discipline of the church. The congregation readily agreed that children should retain their membership when they became adults; but, despite several church meetings, they reached no agreement on the extension of baptism. Salem debated the issue sporadically for thirteen years before it finally adopted the half-way principle in 1665.[22]

Ipswich considered the enlargement of baptism in the same year. Nathaniel Rogers, pastor of the church, wrote Mather in the winter of 1652-1653, "we are this week to meet in the Church about it, and I know nothing but we must speedily fall to practice."[23] Roger's plan received the endorsement of his colleague John Norton, who in 1647 had supported Mather's proposals and in 1654 was to prepare a careful defense of the principle of broad baptism. But Rogers and Norton, like many other ministers in these years, discovered that church members were less receptive to the innovation than they had anticipated. Despite the encouragement of both teachers, Ipswich clung to orthodoxy.[24]

Thomas Cobbett, preaching in Rogers' place at

[21] Peter Prudden to Richard Mather, June 12, 1651, *First Principles*, p. 25.

[22] Salem Church Records, typescript copy in the possession of First Church of Christ in Salem, 2, p. 234.

[23] *First Principles*, p. 23.

[24] *ibid.*, p. 15.

Ipswich in 1656, reintroduced the subject of baptism. This time the congregation heeded its minister's advice and voted that the children of members in full communion were real members and subject to the watch and discipline of the church.

> 4. We look upon it as the Elders' duty to call upon such children, being adults, and are of understanding and not scandalous, to take the covenant solemnly before our assembly.
> 5. We judge that the children of such adult persons be baptized.
> 6. . . . yet we judge that these adult persons are not to come to the Lord's Supper, to act in Church votes, unless they satisfy the reasonable charity of the Elders or Church that they have a work of faith and repentance.[25]

Ipswich probably became the first church in New England to practice the half-way covenant, but the loss of the church records makes the evidence inconclusive. Several churches voted favorably on the *principle* of extending baptism and then failed to implement the decision because of continued opposition within the congregation.

Roxbury considered adopting the half-way covenant in 1653 and asked for advice from Jonathan Mitchel, pastor at Cambridge and in 1662 the most articulate advocate of the innovation. But at this point, as yet unsure himself, Mitchel requested "that it

[25] Ipswich Church Records, quoted in Joseph B. Felt, *The Ecclesiastical History of New England*, Boston, 1862, 2, p. 141; Walker, *Creeds and Platforms*, p. 256.

might not yet be pressed." Mitchel's hesitancy apparently dissuaded Roxbury; the church records give no indication that the matter ever came to a vote.[26]

We know with certainty of only one church that adopted the half-way covenant before 1657. In the winter of 1656-1657, after several months of agitation, the Chelmsford church voted, "all they that are in Ch: C[o]v[enan]t are Ch: Members . . . Bapt. belongs of right to all such." A week later the church amplified its decision. The church covenant included all children under fourteen at the time when their parents joined. These children had an obligation to "acquaint themselves betimes with God and with his will" and "such of these as have attayned the knowl. & understanding of the principles of Religion & are without just Scandall are to be Encouraged to lay hold on & so owne there P[ar]ents Covt psonally." Evidence of faith and repentance remained prerequisites for the Lord's Supper and voting in the church.

Chelmsford sent letters to Concord and Woburn to acquaint them with the church's decision. Unlike Dorchester, Chelmsford announced plans; it did not ask for advice. Without waiting for answers, the church set the principle into practice. On February 1, 1657, the members presented for baptism seventy-five children ranging in age from several months to twenty-two years. Multiple baptisms accounted for two-thirds of the total; families brought four, five, and six children to receive baptism together. Late in February the Concord church wrote to Chelmsford

[26] Mather, *Magnalia*, 2, Bk. 4, p. 99.

"Testifying that we proceeding according to these sd. ppos. it shall not be offencive to them &c." Woburn's letter demanded "or scr[ipture] grounds to the sd. propositions." But Woburn's scruples did not deter Chelmsford: what it had started, it continued.[27]

Coincident with Chelmsford's action, First Church Boston accepted part of the revisionist program. The church considered the question: "Whether the relation of Immediate children, of church members be such, as giveth the church a church-power over them . . . That their knowledge and life may be answerable to the Ingagement of their relation?"[28] The congregation voted affirmatively. This extension of discipline marked the first step toward a broader conception of membership and an enlargement of baptism. Perhaps First Church's ministers, John Wilson and John Norton, recognized the danger involved in attempting to implement the entire revisionist program at one time. Too often when a congregation confronted enlargement of baptism it drew back. Norton and Wilson probably hoped a patient course of attack would achieve more with less resistance.

The number of ministers attempting to implement the half-way covenant gave the revisionists hope that the tide had turned in their favor, and in the fall of 1656 they received a windfall. The Connecticut General Court sent its counterpart in the Bay "several questions of practical concernment" about church

[27] Notebook of the Reverend John Fiske, typescript copy, Essex Institute, pp. 185-189.

[28] Richard Pierce, ed., *Records of the First Church in Boston; 1630-1868*, CSM *Publications*, Boston, 1961, *1*, pp. 55-56.

membership and baptism and requested the aid of Massachusetts in resolving them.[29] What precipitated Connecticut's inquiry cannot be determined. The Hartford church was torn by internal strife, but this was more a matter of personality than doctrine, and baptism never became more than a peripheral issue in it. Most likely the Court recognized the diversity of opinion among ministers and simply chose this time to seek a resolution.

The Massachusetts General Court responded to Connecticut's request by calling for a ministerial assembly to meet in Boston the following June and resolve the questions. To represent Massachusetts the Court selected thirteen ministers, four from each county plus the President of Harvard College.[30] Connecticut, in turn, appointed four ministers to attend and "returne to Gen: Court of the issue of their consultations."[31] New Haven rejected an invitation to participate. The New Haven General Court complimented Massachusetts for "readiness to afford help when the case requires it," but it felt the elders of Connecticut "had bine fully sufficient to cleare and maintayne the truth . . . without calling a synod . . . which in such times may prove dangerous to the purity of these churches." No minister from New Haven would attend, the Court wrote. Even Davenport had

[29] The questions have been lost, but they probably corresponded closely to the questions answered in *A Disputation Concerning Church Members and Their Children in Answer to XXI Questions*, London, 1659.

[30] *Massachusetts Records*, *3*, p. 419.

[31] J. Hammond Trumbull, ed., *Public Records of the Colony of Connecticut*, Hartford, 1850, *1*, p. 288.

excused himself because of the probable heat. But the Court prayed "God to bless the meeting" because without His help "such a meeting . . . may produce sad effects."[32] Plymouth never responded to the invitation and took no part in the proceedings.

New Haven was well aware that many of the representatives to the assembly hoped to accomplish major revisions in congregational polity. The questions proposed for discussion plainly dealt with enlarging baptism, and revisionists dominated the assembly. At least six of the Massachusetts delegates had already endorsed the half-way principle: Richard Mather of Dorchester, John Norton of Boston, Edward Norris of Salem, Jonathan Mitchel of Cambridge (between 1653 and 1656), Thomas Cobbett of Ipswich, and Peter Bulkeley of Concord. Six other representatives ultimately supported the principle and probably inclined toward it before the assembly convened. The only declared opponent of the half-way covenant from Massachusetts was Charles Chauncy, then President of Harvard College, who, while minister at Scituate, had successfully combined with Davenport to override the majority at Cambridge. The Connecticut delegation included Stone and Warham, who had both championed the liberal measure in that colony. Before the assembly met, the revisionists lacked a majority by no more than one vote and in fact probably already had a sizable majority. New Haven had warned the Massachusetts Court of the danger: "We heare the petitioners, or others closing

[32] Charles J. Hoadly, ed., *Records of the Colony or Jurisdiction of New Haven; 1653-1664*, Hartford, 1858, 2, pp. 196-197.

with them are very confident they shall obteyne great alterations." To counter the forces of apostasy, Davenport prepared arguments denying the scriptural grounds for enlarging baptism.[33]

Despite the admonitions of New Haven and the indifference of Plymouth, the Ministerial Assembly convened June 4, 1657, in Boston. In less than two weeks it completed its work and forwarded the results to the General Courts. *A Disputation Concerning Church Members and Their Children in Answer to XXI Questions*, written by Richard Mather, embodied the assembly's decision and included all the features of the half-way covenant:

> It is the duty of those Infants when grown up to years of discretion, though not yet fit for the Lords Supper, to own the Covenant they made with their Parents, by entring thereinto in their own persons, and it is the duty of the Church to call upon them for the performance thereof. . . . Being accordingly called therunto, if after Church admonition and other due means with patience used they shall refuse . . . it is the part of the Church to proceed with them to the censure of excommunication. In case they understand the grounds of Religion, are not scandalous, and solemnly own the Covenant in their own persons, wherein they give up both themselves and their children unto the Lord, and desire Baptism for them, we (with due reverence to any Godly Learned that may dissent) see not

[33] *Ibid.*, p. 196.

> sufficient cause to deny Baptism unto their children. . . Though the persons forementioned own the Covenant according to the premises, yet before they are admitted to full communion they must so hold forth their faith and Repentance. . . .[34]

One powerful member of the "Godly Learned" did dissent. Charles Chauncy denounced the proposals, but to no avail. In 1648 Chauncy had withstood the pressure of the majority and had fought the synod to a standstill. This time, despite his increased prestige as President of Harvard College, the majority carried the day.

It is doubtful that the arguments of either side had changed significantly since 1648; what had changed were the circumstances. The majority no longer acceded to a strident minority for the sake of peace and harmony in the churches. The cry "innovation" no longer frightened the ministers. They had confidence built on common goals and the rectitude of their course. Some of them had corresponded and discussed the question for more than a decade. On one side these ministers saw the continued life of Congregational churches that ministered to the needs of the people; on the other side they saw the unbaptized and an increasing chasm between the church and the community. The half-way covenant meant the preservation of the purity of the Lord's Supper *and* the continued institutional existence of the church.

The Ministerial Assembly of 1657 provided the

[34] *A Disputation Concerning Church Members*, pp. 20-24.

first real sanction of extended baptism but hardly resolved the crisis. Revisionists pointed to the assembly; strict Congregationalists fell back on the *Cambridge Platform*. Even with the assembly's endorsement it was an open question whether the ministers could convince their heretofore reluctant congregations to accept the half-way covenant.

The meeting had barely adjourned before several ministers found the answer. John Warham, one of Connecticut's four representatives at the Ministerial Assembly, led the way; and in January 1658 his Windsor congregation implemented the half-way principle. Surprisingly, Warham later reversed his position, halted the practice in Windsor, and became a supporter of John Davenport.[35] Rev. Richard Blinman of New London discovered that the assembly's recommendations not only could help a minister convince a reluctant congregation, but also could be used by the laity against a reluctant minister. Blinman, who opposed the half-way covenant, returned to New London from the Ministerial Assembly determined to prevent introduction of the innovation. Unfortunately for him, the assembly's proposals, particularly the tenth proposition, which called for the extension of baptism, became the subject of public discussion. Jonathan Brewster, son of the famed Elder Brewster of Plymouth, debated the merits of this proposition with Blinman. Brewster, reflecting his Separatist heritage, defended the broader conception of membership while Blinman stood fast by the "old ways." As a

[35] Henry R. Stiles, *The History and Genealogies of Ancient Windsor*, Hartford, 1891, *1*, pp. 196.

result of the debate "some of the town manifested, that except he [Blinman] would practice that conclusion, the[y] would not paie his maintenance."[36] Blinman blustered and threatened to desert the town, but remained. He refused to enlarge baptism and in several sermons railed against his critics and their principles. The controversy in New London ultimately provoked Blinman to resign and migrate to Newfoundland. As his successor the church elected the liberal Gershom Bulkeley.

In the fall of 1658 John Eliot and Samuel Danforth partially converted the Roxbury church to the revisionist principle. The congregation adopted five propositions which included all the recommendations of the assembly. But the church records suggest Roxbury's halting progress toward the half-way covenant:

> Upon many agitations of disquisition amongst ourselves, upon much advice and counsell and especially that of the first Synod at Cambridge (1647) And the late councill at Boston (1657) and after more than ten years time of consideration about these points in hand, we, the church of Roxbury are at last come up to this resolution that we judge in our consciences that these 5 propositions are agreeable to the truth of God and rules, wch we now are to walk by.[37]

[36] Jonathan Brewster to John Winthrop, Jr., 1657, *Winthrop Papers*, MHS *Collections*, Boston, 1865, 37, pp. 84-85.

[37] Charles M. Ellis, *The History of Roxbury Town*, Boston, 1847, p. 29; Walter E. Thwing, *History of the First Church in Roxbury*, Boston, 1908, p. 11. Both authors cite the church records as the source of this quotation; however, the published rec-

Actual implementation of the half-way covenant lagged well behind the resolution to practice it. Although Roxbury considered the innovation for a decade, not until 1660, seventeen months after the vote, did the first member "personally & solemnly own the Covenant & thereupon had her child Baptised."[38] By 1664 exactly three women had owned the covenant, hardly an overwhelming response on the part of the congregation.

Although actual use of the half-way covenant came slowly, an increasing number of ministers publicly endorsed the principle. Thomas Allen, pastor at Charlestown, in the preface of Thomas Shepard's *Covenant of Grace* (London, 1659) wrote that the children of members not in full communion "being within the Covenant, they may be partakers of the First Seal of the Covenant."[39] This was the point the revisionists consistently emphasized: the covenant relation continued until willfully broken by the member. The Charlestown congregation seemed less sure of this interpretation and refused to accept the half-way covenant until 1663, although Allen had long maintained this view.[40]

Fortunately for Richard Mather the revisionist cause did not depend on the success of his own

---

ords of the church have no reference to this vote. *Roxbury Land and Church Records, Report of the Record Commissioners*, Boston, 1884, *6*.

38 *Roxbury Church Records*, p. 88.

39 Mitchel, "Preface," p. 306.

40 Thomas Allen to John Cotton, Felt, *Ecclesiastical History*, *I*, p. 480.

attempts at Dorchester; his own congregation proved remarkably intractable. Mather made an attempt to use the half-way covenant in his church in 1657 on the grounds that the congregation had accepted the principle two years earlier and had simply delayed because of the reservations of other churches. But even the records of the unknown church clerk who set down the proceedings reveal the resistance Mather confronted. "Martha Minott p'sented by her father—though he was noe member accordinge to our church order: but a Corruption Creepinge in as an harbenger to old england practice viz. to make all members: (wch god prvent in mercye)."[41] God and reluctant members kept Martha Minott out.

Mather refused to surrender to his recalcitrants and kept the issue before the church. He reminded the members in the spring of 1660 that the elders still considered that the children of the church "are to be lookt at as members" and that they should not think "it is forgotten or their [the elders] minds changed." As a first step he recommended that the brethren start exercising proper church watch over the children. The children, in turn, ought to start behaving as ones liable to "account in casse of defect."[42] Several months later Mather announced to a church meeting that the wife of James Minott still desired baptism for her children and that she was willing to own the covenant to qualify them. "To this divers of the Church shewed their Consent but some weer unsatisfied & therefore it was defered. . . ." Twice in the next three weeks

[41] *Dorchester Church Records*, p. 168.
[42] *ibid.*, p. 33.

Mrs. Minott's request came up, but continued opposition forced postponement. The next Sabbath, after evening service, Elder Withington announced that "some of the breatheren had been with them that weeke & told them that they aprhended mr. mathers Arguements for baptizing of such children" and desired "it might be now spoken unto." Several members presented arguments in favor of the innovation, "but nothing fully concluded: though thes arguments unto some weer not answered to ther aprhention: & some weer still unsatisfied."[43] Since Dorchester did not require unanimity in church votes, Mather apparently chose peace and harmony in the church over implementation of the half-way covenant. He deserves credit for his tenacity, but credit must be shared with the handful of members who had become so artful in the tactics of delay.

In Boston, Norton and Wilson almost succeeded where Mather had failed. In 1657 First Church had extended discipline, and in 1661 it considered enlarging the covenant. The members voted that the elders should call on all the adult children of the church "to see whether they would own and take hold of the covenant of their fathers (which had been thus long, for the most part neglected)." John Hull, master of the mint for Massachusetts Bay Colony and a member of First Church, recorded in his diary that "a great willingness appeared, both in youth, maides, men and women." On two succeeding Sabbaths "being called by their names, in the face of the whole congregation, [they] did openly manifest their desire to

[43] *ibid.*, pp. 33-36.

acknowledge their relation to the church according to the covenant of God which they plighted in their parents." The decision upset at least two prominent merchant members, Edward Hutchinson and Anthony Stoddard. Hutchinson had agreed to remain quiet even though he disapproved, but when the children stood up he turned his back to the church. In fact, Hutchinson requested dismissal from the church, probably to join Boston's Second Church, where such innovations had not yet been broached. But most of the members, "with general satisfaction and cheerfulness, attended the work."[44]

First Church had not adopted the half-way covenant; it had only explored the possibility. Polled "to see whether" they wanted the half-way covenant, the children of the church had "manifest[ed] their desire to acknowledge" their covenant. Undoubtedly, Norton and Wilson intended to follow this expression of interest by implementing the half-way principle, but they were disappointed. First Church had gone as far as it would under their leadership. The church records support the interpretation that this was only an exploratory procedure designed by Norton and Wilson to put additional pressure on the congregation. Multiple baptism, where more than one child in the same family are baptized at the same time, usually follows implementation of the half-way covenant. This occurred only once in First Church in the succeeding months and in that instance one parent had just recent-

[44] John Hull, "The Diaries of John Hull," *Transactions*, American Antiquarian Society, Boston, 1857, 3, p. 198.

ly joined in full communion.[45] In fact, there is nothing in the church records—no votes, no baptisms, no names—to substantiate any of the events Hull described in his diary.

Although slow progress toward the adoption of the half-way covenant appears to have been the rule, the remarkable element in the years after the Ministerial Assembly is the grudging retreat of the church members from "orthodoxy." In church after church ministers found gradualism the only practical approach; even when a church adopted the half-way covenant in a single step, the minister often spent several years trying to convince members to use it.

Salem reconsidered the question of baptism in the fall of 1661. A half-dozen years earlier the church had accepted the proposal of Edward Norris that the children of the church still be accounted real members when they reached maturity. The congregation now reaffirmed that vote and under the guidance of Rev. John Higginson took the revisionist program one step further. They placed the children of the church "under the watch and care of the Elders . . . [and] of the whole church." Despite Higginson's admonitions, Salem refused to carry the concept of membership as far as the Ministerial Assembly recommended; children of the church still could not present their children for baptism.[46]

Seaborn Cotton, John Cotton's son, was more fortunate than Higginson. The Hampton church gave him liberty to follow his conscience regarding baptism

[45] *Boston First Church Records*, *1*, pp. 58-60.

[46] Salem Church Records, *2*, pp. 223-224.

and he took advantage of this opportunity by introducing the half-way covenant in 1662. He exercised his prerogative with such relish that a year later one parishioner charged, according to Cotton's account, "that I would baptize all the heathen in the country if there were water enough," and that I "might as well have cast the water upon a beasts face."[47] The indictment may simply have been the complaint of a disgruntled traditionalist, or it may indicate that Cotton had moved beyond the half-way covenant toward a more inclusive parish.

The phrase "own the covenant" has frequently appeared; what did it mean to own the covenant? Although we know a great deal about the practice in the eighteenth century when it had often become a mass ritual, the record of the earlier years is slim. The best example involves a young scholar from Chelmsford about to depart for Harvard College. Moses Fiske, the son of the church's pastor John Fiske, was called before the church, and the elders inquired if any "had aught ag[ainst] him for matter of offence." When no one responded, the elders posed the following questions to him:

> You Moses doe her[e] before the Lord, his Angells, & us his people promise & engage yorself psonally to own & stand to yor parents covt with this church & in ptic:
> 1. To owne no other God . . . & doe give up yorself unto him.

[47] Samuel E. Morison, "The Reverend Seaborn Cotton's Commonplace Book," CSM *Publications*, 1931, 32, pp. 330-331.

2. To owne the Lord Christ in all his offices. . . .
3. To walke according to the holy Order & Rule of the Gospel according to yor best light. . . .
4. And you doe heere by your owne psonal Act give this yorself to the watch & care of his church. & all this by the help of Gods sp[ir]it & grace.

After Moses answered each question in the affirmative, the church voted "to pforme unto you her duty of Church Inspection & care And also to be ready to owne you afterward to further privileges in the church, as the Lord shall qualify you thereunto." The congregation then prepared a letter to the church at Cambridge commending Moses to its careful watch while he was in college. Had Moses' circumstances been different he might have proceeded to have his children baptized at the same time.[48] Roxbury defined owning the covenant as "personally, publickly and solemnly to avouch the Lord in an ecclesiasticall way to be their God according to the Covenant of Grace, and to submit themselves to the power and government of Christ in his church."[49]

One recurring misconception about the half-way covenant needs to be laid to rest. Historians have often charged that a relationship existed between the franchise and the demand for extending baptism. Some have implied that sinister forces undermined religious purity for political gain; more secular historians make the claim to prove the narrowness of the

[48] Notebook of Rev. John Fiske, p. 205.
[49] Thwing, *Roxbury*, p. 11.

franchise in the Puritan colonies.[50] Williston Walker denied any connection between the franchise and the half-way covenant three-quarters of a century ago, but apparently without effect.[51] Of the four holy commonwealths, only for Massachusetts could this charge have had validity. Neither Connecticut nor Plymouth made church membership a prerequisite for freemanship. In 1665 New Haven Colony merged with Connecticut and adopted that colony's standards for admission to the franchise. It is doubtful that prior to the union any church in New Haven Colony had even debated the half-way principle, much less put it into practice. In New Haven the franchise was limited to visible saints, and Davenport so effectively dominated the theological life that latitude in baptism never became an issue.

In Massachusetts, however, admissions to freemanship had been limited to church members since May 1631, and five years later the General Court specified that only members of churches that had been approved by the elders and magistrates were entitled to the franchise.[52] As the number of adult members not qualified for communion increased, it is possible

[50] Leonard Bacon, *Thirteen Historical Discourses*, New Haven, 1839, p. 141; Henry M. Dexter, "Two Hundred Years Ago in New England," *Congregational Quarterly*, 1862, *4*, p. 288; C. C. Goen, *Revivalism and Separatism in New England*, New Haven, 1962, p. 4; Elisha Douglass, *Rebels and Democrats*, Chicago, 1965, p. 3; Clarence Ver Steeg, *The Formative Years*, New York, 1964, p. 87.

[51] Williston Walker, *A History of the Congregational Churches in the United States*, New York, 1894, pp. 172-173.

[52] *Massachusetts Records*, *1*, p. 168.

some confusion existed regarding eligibility to vote. The critical point was the legal definition of "member." If the Court had chosen to interpret the law of 1631 broadly, every baptized adult male in the Massachusetts churches could have qualified, communicant or not. But the Court had no such intention. "No man whosoever shall be admitted to the freedom of this body politic but such as are members of some church of Christ, *and in full Communion*" (italics mine). This, said the Court in 1660, was "the true intent of that ancient law."[53] Agitation over membership probably precipitated the clarification, but since churches prohibited members who had merely owned the covenant from voting in church affairs, it seems doubtful that anyone would have considered them qualified to vote in colonial affairs. Nowhere in the debate over the half-way covenant was the franchise mentioned. If there were unrecorded political motives, the General Court eliminated them two years before the Half-Way Synod convened. Not until the Court modified the qualifications for freemanship in 1664, to mollify the King's Commissioners, could anyone other than communicants acquire political rights.

After 1648 the ecclesiastical situation in New England was in flux. The *Cambridge Platform* provided one answer for baptism; the Ministerial Assembly of 1657 provided another. Churches debated, procrastinated, defied their ministers, or bowed to clerical pressure, but without resolving the problem. Order and unity disappeared and each day things became more unsettled. To compound the difficulty, the

[53] *ibid.*, 4, Part 1, p. 420.

restoration of Charles II in 1660 jeopardized the Puritan cause everywhere. Now more than ever New England had to close ranks. That marvelous intellectual construct, the New England Way, was foundering on the rocks of baptism.

Again the Massachusetts General Court took the initiative. In December 1661 the Court issued a call for a synod to meet in Boston the following March "for settling of the peace . . . in these chhs of Christ." The question the Court wanted resolved was: "Who are the subjects of baptism?"[54] The Court undoubtedly hoped a full-scale synod would provide a conclusive answer to the problem which beset Congregationalism.

[54] Massachusetts Archives; Ecclesiastical, *10*, 193b; *Massachusetts Records*, *4*, Part 2, p. 38.

TWO

The Half-Way Synod

IN MARCH 1662 more than eighty ministers and laymen gathered in Boston's First Church for the opening of the Half-Way Synod.[1] Despite the wintry season, leaders from most of the thirty-four churches in Massachusetts had come to attack New England's most pressing ecclesiastical question. The number sent by each church varied widely: First Church Boston, the host, sent six; Salem sent three; Dorchester, two. But each messenger had a vote; and in number, if not in influence, laymen dominated the synod. Many of those who arrived must have been disappointed to find the other colonies had ignored the General Court's invitation to send representatives. Some would sorely miss the conservative influence of John Davenport, but Davenport faced a serious problem at home. (By the terms of the new royal charter, the colony which he had founded and sustained was to be absorbed by Connecticut.) Other men at the synod regretted that the Connecticut elders who had supported the extension of baptism in 1657 had decided

[1] This figure is based on Cotton Mather's report that the vote was seven to one in favor; *Magnalia*, 2, Bk. 5, p. 528; and Eleazar Mather's estimate that not more than ten or twelve voted against the proposals; Eleazar Mather to John Davenport, July 4, 1662, *Mather Papers*, MHS *Collections*, 1911, 67, p. 192.

against coming to Boston. Massachusetts would have to solve the problem alone, without the aid of ministers from the other colonies, but repercussions would be felt all over New England.

The advocates of the half-way covenant wasted little time before opening the debate. As soon as they had elected a moderator, they introduced for the synod's consideration seven propositions based on the conclusions reached by the Ministerial Assembly. The initial response was as inauspicious as the March weather. On the first vote the propositions "were (some of them) disliked by 8 ministers, and sundry messengers. Thereupon the Synnod was ajourned to the 10th of June next."[2] The first session of the synod had lasted only eleven days, but the lines of debate, had they ever been in doubt, were now clearly drawn. The seven propositions outlined the liberal position by calling for the recognition of the membership of children of church members and the right of the succeeding generation to baptism, if the parents displayed historical faith and sincere attachment to the covenant. The three-month interval between the first and second sessions gave the conservatives time to prepare their answers and marshal support.[3]

For the conservatives the opening days of the second session were a portent of things to come. When the synod reconvened on June 10, it set aside the following day for prayers to seek the Lord's aid in

[2] Increase Mather to John Davenport, Spring, 1662, *Mather Papers*, p. 192.

[3] Walker, *Creeds and Platforms*, p. 265; Felt, *Ecclesiastical History*, 2, p. 292; *Roxbury Church Records*, p. 199.

breaking a drought which had beset the country. Some people in the colony had attributed the drought "to the sitting of the synod; but he was pleased to bear witness ag[ain]st their rashnes; . . . the day following God sent showers from heaven."[4] With God favorably disposed toward them, the messengers renewed debate.

The seven proposals were once again put before the synod and the question of baptism was fully considered. When the proposals came to a vote "not above 10 or 12 appeared to act contrary to what the Assembly had voted."[5] What had appeared to be a formidable number of opponents in March was reduced to one man in eight by late June. Eleazar Mather, frustrated by the changed temper of the synod, tried to explain to John Davenport the reasons for the shift: it was "because they would allow everyone his interpretation in debate, & thence sundry inconsiderately voted for that which when it was too late they wished they had not done." Nor had the revisionist ministers confined their arguments to the merits of the case. "All dissenting is esteemed intolerable & dissenters are accounted & charged to be Breakers of the peace of the churches,"[6] and these *ad hominum* tactics added to the defections from the conservative ranks.

Although the overwhelmingly favorable vote meant that the revisionist ministers had cleared a major hurdle, the work of the synod was not com-

[4] *Roxbury Church Records*, p. 200.

[5] Eleazar Mather to John Davenport, July 4, 1662, *Mather Papers*, p. 192.

[6] *loc.cit.*

pleted. The messengers had adopted the proposals only in tentative form; final propositions still had to be written and approved. Also, the second question posed for the synod by the General Court, whether there should be a consociation of churches, had not yet been broached. Rather than continue the session any longer in Boston's summer heat, the synod recessed July 4 for the second time and set September 9 for the start of the third session.

As soon as the meeting adjourned, opponents of the half-way covenant sent Davenport details of the events. Both Increase and Eleazar Mather kept in touch with him during every phase of the synod. When he heard the news from Boston, Davenport prepared an attack on the tentative recommendations, "A Reply to the 7 Propositions Concluded By the Synod," to which his colleague in the New Haven church, Nicholas Street, added a short supporting essay.[7] Davenport visited Boston late in the summer and left the two essays with Charles Chauncy "with a Condition from him to bring them into public view, as the testimony of himselfe, and his Judicious Col-

[7] These two essays can be found in a transcription of manuscripts made by David Pulsifer in 1843, now in the Dexter Collection at Yale University. Street's essay appears unchanged in *Another Essay for the Investigation of the Truth*; Davenport changed his "Reply" considerably before *Another Essay* was published, although the thrust of the argument remained the same. Also contained in Pulsifer's transcriptions are "Plain Proposalls," the preface which the dissenters addressed to the General Court in October, and "Judgement of the Dissenting Brethren," which appears to be an early draft of *Anti-Synodalia Scripta Americana.* Dexter listed these essays in his catalogue of 1890 as lost, and Walker doubted that they had ever existed.

legue concerning these controverted Points."[8] Since there was not time to have them printed before the synod met, Chauncy kept them to himself until September.

The messengers reconvened on September 9 and began individual consideration of the seven propositions. Each one was debated and redrafted, and great care was taken that the phrasing was clear. Surprisingly Charles Chauncy formulated the final version of the third proposition, which asserted that the children of church members, when adults, retained their membership and remained subject to church discipline. "One of the chief of our Dissenting Brethren did propound, and earnestly promote [it]," John Allin reported.[9] Many persons in the synod, including Jonathan Mitchel, thought the third proposition carried the entire cause.[10] Chauncy may have realized the risk he ran, but the exclusion of the children from church discipline in the past had worked to the advantage of the liberals. With his back to the wall in the synod, Chauncy may have hoped the extension of church watch would forestall more radical innovations.

The controversial fifth proposition caused the major debate of the synod. Three drafts of this proposal, which permitted the children of the church to have their children baptized, were prepared. The final one, Chauncy lamented, "swerves further off from the

[8] Chauncy, et al., "Preface to Two Essays," p. 56.

[9] John Allin, *Animadversions Upon the Antisynodalia Americana*, Cambridge, 1664, p. 13.

[10] Jonathan Mitchel, "An Answer to the Apologetical Preface," *A Defence of the Answer*, Cambridge, 1664, p. 3; Walker, *Creeds and Platforms*, p. 268.

Scriptures then both the former."[11] The support of the lay majority was essential to the conservatives. With the clergy supporting the proposition five to one, their only hope was to enlist broad support among the less theologically sophisticated laymen. But far too few shared Chauncy's sentiments. Although the moderator counted more negative votes on this proposition than on any other, "*there were not Five twice told.*"[12] Chauncy, like Eleazar Mather, blamed the defeat on the naïveté of the laymen. "Divers of the Messengers being no Logitians, and so unable to answer Syllogismes, and discern Ambiguities, were overborn."[13] Perhaps if Davenport had attended, he might have won additional votes, but most of the messengers were not even familiar with his arguments. When Increase Mather "offered the synod" the essays by Davenport and Street to be read aloud, "Mr. Norton advised them not to suffer me." The synod accepted Norton's advice, and a handwritten copy of the essays had to be circulated privately.[14] If the lay representatives were initially as hostile as Chauncy and Mather seemed to think, the dissenting ministers had only themselves to blame for their defeat. The dissenting "Logitians" apparently had not provided sufficient intellectual ammunition and encouragement to prevent the laymen's defection. In

[11] Chauncy, et al., *Anti-Synodalia Scripta Americana*, London, 1662, p. 5.

[12] Mather, *Magnalia*, 2, Bk. 5, p. 258.

[13] Chauncy, *Anti-Synodalia*, p. 5.

[14] Increase Mather to John Davenport, October 21, 1662, *Mather Papers*, p. 205.

fact, it is doubtful that the dissenters ever represented close to a majority of the synod.

Late in September the seven propositions were finally "Voted and Concluded by the Assembly in the particular terms. . . ."[15] The question, "Who are the subjects of baptism," had been answered and Massachusetts had a new orthodoxy. The Cambridge Synod had evaded the issue; the Ministerial Assembly had outlined the principles; the Half-Way Synod placed the full weight of a synodical decision behind the extension of baptism and gave new meaning to the church covenant.[16]

Leading the synod to its decision were the same ministers who had championed the half-way covenant in the previous decade. For Richard Mather the Half-Way Synod was a personal triumph, a vindication of his "Model of Church Government," and the culmination of a fifteen-year campaign. In the final month of the synod John Norton, just returned from his mission of appeasement at the court of Charles II, stood by Mather's side and frustrated the attempt to introduce Davenport's essay. Among the other ministers in attendance were John Higginson, John Fiske, John Eliot, John Wilson, and Thomas Cobbett, whose churches had already adopted all or part of the synod's recommendations. One new figure came to the forefront in the synod. Jonathan Mitchel of Cambridge, perhaps the most charismatic of the second generation of ministers, became most clearly identified with the decision of the synod. In 1657 he had partici-

[15] Mitchel, "Preface," pp. 312-313.

[16] Walker, *Creeds and Platforms*, pp. 313-314.

pated in the Ministerial Assembly but had played a minor role. In 1662 he drafted the propositions for the press, wrote the preface, and then defended them in the postsynod debate by answering Increase Mather's attack. Ten years later when Increase recanted and endorsed the half-way covenant he credited Mitchel with his conversion.

The burden of dissent in the synod fell on three ministers, an old man of seventy and two young men only six years out of Harvard College. Even at seventy Charles Chauncy as President of Harvard and one of New England's leading scholars commanded the synod's attention, but he could not command its votes. In 1662 he was confronting Richard Mather and the advocates of the half-way covenant for the third time. Chauncy was a stickler for literal interpretation of the Bible. In the past he had insisted on baptism by immersion (an uncomfortable practice in New England) and had refused to administer the Lord's Supper except in the evening. His attempt to implement these ideas in Scituate had caused a church schism. At the time of his election as President of Harvard in 1655 he had agreed to remain silent about his peculiar views.[17] In a way his aversion to the half-way covenant may have reflected his literalness.

The two youthful critics of the synod were Increase and Eleazar Mather, sons of Richard Mather, the man most responsible for the synod's decision. Increase had been graduated from Harvard in 1656 and after preaching briefly in New England had gone

[17] Samuel E. Morison, *Harvard College in the Seventeenth Century*, Cambridge, 1936, *1*, pp. 322-323.

to England in 1657. He took his M.A. at Trinity College, Dublin, held several chaplaincies in England, and then returned to New England after the restoration of Charles II. When the synod met for the first time, Increase had been back in Boston for only six months. Although he had left for England before the Ministerial Assembly had finished its work, he was certainly familiar with its recommendations.

Why Increase Mather opposed the synod remains unclear. Possibly John Mayo, the pastor of Second Church Boston, influenced him. Mayo voted with the dissenters from the beginning and added his name to the tracts attacking the synod which appeared in 1663. Since he had returned from England, Increase had preached in Second Church on a trial basis and had had considerable contact with Mayo.[18] But Increase's stance marked a sharp divergence from the views of John Norton, his former tutor at Harvard, whose ideas we know decisively affected Mather.[19] The condemnation of the synod's propositions may have signaled Increase's intellectual declaration of independence from his father. At twenty-three and about to embark on his own career in New England (he sat in the synod as a delegate from the same church as his father), Increase probably considered his stand a sign of freedom. It is noteworthy that Increase Mather reversed his opinion about the half-way covenant the year after his father died.

The reasons for Eleazar Mather's opposition are

[18] Chandler Robbins, *History of the Second Church*, Boston, 1850, p. 20.

[19] Pettit, *The Heart Prepared*, pp. 199, 204.

equally veiled. Although Eleazar was two years older than Increase, both had taken their degrees from Harvard in the same year. When Increase went to England, Eleazar moved to the frontier settlement of Northampton and became its first pastor in 1658. He never deviated from his opposition to the half-way covenant, despite pressure from his congregation, and his premature death in 1669 antedated his brother's recantation by two years. It is clear that the younger Mathers worked in concert during and after the synod to defeat the propositions, and Eleazar may have shared a desire to assert his independence. Perhaps the influence of Charles Chauncy, under whom the brothers had studied in their final years at Harvard, was a decisive factor. Surely members of the minority courted both of them assiduously, and conspiring with the President of Harvard and the founder of New Haven Colony to thwart the synod must have had a heady effect. But it is still ironic that Richard Mather should find his sons among the small number of ministers lined up against him in the synod.

The identification of the lay members of the synod who voted with Chauncy, Mayo, and the younger Mathers is largely speculative and based on their actions after the synod concluded. Major William Hathorne and ruling elder Henry Bartholomew, who sat in the synod as messengers from the Salem church, figured in an important way in the anticlerical report the Massachusetts deputies prepared in 1670 condemning innovations in religion as a primary cause of God's displeasure toward New England. Hathorne, an assistant from 1663 until his death, consistently hampered the advocates of the half-way covenant. William Penn of First Church Boston almost certainly supported the dissenting ministers. When John Davenport came to First Church in 1668 to personally lead the fight against the half-way principles, Penn became one of his staunchest allies. As ruling elder of the church Penn bitterly contested the attempt by supporters of the half-way covenant to secede from First Church and establish their own congregation.

The final dissenting votes may have come from the men representing the Woburn church, including the minister Thomas Carter. The Woburn church had attempted to deter John Fiske from introducing the half-way covenant in Chelmsford several years earlier, and it was one of the few churches in the colony that consistently opposed the establishment of Third Church Boston. It is unlikely, given the tenor of the debate over Third Church, that Woburn sympathized with the extension of baptism. Woburn's most prominent layman, Captain Edward Johnson, twice voted in the General Court to condemn innovations in religion. If each of the ministers and laymen discussed above did, in fact, vote against the propositions, every negative vote would be identified.

Within a few days of the synod's adjournment, the General Court received the final draft of the seven propositions from four of the ministers, John Wilson, Richard Mather, John Allin, and Zechariah Symmes. After considering the synod's proposals "the Court, on their perusall, judged it meete to commend the same unto the consideration of all the churches & people of this jurisdiction, and for that end ordered the printing thereof."[20] Now both church and state stood behind the half-way covenant.

At the same time the propositions were presented, several dissenting ministers appeared to apprise the Court of their objections. They entreated the Court "that the Determinations of the Major part of the Assembly may not be imposed on others." To avoid such impositions they had "lefte the land of our fathers . . . to enjoy God, & our consciences in this wilderness."[21] They also set before the Court the grounds of their dissent. Increase Mather wrote John Davenport in New Haven: "I have given in yours & Mr. Streetes Testimony Unto our Gen: Court, with a preface subscribed by Mr. Ch[auncy,] Mr. Mayo, my Brother & myselfe, in the name of others of the Dissenting Br[ethre]n in the Synod, wherein we declare that wee fully concurr with what is asserted by your selves."[22]

If the dissenters had hoped to dissuade the Court from accepting and recommending the synod's proposals, they were disappointed, but the attempt was not entirely in vain. "Some of the Court would very faigne have had them throwne out againe, without soe much as reading them, but the major part were not soe violent. . . . it was moved allsoe that what yourselves & wee have done might be printed." As Increase Mather told Davenport: "wee must count

[20] *Massachusetts Records*, 4, Part 2, p. 62.

[21] "Plain Proposalls," p. 64.

[22] October 21, 1662, *Mather Papers*, p. 205.

it a favour that wee were not Commanded to be silent. It is our purpose therefore to print what wee have given in to the Court, of yours & ours, many that are true to the cause desiring us soe to doe."[23] The long essay, "The Judgement of the Dissenting Brethren of the Synod," which the four leading critics had presented to the General Court, appeared from the press in London the following year as *Anti-Synodalia Scripta Americana*.[24]

Although *Anti-Synodalia* was published in England, the General Court's decision to permit the publication of dissenting opinions resulted in the most controversial series of pamphlets yet published in New England.[25] Through them minority views

[23] *loc.cit.*

[24] The only changes in the essay were made because "now we are to speak to many meaner persons." The preface attributed to Chauncy in *Anti-Synodalia* is the same as the "Plain Proposalls" presented to the General Court by the dissenters in October 1662.

[25] The major works defending the synod were Mitchel's "Preface" to the *Propositions*; John Allin's *Animadversions Upon the Antisynodalia Americana*; Richard Mather and Jonathan Mitchel, *A Defense of the Answer and Arguments of the Synod*, in which they answered Davenport and Increase Mather; Thomas Shepard, *The Church Membership of Children and Their Right to Baptism*, a manuscript given to the press by Thomas Shepard, Jr., to add the weight of another founder to the synod's conclusions. The pamphlets opposing the synod include Chauncy, et al., *Anti-Synodalia Scripta Americana*; John Davenport, *Another Essay for the Investigation of the Truth*, and "A Vindication of the Treatise Entituled Another Essay." The latter circulated in manuscript through the offices of Increase Mather and is now in the American Antiquarian Society collections. Increase Mather wrote a long "Apologeticall Preface" to *Another Essay* and Nicolas Street's "Considerations" was appended to the same volume. The final word on the subject, at least until the middle of the next

received far wider circulation than they might otherwise have expected. The effect was to undermine the "official" status of the synodical decision and encourage laymen to resist introduction of the half-way covenant. The General Court had given its imprimatur in fact, if not in spirit, to the publication of conclusions diametrically opposed to the propositions of the synod. The Court's decision probably reflected the ambivalence felt by many of the deputies toward the recommended innovation. After the synod had reached these conclusions by a large majority, the members discovered that they faced a renewed attack from an articulate minority which commanded respect in the colony.[26]

The dissenters focused their condemnation of the synod on four primary issues: innovations in religion; pollution of the churches; inability of the children; and, willful breaking of the covenant. The extension of baptism, they said, would fundamentally alter the church polity established by the founding generation, and they considered themselves bound "by covenant and oath of God unto that order and dispensation of word which hath been hitherto received and peaceably practiced amongst us thes thirty yeeres. . . ." The synod's innovations would open the churches to the unfaithful and ultimately lead to defilement of

century, was Increase Mather's recantation, *First Principles of New England.* Since all the essays provoked by the decision of the synod except *First Principles* appeared within two years and varied very little on each side, they have been treated as a common source.

[26] Perry Miller, *From Colony to Province*, p. 94.

the Lord's Supper. "It is apparent unto all what a corrupt masse of unbelievers shal . . . thronge into the communion of Gods people: and the children of strangers uncircumcised in heart shall bee brought into Gods sanctuary to pollute it."[27] Owning the covenant, the critics charged, was a mockery, since only persons with saving faith could fulfill the required pledges. The final assertion advanced by the dissenters was the most radical. Children of the church, by their failure to take up the promises offered in baptism, had deserted the covenant and were incapable of passing membership to the next generation. Underlying all these objections was the distinction the dissenters made between mediate and immediate membership. The failure of the synod to distinguish the degrees of membership, they felt, had been its primary error and the source of its unscriptural innovations. In each of the relevant propositions the dissenters took pains to clarify their understanding of membership.

The critics of the half-way covenant summarized their objections eloquently. "That practice that exposeth the blood of C[hris]t to contempt, and bap[tism] to p[ro]fanation, the Church to pollution and the Commonwealth to confusion is not to be admitted."[28] God's blessings on New England had been many and great, "But since the motion of this change what the Lords dealing hath bene and still is, we leave it to the prudent to judge."[29] "We have not

[27] "Plain Proposalls," p. 24.
[28] "Judgement of the Dissenting Brethren," p. 29.
[29] "Plain Proposalls," pp. 5-6.

falne hitherto in 30 or 40 yeeres into apostacy, unlesse that now we fall into it."[30] The best way to prevent irreligion and apostasy, Davenport said, was to have "the Porter look well unto the Doors."[31]

Advocates of the half-way covenant proclaimed that their policy would preserve the New England Way and protect the purity of the churches. Extending baptism had not betrayed the principles of the founders, the majority said. "The Points herein which may be most scrupled by some are knowne to have beene the judgement of the generality of the Elders of these Churches for many years." Mitchel recounted the events at the Cambridge Synod and produced excerpts from Richard Mather's correspondence and his own gleanings from the published and unpublished writings of the first generation to prove his point. Even had the revered founders of New England not endorsed the principles put forward by the synod, it was "not so much what hath been held or practiced as what should be."[32]

The majority contended that the half-way covenant would insure the purity of the Lord's Supper. Parents who had not experienced effectual calling would not have to resort to dissimulation and pretense in order to have their children baptized. Nor would churches be tempted to ease the requirements for admission to full communion to insure that the rising generation would have the blessings of the covenant. It was the critics who endangered the Lord's table; "We believe that time will show that that Principle that over

[30] "Judgement," p. 45.
[31] *Another Essay*, p. 15.
[32] Mitchel, "Preface," p. 305.

inlargeth full Communion . . . will prove a Church-corrupting Principle."[33]

Although the fifth proposition was the most controversial, the majority had erected its arguments like building blocks, each proposition resting on the one preceding, and this structure forced the dissenters to begin their critique at the foundation. The initial proposition stated: "They that according to Scripture, are Members of the Visible Church, are the subjects of Baptisme." Had they had their way the dissenters would have altered it to read: "Visible Believers and Converts in full Communion in an instituted Church together with their next seed in Minority, are the proper and immediate subjects of Baptism."[34] This alteration placed more emphasis on visible faith as the qualification for membership than the synod had. The critics thought the synod had weakened the proposition when the second session deemphasized membership in particular churches.[35]

Both factions accepted the phrasing of the second proposition. "The Members of the Visible Church according to scripture, are Confederate visible Believers, in particular Churches, and their infant-seed, i.e. children in minority, whose next parents, one or both, are in Covenant." The differences of opinion on this proposition stemmed from divergent definitions of the terms. "We all own, that only visible Believers, or visible Saints, are to have their Children Baptized; but the Question is, *who* are to be accounted visible

33 Mitchel, "An Answer," p. 24.

34 *Anti-Synodalia*, p. 16.

35 *ibid.*, p. 19; Davenport, "Reply to 7 Propositions," p. 67.

Believers?"[36] The synod maintained that church members and their children qualified as visible believers according to the covenant promises in Genesis 17:7-14. The church seed were federally holy and in covenant; when they grew up they remained visible believers.

Critics demanded a clearer distinction between "confederate believers and their infant seed." Although the covenant extended to the children, "yet they are not in any scripture, that we know of, called believers."[37] Churches in the New Testament, unlike Abraham's family, "are by Christs appointment cast into a Congregationall and more Spiritual Form; and therefore, are not capable of being propagated and continued, in a lineal succession by natural generation."[38] Opponents of the half-way covenant denied that Genesis provided a precedent for the continuing covenant which the second proposition suggested. "Circumcision was first appointed for a Domesticall, and then for a National Church, whereas Baptisme is appointed for a Congregationall. . . . in some respect Baptisme may be called Gospel-Circumcision . . . yet the similitude runs not upon four feet."[39] We must not look at "every subject of Circumcision as the subject of Baptism," Davenport told his readers, because "the former was more external and carnal, the latter more internal and spiritual."[40] Although both baptism and circumcision sealed the same covenant, "Baptism is an Ordinance

[36] Mitchel, "An Answer," p. 24.

[37] "Judgement," p. 12.

[38] *Another Essay*, p. 6.

[39] *Anti-Synodalia*, p. 14.

[40] *Another Essay*, p. 3.

and seal of the New-Testament, and must therefore be administered, as for the manner of it, according to Gospel-rules."[41] As the dissenters interpreted the Scriptures, continuation of the covenant from generation to generation required personal affirmation of faith in each person; familial entailment was not sufficient.

The development of the dissenters' arguments on circumcision threatened one fundamental tenet of Congregationalism. God's command to Abraham to circumcise his seed had served the Reformed tradition for generations as the strongest scriptural justification for infant baptism. By criticizing the applicability of this section of Genesis to New Testament churches, the dissenters substantially undermined the basis for including children in the covenant. John Allin quickly recognized the danger—"our Dissenting Brethren give great advantage to the Antipoedobaptists."[42] In their effort to keep out some of the children of the church, the antisynodists unwittingly abetted those persons who wanted to exclude *all* children.

In its third proposition the synod asserted: "the Infant-seed of confederate visible Believers, are members of the same Church with their parents, and when grown up, are personally under the watch, discipline and government of that Church." Although Charles Chauncy had drafted this proposal and the synod had approved it without dissent, the critics now had some second thoughts. "We take liberty to shew our owne meaning . . . wch we see hath bene misinterpreted."

[41] *Anti-Synodalia*, p. 13.

[42] *Animadversions*, p. 42.

They had not meant that the children of the church "have a personall, and immediate membership . . . but only, that the church watch . . . should reach unto ther p[er]sons."[43] The children had only a "mediate membership" through their parents which made them subject to church admonition, but not to excommunication.[44]

Only John Davenport publicly challenged the fourth proposition, although some of the dissenters must have privately agreed with his logic. This proposition had explicitly excluded the children of the church from the Lord's Supper. "These Adult persons, are not therefore to be admitted to full Communion, meerly because they are and continue members, without such further qualifications as the Word of God requireth thereunto." Communicants must "be able *to examine themselves, and to discern the Lords body*; else they will . . . *eat and drink damnation* . . . *to themselves*."[45] Davenport's understanding of personal membership, as distinct from mediate membership, led him to conclude, "Whosoever are members of the Church personally . . . they have a p[er]sonall right to all Church privileges, & may exercise it."[46] Davenport, of course, never intended that the children of the church should be admitted to communion without evidence of saving faith. Neither faction would have tolerated that. He was attempting to prove through a striking example what personal or

[43] "Plain Proposalls," p. 4; "Judgement," p. 17.

[44] "Judgement," p. 17; *Another Essay*, p. 73.

[45] Walker, *Creeds and Platforms*, p. 327.

[46] *Another Essay*, pp. 73-74.

immediate membership meant and to point out the synod's critical error. Both Charles Chauncy and Increase Mather avoided applying their concepts of membership to the fourth proposition the way Davenport had. Probably both of them feared that the unsophisticated would misinterpret their meaning, and the prospect of open communion chilled them.

All the synod's critics reserved their heaviest barrage for the heart of the innovations, the fifth proposition:

> Church members who were admitted in minority, understanding the Doctrine of Faith, and publickly professing their assent thereto; not scandalous in life, and solemnly owning the Covenant before the Church, wherein they give up themselves and their children to Christ in the Church, their children are to be Baptised.

The dissenters directed their attack at the first two words of the proposition. All membership was not the same, "some being only federally holy, as the infant seed, other[s] sanctifyed in the name of Lord Jesus, some having publickly and p[er]sonally laid hold on the covenant, other[s] having only parentall and partiall right."[47] Although Adam had stood as the representative of all men, no parent could act as a representative person "Covenanting for all his posterity."[48] The critics claimed that unless one distinguished between the types of membership, parents would entail the covenant for generations. Parents and children held distinct memberships: "the parents

[47] "Judgement," pp. 12-13. [48] *Another Essay*, p. 40.

are members federally *per se*, by themselves Covenanting for themselves, their infant seed are members federally *per alium*, by their parents covenanting for them, which seemes to me to be best cleared by that distinction of immediate and mediate members."[49] Since the membership of children is *Mediante Parentum foedere*, the dissenters said that when the children grew up they "must be admitted into immediate fellowship and full communion with the Church by their personal faith held forth . . . and by taking hold of the Covenant for themselves."[50] The membership of children was so inextricably related to the parents' membership "as to live and dy therewith."[51]

Jonathan Mitchel rejected the critics' sense of membership. Children of the church "are personally and formally members." Membership was membership and additional privileges such as voting and partaking of the Lord's Supper were only adjuncts to it. To the majority of the synod, the assertion that a child's membership was bound so completely to his parents' would make the child subject to excommunication with his parents. Can the parents' sin cut off the child, they asked the dissenters.[52] Children of the church, the synod had admitted, held mediate membership because they became members by their parents' covenanting for them, "but that doth nothing vary or diminish *the essence* of their membership." Parents are the "efficient," but "divine Institutions giveth or

[49] "Reply to 7 Propositions," p. 68.

[50] *Another Essay*, pp. 5, 36-43.

[51] Chauncy, et al., "Preface to Two Essays," p. 59.

[52] Mitchel, "An Answer," pp. 8, 9, 34.

granteth a real and personal membership unto them." There was no distinction between mediate and immediate membership which "put a *medium* between these two."[53] The dissenters' contention that membership "do admitt of a diversity of degrees,"[54] Richard Mather had denied absolutely. "Membership is a Relation, and therefore admits not of magis and minus, more or lesse: Members are better or worse, and communion is more or lesse; but membership admits not of degrees."[55]

Jonathan Mitchel thought that the anti-synodists had based their entire argument on the distinction in membership and that their case would collapse if it could be disproved.[56] But substantial disagreement about the nature of the covenant and baptism underlay this controversy and probably made it irreconcilable.

As the dissenters interpreted Scripture, only repentance and saving faith could transform the mediate membership of the children into the immediate, personal membership required to transmit baptism. "That which will not make a man capable of Baptism himself, in case he were unbaptized, doth not make him capable of transmitting right of Baptism to his childe."[57] Being in covenant was not enough, "for thus the Covenant and Baptisme are entailed to a

[53] *Propositions*; Walker, *Creeds and Platforms*, pp. 332-333.

[54] "Judgement," p. 13.

[55] Richard Mather, *Disputation Concerning Church-Members and their Children*, in Walker, *Creeds and Platforms*, p. 297; *Propositions*, p. 332.

[56] *First Principles*, p. A2.

[57] Mather, "Apologeticall Preface," p. A12.

thousand generations."[58] The main ground of baptism, the critics argued, was not the covenant but faith.[59] God had not given faith indefinitely in the promise sealed in baptism, but had made it contingent. Unless the parent qualified for the Lord's Supper, no scriptural warrant existed to baptize his children.[60] "It is not Meer Membership but qualified membership that gives right unto Baptism."[61] The covenant relation of the children, as the dissenters developed it, was limited, dependent, and conditional. Children shared in the covenant only if their parents were effectually called. Thus, they made the covenant contingent upon faith.

The synod justified the extension of baptism through a much more inclusive sense of the covenant and by a denial of the necessity for saving faith. Children whose parents were included in the covenant, even if the parents had not experienced saving faith, had as much right to baptism as children of the visibly regenerate. "Interest in the Covenant is the main ground of title to Baptism, and this these children have. . . . Because *if the parent be in the covenant, the childe is also*." Contrary to what the dissenters claimed, saving faith was unnecessary "because the

[58] "Judgement," pp. 13-14.

[59] Davenport's views of baptism had been quite different in 1633 when he was in Leyden. At that time he required parents to answer satisfactorily only three questions: what was their religion; to what church did they belong; and, in what faith would they educate their children. *A Just Complaint*, MHS *Proceedings*, 1910, *43*, p. 50.

[60] *Another Essay*, p. 29.

[61] "Apologeticall Preface," pp. A10, A12.

tenor of the covenant is *to the faithfull and their seed after them in their generations* even to a *thousand generations*, i.e. conditionally, provided that the parents successively do continue to be *keepers* of the covenant. . . ."[62] Although the parent acted for the minor child in baptism, "the child is baptized by vertue of his own membership, and not by vertue of his Parents membership."[63] Each generation of covenanted parents kept the covenant alive for the next generation.

The dissenters challenged the synod's meaning of "keepers of the covenant" and claimed that the messengers had accepted a narrower definition during the sessions, but had refused to incorporate it in the propositions. "Wee intreated & begged that this which they sayd was true might be expressed & yet we could not by any meanes obtaine it."[64] The critics conceded that the acts required by the fifth proposition *might* imply faith, but such slight qualifications made it impossible to determine with any certainty whether faith existed or not.[65] "A man may do and be all that is there required yet have no faith in Christ, but be an unregenerate person."[66] It was a sham to call it owning the covenant, "when they assent only, who know not what the Covenant is, or are not qualified to take hold of it according to God."[67] Past experience with the half-way covenant had demonstrated to

[62] *Propositions*, pp. 328-329.
[63] *Disputation Concerning Church-Members*, p. 297.
[64] "Preface to Two Essays," p. 61.
[65] "Judgement," p. 24.
[66] *Another Essay*, p. 25.
[67] *ibid.*, p. 77.

the dissenters the futility of such proceedings: "when some of them having publickly said they own it, being afterward asked in private, What is the Covenant which you owned? answered, I do not know."[68]

Chauncy thought the third and final draft of the fifth proposition strayed the furthest from orthodoxy because it required the least from the children of the church. In the first draft "ther was required of thes children that they should understand the grounds of religion," but the synod's final version accepted children with "no knowledge of sin . . . no knowledge eyther of the dutys of holynesse. . . ." The second draft had required the children to give satisfaction for any offense instead of being merely "Not scandalous in life." It had also specified that the children "personally and publickly owne the covenant of God with them and in their parents." This wording would have admitted that "the covenant of God with them is only in & wth ther beleeving parents."[69]

If Chauncy had raised the same objections during the synod, that would explain the changes in the text. The majority wanted the language explicit enough to avoid misinterpretation, deliberate or accidental. To most ministers, owning the covenant constituted a solemn acceptance by an individual of his obligations to man and God, and a declaration of intent to meet those obligations as far as it was humanly possible unaided by grace.[70] Owning the covenant was not intended to demonstrate saving faith. When the dissenters failed to "raise" the requirements set by the

[68] *ibid.*, p. 26. [69] "Judgement," pp. 22-25.
[70] Walker, *Creeds and Platforms*, p. 278.

synod, they denigrated them as totally unsatisfactory to separate the wheat from the chaff.

The dissenters suggested in fact, contrary to what the synod had asserted, that these children not only could not renew the covenant, but might no longer even be included in it. "It remains to be proved that the Parents in question are children of the covenant."[71] The synod had claimed that only notorious sin could cut the covenant bond. The critics advanced a more radical notion:

> these Parents, in not taking hold of the Covenant personally & immediately—it may easily & abundantly be proved that such as have bin Baptised in the Church, & have lived under the precious meanes & great light untill they are Married & have Children, & all this while have neglected the maine thing that doth Concerne them, which is to beleeve, & upon their beleeving personally for themselves to take hold of the Covenant are under very great sin & offence.[72]

The idea that membership could be terminated only by church censure applied solely to communicants.[73]

Children of the church might be discovenanted without any church act. "I deny that that Membership continues in adult age . . . because then the reasons of their mediate Membership ceaseth, they being by age capable of covenanting for themselves," John Davenport announced.[74] By "covenanting for them-

[71] *Another Essay*, p. 28.

[72] Street, "Considerations," p. 86.

[73] *Anti-Synodalia*, pp. 24-25.

[74] *Another Essay*, p. 42.

selves" Davenport clearly meant meeting the qualifications for full communion. If they could not demonstrate a conversion experience, they became nonmembers by their own defection; they had refused Christ when the means were available.[75] Davenport called this desertion of the covenant.[76] "The Lord himselfe discovenants them," the dissenters stated. "A man may reject the counsell of God against himselfe . . . to their hurt and destruction. . . . so persons may bee *fellones de se*."[77] The children of the church could not transmit their covenant relation because it no longer included them. ". . . such Christ accounts to bee against him, as he saith he that is not with me is against mee."

The dissenters were vague about the critical point at which these children became *fellones de se*. But sometime after they reached maturity, married, and started a family God cut them off from the covenant without either the church or the children knowing it. However, even this rough schedule went against past experience—"those whom God doth call, it is most commonly in their middle age. . . . he calls many before, some after, but most then." In maturity "the workes of reason put forth themselves. . . ."[78] The anti-synodists were condemning the children of the church for failing to achieve a goal that lay beyond

[75] "Apologeticall Preface," pp. A4, A6; *Another Essay*, p. 47; *Anti-Synodalia*, p. 21; "Preface to Two Essays," p. 60.

[76] *Another Essay*, p. 45.

[77] "Judgement," p. 35.

[78] Thomas Hooker, *Preparing for Christ*, pp. 198-200, quoted in George L. Walker, *History of the First Church Hartford*, Hartford, 1884, pp. 140-141.

the power of an individual. Saving faith came not from human initiative but as a divine dispensation. These children led moral, honest, God-fearing lives; they attended the preaching of the word and waited for a conversion experience. The conclusion drawn by the dissenters that unregenerate children cut themselves off from the church may have marked a logical step in the purification of the temple, but to most New England divines this march further out of the world in the search of purity represented the *reductio ad absurdum* and a denial of the "errand into the wilderness."

The final two propositions of the synod,[79] derived from the fifth, received no notice from the dissenters. They had built their case carefully from the first to the fifth proposition to insure that their interpretations were clear. The final propositions would stand or fall with the fifth.

[79] "6. Such Church-members, who either by death, or some other extraordinary Providence, have been inevitably hindred from publick acting as aforesaid, yet have given the Church cause, in judgement of charity, to look at them as so qualified, and such as had they been called thereunto, would have so acted, their children are to be Baptised."

"7. The Members of Orthodox Churches, being sound in the Faith, and not scandalous in life, and presenting due testimony thereof; these occasionally comming from one Church to another, may have their children Baptised in the church whither they come, by virtue of communion of churches: but if they remove their habitation they ought orderly to covenant and subject themselves to the Government of Christ in the church where they settle their abode, and so their children to be Baptised. It being the churches duty to receive such unto communion, so farr as they are regularly fit for the same." Walker, *Creeds and Platforms*, p. 314.

The second question posed by the General Court, "Whether there ought to be a consociation of churches," the synod had resolved in terms which duplicated those of the *Cambridge Platform*. For this reason almost all the dissenting literature ignored consociation. Only Davenport recognized it as a threat. Taken in conjunction with the decision regarding baptism, the promise "to take notice of the Troubles and Difficulties, Errours and Scandals of another Church," boded ill for the anti-synodists in Davenport's opinion.[80] (His warning was prophetic; within a few years Davenport was engaged in a battle against the ministers and church councils of Massachusetts.) When he came to Davenport's attack on consociation, Richard Mather departed for the first time from his point-by-point refutation of *Another Essay* "because there appeared no Dissent or Dissatisfaction in the Synod about that matter."[81]

The controversial tracts, by bringing debate over the half-way covenant into public view, aggravated the problem most of the ministers faced and therefore represented a partial victory for the dissenters. Jonathan Mitchel was deeply disturbed by the events, and he considered the role of the critics particularly irritating. Examination for further truth, if it was "done Orderly and Peaceably," had virtue, but "to Amuse and trouble the People" by publishing attacks on the synod had no merit at all. "It makes the People Judge of the Case, who are incompetent."[82] Several years later Mitchel warned Increase Mather,

[80] *Another Essay*, pp. 51-64.

[81] *A Defence*, p. 99.

[82] "An Answer," pp. 1-3.

"yourself and those few in the Ministry here, that dissent, do bear a greater weight then it may be you are aware of, For the People in the Country have in a manner no Arguments to object but this, some of the Ministers are against it."[83] Undoubtedly this is what the minority had hoped would happen. They had lost the debate with their peers in the synod so they carried the fight to the laymen in the churches. "I hope some in New England will with clear light stand up against the enlarging of Baptisme," Increase Mather told his readers.[84] A decade later he regretted that so many had taken his advice.

Despite the decision of the Half-Way Synod and the recommendation of the General Court, Congregational polity insured that each church would make its own judgment about the extension of baptism. In the synod the combined voices of the ministers had won over the hesitant lay messengers, but back in his own church the minister spoke alone. If the laity could be convinced that the half-way measures represented unwarranted innovation and apostasy, implementation of the synod's propositions would be stopped dead. The pamphlets that followed the synod were part of the difficult battle for the lay mind.

In spite of the sobriquet of derision attached to the work of the Half-Way Synod, the half-way covenant was a necessary adjustment in the New England Way. The synod realistically faced and solved a problem unforeseen when the founders introduced testified

[83] *First Principles*, p. A7.

[84] "Apologeticall Preface," p. A14.

regenerate membership, and it preserved two central tenets of Congregationalism: limitation of the Lord's Supper to the visible saints, and infant baptism. The synod considered the alternatives to its solution untenable. In one direction lay the inclusive parish, advocated by Noyes and Parker, which would end all semblance of regenerate membership. In the other direction lay the unacceptable program of the dissenters, which would keep the churches pure but exclude good baptized Christians and their children. The synod took the only viable course it saw to preserve the essence of the New England Way and to keep the churches open to the children of the faithful.

THREE

Connecticut Confronts the Problem: 1664-1668

THE Half-Way Synod had no official impact on Connecticut, since no one had represented the colony in Boston. But differences of opinion about baptism and church membership divided Connecticut's churches and ministers just as sharply as they had in Massachusetts. After 1664 disputes over these issues increased alarmingly, and for a half-dozen years the churches were torn by factional strife. Schism, virtually unknown in Massachusetts churches, became the most common solution for Connecticut's church quarrels. From the outset the Connecticut General Court actively intervened in ecclesiastical affairs in the search for a settlement. In 1664 the Court recommended a new admissions policy to the churches and made some overtures toward enforcing the plan. Between 1667 and 1669 it directed the ministers to devise a solution, and when they failed, the Court announced its own program for reconciliation.

In Massachusetts the baptism of members' children was the central issue, but in Connecticut baptism was only the symbol. The controversy surrounding the half-way covenant camouflaged a more fundamental conflict between Congregationalists and presbyterialists.[1] At stake was the New England Way.

When John Norton returned from his embassy in England in the summer of 1662, he carried a letter from Charles II advocating changes far beyond anything contemplated by the elders in the Half-Way Synod. "All persons of good and honest lives, and conversations" should be admitted "to the sacrament of the Lords Supper, according to the said booke of common prayer, and their children to baptisme," the King directed.[2] Massachusetts ignored the recommendations, but in Connecticut William Pitkin and six other men formulated a petition to the General Court based on the king's letter. They complained of their continued exclusion from "those ordinances that we

[1] Even though this faction in Connecticut was moving toward Presbyterianism and was often so labelled by contemporaries, the term presbyterial is used to distinguish their views from a fully developed and integrated Presbyterian polity. The presbyterialist occupied a half-way house between Congregationalism and Presbyterianism. They were striving for a more inclusive form of church membership that would bring more people into the church, but the expanded membership was not always admitted to full communion. Although these men may have recognized the validity of standing synods and highly structured interchurch relations, they concentrated on transferring control of church affairs from the hands of the laity into the hands of the elders. Also, unlike Presbyterian clergymen, these ministers renewed their ordinations in each church which they served. They were, in effect, crypto-Presbyterians. For a brief but lucid contrast of Congregational and Presbyterian polity see Leonard J. Trinterud, *The Forming of an American Tradition*, Philadelphia, 1949, pp. 15-21.

[2] June 28, 1662, quoted in Walker, *Creeds and Platforms*, p. 271.

stand capable of, as the baptising of our children, our being admitted . . . to the Lord's Table," and they requested exemption from ecclesiastical taxes as long as the churches continued to "neglect or refuse to baptise our Children & to take care of us. . . ."[3]

A young English lawyer, William Pitkin had only recently emigrated to Connecticut, but he was already held in high esteem. In 1662, at the same time the General Court admitted Pitkin to freemanship, it also appointed him to act as its attorney in a case then pending. As a promising and favored young man, Pitkin must have found exclusion from the church particularly galling. Perhaps because of Pitkin's status the Court proved surprisingly receptive to his petition. ". . . haveing duely considered [we] commend it to the ministers whither it be not their duty to enterteine all such persons, whoe are of an honest and godly conversation, haveing a competency of knowledg in the principles of religion, and shall desire to joyne with them in church fellowship. . . ." The Court further recommended "that all children of the church be accepted and acco[un]td reall members . . . and that the church exercise a due christian care and watch over them."

The Court's proposals were radically revisionary and went far beyond the limited innovations of the Half-Way Synod. Had the Connecticut churches implemented the Court's program, they would have eliminated the Congregational principle of restricted membership elaborated by the *Cambridge Platform*,

[3] "Pitkin Petition to the General Court," Ecclesiastical Affairs Manuscripts, Conn. State Library, *1*, Part 1, p. 160.

and erected in its place more comprehensive parish churches. The Connecticut General Court was turning back toward the admissions policies which existed prior to the introduction of regenerate membership. The Court was so confident of its course that it asked the elders "whither it be not the duty of the Court to *order* the Churches to practice according to the premises, if they do not practice without such an order."[4] Certainly authority existed to do this; the laws of 1650 gave the civil government coercive power "to see the peace, ordinances and rules of Christe bee observed in every Church."[5] But who determined the "rules of Christe" the law did not specify. The Court asked any ministers who felt aggrieved by the recommended course to present their views to the next session.[6]

Thomas Hanford of Norwalk and Adam Blakeman of Stratford immediately challenged the Court. Together they prepared a sixteen-page rebuke to the suggested policies. Blakeman was adamant. He promised until his "dying day to adhere to that forme of Church Discipline agreed on . . . in the year of 49 [48?]."[7] Hanford and Blakeman may have dissuaded the General Court from its original intention, because when it met again the Court failed to pursue the proposals. It neither withdrew its recommendations nor made any attempt to implement them.

[4] *Connecticut Records*, *1*, pp. 388, 437-438.

[5] *ibid.*, *1*, pp. 524-525.

[6] *ibid.*, *1*, p. 438.

[7] Walker, *First Church in Hartford*, p. 198; Walker, *Creeds and Platforms*, p. 272.

While the General Court groped for its own solution, an acute ecclesiastical situation was developing within Connecticut's parishes. Several of the larger towns in the colony openly divided on the question of church membership. In addition to the familiar debates among church members over the extension of baptism, inhabitants without membership in the Congregational churches sought innovations in polity which would open church membership to themselves and their children. The appearance of a new generation of ministers in the 1660's compounded an already complex problem. The first generation of ministers, widely respected men associated with the establishment of the towns, were dying or going into partial retirement. When the time came to choose a successor or an assistant, the differing views of church membership burst into the open and disrupted the churches.

Events in the Windsor church suggest the fluidity of the situation in Connecticut and some of the problems involved. John Warham had led the way in Connecticut when his congregation adopted the half-way covenant in 1657. Yet in March 1664 he abruptly discontinued the practice. He announced to a startled congregation that he had met with such unanswerable arguments against the half-way covenant that he dared not continue. Not that he intended to cast it off permanently, he told them, but simply to forbear until he could resolve the conflict in his own mind.[8]

In light of local circumstances Warham's decision

[8] Henry R. Stiles, *The History and Genealogies of Ancient Windsor, Connecticut, 1635-1891*, Hartford, 1891, p. 196.

appears particularly unfortunate. A large segment of Windsor's population wanted a liberalization of the church's admission policies beyond those initiated by the half-way covenant. These people felt that communion should be opened to former members of the Church of England and to any other godly men, without regard to public confessions and relations of conversion. Two signers of the Pitkin petition, James Eno and Michael Humphrey, requested Warham to admit them to the Windsor church and baptize their children on the basis of their membership in the Anglican Church.[9] Although Warham denied their application, Eno and Humphrey had raised a serious question. Fewer than one in three of Windsor's adult males were communicants in the church. Countless respectable, God-fearing men and women were denied the sacraments and could not have their children baptized.[10] Although the half-way covenant had not been devised for those outside the church, Warham's return to a more conservative and restrictive stance must have further alienated Anglicans and Presbyterians in Windsor. It appeared to be another example of Congregational rigidity. The General Court was recommending liberalization of membership, but the church was moving in the opposite direction. Warham's decision gave further impetus to a group of Windsor inhabitants, including Eno and Humphrey, who left the town shortly thereafter and established the town of Simsbury. Virtually all of Simsbury's first

[9] *ibid.*, pp. 190-194.

[10] Job Drake to John Winthrop, Jr., *Wyllys Papers*, CHS *Collections*, 1924, *21*, p. 161.

settlers were Anglicans from Windsor, and in their new parish they could practice a more inclusive church way.[11]

Since the Windsor church was already looking for an assistant to relieve the burden carried by the aged Warham, a more judicious course might have been to maintain the status quo until that matter was settled. But clerics, and Puritan clerics most of all, rarely shy from ecclesiastical debate. Where the minister's conscience led, the congregation followed, however reluctantly. Within a few years the controversy sparked by Warham's elimination of the half-way covenant culminated in schism and the formation of Second Church Windsor.

A similar situation developed in the Stratford church where Adam Blakeman held the church and town together until his death in 1664. When the church elected as his successor, both to the mantle and strict Congregational polity, Charles Chauncy's son Israel, the differences suppressed under Blakeman came to the surface. Despite opposition within the church and from some inhabitants who were not members, Chauncy was called to preach for one year and ordained pastor in the spring of 1665. Chauncy recognized his tenuous position in the parish and made an agreement with the minority that opposed him that if at the end of the year they remained dissatisfied with him they could call another minister to share the pulpit. This concession probably reflected Chauncy's awareness of the power held by Connecticut's

[11] John E. Ellsworth, *Simsbury: 1642-1935*, Simsbury, 1935, pp. 17, 133-134.

town meeting over such church matters as the minister's salary and tenure. In the town meeting all male inhabitants, church members and nonmembers alike, shared in these decisions.

At the end of his first year Chauncy received from the freemen suggestions that he modify the requirements for church membership:

> we desire that all they that profess fayth & obedience to the rule of Christ not scandalous in life and present themselves in owning the covenant . . . may be admitted and accounted members of the church . . . and have their children baptized. . . . we desire also that the children of church members may be accounted church members as well as their parents and that they doe not cease to bee members . . . untill according to the rules of Christ they be cast out . . . and that they should have their children baptized notwithstanding that present unfittness for partaking of the Lords Supper.[12]

The freemen were calling for an enlargement of church membership that would include most inhabitants, not just the extension of baptism to the children of church members. Any person in the community of civil life and having knowledge of the faith should be able to own the covenant and have his children baptized. Clearly Chauncy had not initiated the half-way covenant in his brief tenure; nor did he

[12] William Cothren, *History of Ancient Woodbury, Connecticut; 1659-1854*, Waterbury, 1854, p. 119.

start then, despite the town's pressure.[13] Chauncy faced an unpleasant dilemma; he could satisfy the freemen only at the risk of alienating the majority of his own congregation.

When Chauncy refused to accept the recommendations of the town meeting, the minority in the church who had initially opposed him called Zechariah Walker to minister to them and their families. Technically the Stratford church had not split; but the town had two ministers and two congregations whose only common ground was sharing the same meeting-house. Walker's smaller congregation was allotted two hours in the Sabbath midday for services and Chauncy bracketed this with the two regular church meetings. This situation proved untenable and open hostility replaced the initial toleration. When Walker made some overtures for reunion, Chauncy's congregation rebuffed him. "We should meet separately . . . that we might enjoy the ordinances of God according as we are persuaded without disturbance each to other. . . . Though our difference be not about fundamentals . . . yet it reaches to the fundamentals of order in church administration."[14] The obstinance made the split almost irreconcilable.

In Hartford, as in Stratford, the death of a long-time pastor enmeshed the church in controversy over

[13] Samuel Orcutt, *A History of the Old Town of Stratford*, New Haven, 1886, p. 172. Orcutt obviously erred when he claimed, "This Half-Way Covenant . . . had been used for years in the Stratford Church when Mr. Chauncy came here."

[14] Cothren, *Woodbury*, pp. 32-33; William Wilcoxson, *History of Stratford, Connecticut; 1639-1939*, Stratford, 1939, p. 149.

church membership. Dissension and schism were no strangers to the Hartford church; from 1653 to 1659 followers of the Reverend Samuel Stone and the ruling elder William Goodwin had engaged in a rancorous debate. Although primarily a clash of personalities, the fight focused on the selection of a pastor to succeed Thomas Hooker. Peace returned only when Goodwin and many of his faction migrated to Hadley, Massachusetts. Stone still needed an assistant, and in 1660 the church chose John Whiting. A Harvard graduate in 1653, Whiting had assisted Edward Norris in Salem prior to his call from Hartford. Both Stone and Norris advocated adoption of the half-way covenant and, although their churches had not yet accepted it, there is no evidence that Whiting's relations with either man were anything other than harmonious. But when Stone died in 1663, the election of the Reverend Joseph Haynes as his successor provoked a bitter conflict, ostensibly over the half-way covenant. Haynes had been graduated from Harvard in 1658, and for two years prior to his move to Hartford he had preached in Wethersfield. As the son of Connecticut's first governor Haynes certainly occupied a prominent position in Hartford. Both Haynes and Whiting were young, twenty-three and twenty-nine; both were originally from Hartford and had grown up in the church they now served; both expected to lead the church. These factors alone might have caused competition and jealousy, but their disparate views of church membership made strife inevitable.

In June 1666 Haynes announced to the congregation that on the following lecture day he would explain his ideas about baptism and initiate the half-way covenant. Whiting immediately remonstrated; he refused to bow to the younger Haynes' leadership and searched for means to forestall the innovation. At Whiting's instigation John Warham came down from Windsor to testify against extended baptism. But when Warham started to speak the members interrupted. "What hath Mr. Warham to do to speake in our church matters?" Although Haynes had prepared the water for baptism, the Thursday lecture ended in tumult without beginning the half-way covenant. Haynes then challenged his colleague to debate the question before the entire congregation, and Whiting accepted.[15] It is unlikely the debate proved conclusive or helped resolve the conflict; most minds were already set.

The dissension in Hartford aroused immediate concern throughout the colony. From New Haven John Davenport wrote Governor Winthrop lamenting the recent events. If Thomas Hooker was still alive, "it would be as a sword in his bones" to see his church "thus disturbed, by innovacions, brought in, and urged so vehemently, by his yong successor in office." Davenport thought the strife seriously threatened the Congregational way. "The people there are woefully divided, and the better sorte are exceedingly grieved, while the looser and worser party insult, hoping . . . that the plantacions shall be brought into

[15] Walker, *First Church in Hartford*, pp. 184-185; Davenport to Winthrop, June 14, 1666, Calder, *Letters of John Davenport*, p. 264.

a parish-way. . . ."[16] Davenport raised the spectre of old England to frighten the governor, but there is some evidence his charge was not far from the mark. Increasingly, as the debate progressed, people called Haynes and his supporters Presbyterians. Although Haynes never advocated permanent synods or control of the keys only by the elders, he had a broader conception of church membership and to many persons this was sufficient to label him and his faction Presbyterian.

John Woodbridge, Jr., described the Hartford events to the English Presbyterian divine Richard Baxter as "a dysaster . . . too odious either to be written or concealed." Haynes, he claimed, "having more light in the Regularnesse and conviction of the duty of Baptising more extensively than the former Practice and the judgment of the other" had the support of a majority of the church.[17] Whether at Haynes' instigation or simply as the by-product of the strife, the debate in Hartford soon encompassed the entire question of church membership. Six freemen of Hartford, including William Pitkin, came to Whiting and requested admission to full communion. When the pastor inquired on what grounds they founded their request, "William Pitkin answered they did desire it upon account of a union they had already. . . . I returned answer that I knew of no

[16] Calder, *Letters*, p. 263.

[17] John Woodbridge, Jr., to Richard Baxter, October 14, 1669, "Correspondence of John Woodbridge, Jr., and Richard Baxter," Raymond P. Stearns, ed., *New England Quarterly*, 1937, *10*, p. 565.

such union they had to the Church of Hartford as to entitle them to communion . . . but however I would consider of their motion."[18] Surely Whiting never seriously entertained their appeal. If he had been willing to admit Pitkin and the others without any further qualification than a desire and membership in the Church of England, there would have existed no basis for the heated debates with Haynes.

The Connecticut General Court finally intervened in an attempt to restore peace in the churches. ". . . to bring those Ecclesiasticall matters that are in difference in the severall Plantations, to an issue . . . [we] doe therefore order that a Synod be called. . . ." The Court ordered every settled minister in the colony to attend and requested four Massachusetts ministers, including Jonathan Mitchel, to come and give Connecticut the benefit of the experience gained in 1662. The third Wednesday in May 1667 was appointed for the first meeting. In the interim the Court ordered "the Churches and people in this Jurisdiction to suspend all matters controversall and the practice of them not formerly receaved and practiced in the Churches here until an orderly decision be given by the Synod."[19]

Not all the churches viewed the General Court's interference in ecclesiastical affairs with equanimity. The Court seemed far too willing to countenance innovations. In Branford, formerly part of Davenport's New Haven Colony and recently joined into Connecticut, the church took a radical step to counter the

[18] Walker, *Hartford*, p. 200.

[19] *Connecticut Records*, 2, pp. 53-54.

threats to orthodox Congregationalism. Led by their pastor Abraham Pierson, a majority of the congregation abandoned their homes and migrated to New Ark, New Jersey, in the spring of 1666. There they hoped they could reestablish their church and government in purity. Bereft of a church, those who remained in Branford petitioned the General Court two years later to establish a new church. This appeal, signed by forty-eight men, stressed their adherence to Congregational principles in "the platform of Discipline Agreed on by the Synod in 48" and requested that "an orthodox Minister of that Judgement" be settled among them.[20] Branford wanted no part of the General Court's "open door" policy.

The Connecticut General Court clearly favored adoption of the half-way covenant by the churches, and it had contemplated even more sweeping changes. Each of the Massachusetts elders invited to attend the synod had advocated enlarging baptism. A synodical decision endorsing the half-way covenant would justify *some* of the Court's 1664 recommendations. But the seventeen questions the Court posed for the synod went beyond baptism to such issues as: how to choose a minister; the role of the town inhabitants in ecclesiastical affairs; the proper method for establishing a church; the rights of a minority within a church; and the nature of consociation.

The most remarkable question, however, was the

[20] Walker, *Creeds and Platforms*, p. 273; Ecclesiastical Affairs Manuscripts, January 20, 1667/68, *1*, pp. 17; Branford First Congregational Church Records; 1687-1866, MS, Connecticut State Library, p. 3.

final one: "Whether it be not justifiable by the Word of God that Civil Authority indulge Congregationall and Presbiterian Churches, and their discipline in the Churches."[21] This reopened some of the issues raised several years earlier by the Pitkin petition, but even more important it seemed to constitute a call for the toleration of diversity *within* the established churches. Connecticut had a larger and more articulate presbyterial minority (both inside and outside the churches) than existed in Massachusetts. John Woodbridge, Jr., attributed the evolution of a strong presbyterial party in the colony to the failure of the churches to meet the problem of baptism. "I think the bottome and rise of our contentions is that men of worth and understanding cannot bear it to have their children, orphan-like, deprived of their Legacy that Christ has left them and the others children should be markt for sheep and their owne, as good as the other be lefte out for goates."[22] Woodbridge felt that the half-way covenant alone could not satisfy the demands of the people. Not only the children of church members, but also nonmembers wanted baptism for their children.

Davenport perceived the crisis in quite different terms. "It is the faith and order of the churches of Christ, which we are called to contend for, that they may be preserved intyre and uncorrupted." He thought the New England Way was at stake; and just before the synod was scheduled to meet, Daven-

[21] *Connecticut Records*, 2, pp. 54-55.

[22] "Woodbridge-Baxter Correspondence," p. 578.

port took stock of the Connecticut churches to determine his expected allies:

> The most of the churches in this jurisdiction, are professedly against this new way, both in judgem[en]t and practise, upon Gospel grounds, n, Newhaven, Milford, Stratford, Branford, Gillford, Norwalke, Stamford, and those nearer to Hartford, n, Farmington, and the sounder parte of Windsor, together with theire Reverend pastor, Mr. Warham, and I thinck, Mr. Fitch [Norwich] and his church also. . . .

Davenport welcomed the prospect of a synod; if his calculations proved correct, enough "sound" churches remained to reject all innovations. But time was short, Davenport petulantly warned; "We live in a times and places, where the faces of the Elders are not duly honoured; . . . God will soone take away the most Godly and judicious leaders from so unthanckfull and unworthy people, and leave them to be MISLEAD BY SUPERFICIAL VERBALISTS."[23] It is not difficult to imagine whom the sixty-eight year old Davenport had in mind.

Although the assembly of ministers that Davenport had desired convened in May, the meeting was extraordinarily short and it adjourned until the following October without considering a single question. But even in this brief session the various factions were apparent. Simon Bradstreet of New London recorded in his journal: "This year there was a Synod called

[23] Davenport to John Winthrop, Jr., June 14, 1666, Calder, *Letters*, pp. 263-265.

at Hartford to discusse some points concerning Baptism, and church discipline, but nothing was concluded, the congregationall party, wch was the greatest, violently opposing the presbyterian."[24]

Why the Congregationalists failed to take advantage of their numerical superiority to crush presbyterial encroachments raises several questions. Perhaps they feared an open debate would encourage additional dissent and considered quick recess and silence the safest course. More likely, there existed a more complex division of factions than Bradstreet suggested. At least three distinct groups sat in the synod: strict Congregationalists, who wanted to preserve the original New England Way at any cost; revisionist Congregationalists, who considered the half-way covenant a necessary adaptation; and, presbyterialists, who wanted major departures from traditional polity toward comprehensive parishes. Within this framework no single faction controlled the synod.

The adjourned synod never reconvened. In September the Commissioners of the New England Confederation met in Hartford and voted that when questions of common concern in matters of faith and church order arose "and any of the Collonies shall apprehend it needful to call in the helpe of a Councell or Synode for the orderly Desision thereof; That the Members of such Councell . . . [be] called Indifferently out of all the United Collonies . . . and

[24] "Simon Bradstreet's Journal; 1664-1683," *New England Historic and Genealogical Register*, 1855, 9, p. 44.

the place of meeting to be att or neare Boston."[25] The commissioners may have feared the course that Connecticut might take if left to its own devices and thought any radical changes could be forestalled by calling in ministers from all the colonies. Three Connecticut ministers, John Warham, Samuel Hooker, and John Whiting, all apparently critics of enlarged baptism, immediately appealed to the General Court to cancel the second session of the synod. The synod, they claimed, had desired a "more generall convention of meet persons sent from the churches of the Massachusetts & orselves." The Court acceded to the request and asked the churches to send their elders to join in a meeting with Massachusetts and Plymouth elders, but left the time and place of the synod to the Massachusetts General Court.

Two presbyterialists, Gershom Bulkeley and Joseph Haynes, condemned the decision and told the General Court that the synod had never suggested calling an intercolonial meeting.[26] Which side accurately described events in the synod remains unclear, but when inquiries were directed to the Court regarding the status of the synod it answered that the synod had been superseded by "a more General Convention." The strategy of all this maneuvering is baffling. Why did strict Congregationalists like Whiting risk defeat in a joint meeting with the Bay churches where the half-way covenant had already received synodical endorsement? Conversely, why did Haynes and Bulkeley try to avert this new synod when it ap-

[25] *Acts of United Colonies*, 2, p. 238.

[26] *Connecticut Records*, 2, p. 238.

peared to increase their chances of victory? If the basic division related to questions of church government instead of baptism, it may be that Congregationalists of varying stripes turned to Massachusetts to halt presbyterial inroads.

It is also possible that strict Congregationalists in Connecticut realized that Massachusetts was unlikely to sponsor another synod. The Half-Way Synod of 1662, instead of resolving conflict, had brought it into the open and made it an issue for public debate. Arguments on each side had received wide circulation, and ecclesiastical affairs seemed more unsettled than ever. To compound the confusion in Massachusetts, John Davenport, the most articulate advocate of strict Congregationalism, tentatively accepted a call from First Church Boston in the fall of 1667. Massachusetts had little desire to reopen the entire issue in another synod. When the Massachusetts General Court received the bid to call another synod, it responded without enthusiasm and evaded the proposal.[27] There the matter died. The Connecticut General Court had dismissed its synod, and the Massachusetts Court had denied the call for a successor.

The following spring the Connecticut Court, no closer to a solution than it had been nineteen months earlier, offered a new plan. It appointed James Fitch, Gershom Bulkeley, Joseph Eliott, and Samuel Wakeman to meet at Saybrook on June 8, 1668, "to consider of some expedient for our peace . . . and thereby cleareing up how farre the churches and people may

[27] *ibid.*, 2, pp. 516-517.

walke together . . . not withstanding some various apprehension amonge them in matters of discipline respecting membership and baptisme."[28] Almost a year later the four ministers submitted their recommendations to the Court, and in May 1669 the Court announced its proposal for healing the differences.

> This Court having seriously considered the great divisions that arise amongst us about matters of Church Government, for the honor of God, welfare of the churches and preservation of the publique peace so greatly hazarded, doe decleare that whereas the Congregationall Churches in these partes for the generall of their profession and practice have hitherto been approved, we can doe no less than still approve and countenance the same to be without disturbance untill better light in an orderly way doth appeare; but yet forasmuch as sundry persons of worth for prudence and piety amongst us are otherwise perswaded (whose wellfare and peaceable satisfaction we desire to accomodate,) This court doth declare that all such persons being so approved according to lawe as orthodox and sownd in the fundamentalls of Christian religion may have allowance of their perswasion and profession in church wayes or assemblies without disturbance.[29]

This decision promised to *help* restore peace to the churches, but its implications were revolutionary. For more than a generation the *principle* of uniformity

[28] *ibid.*, 2, p. 84.

[29] *ibid.*, 2, p. 109.

had remained sacrosanct in the holy commonwealths, despite the differences in polity that had always existed. Now the Connecticut General Court admitted that the word of God was not yet clear enough on these issues for the state to promulgate and enforce a single "truth." Although it still considered uniformity a desideratum, Connecticut would recognize diversity and tolerate minority views "until better light in an orderly way doth appeare." Forty years later in the Saybrook Platform the colony thought it had "better light."

Although churches in Connecticut appeared to split over the half-way covenant, in reality two much more fundamental problems divided the ministers and laymen of Connecticut. First was the question of ecclesiastical authority, both within each church and among the churches. Congregational autonomy and lay control of the keys to the kingdom were being seriously challenged by men who thought in terms of presbyteries and rule by the elders. Second was the idea of restricted church membership. Both civil authorities and some of the ministers were questioning the policy that kept so many decent Christians outside of the churches, and they were calling for more charitable tests. Both these issues were partially hidden by the dispute over baptism until the late 1660's; but once in the open, they continued to plague Connecticut churches for the next century.

FOUR

Connecticut's Resolution: 1667-1690

WHILE the Connecticut General Court sought an answer to the questions of membership and baptism, it directed the churches in the colony to "suspend all matters controversall." But the Court moved too slowly, and the issues were too important for the churches to put debate aside for thirty months. Where controversy already existed, the churches simply ignored the Court's injunction. Ostensibly the half-way covenant remained the source of this strife. But as churches argued and then split over baptism, it became obvious that the status of the children of the church was only a superficial issue. Behind the factionalism lay basic conflicts between Congregational and presbyterial polity. The nature of ecclesiastical authority and church membership was the provocation for debating baptism. After 1670 the half-way covenant ceased to be a controversial issue and Congregationalists concentrated on the real threat to the New England Way.

Members of the Hartford church rarely stopped quarreling in those months for which the Court had recommended silence. Although Whiting and his followers continued to condemn Haynes' innovations, the Hartford church introduced the half-way covenant in late 1667 or early 1668. If Whiting's dissenters chose not to use it, that was their affair; but the majority of members, without first qualifying for communion, could now have their children baptized. When the General Court announced its policy of toleration in 1669, both factions agreed to call a church council to help them resolve their differences. The only practical solution the council offered was the separation of Whiting and his followers from First Church Hartford. The fall session of the General Court, after hearing the council's advice, approved the organization of Second Church Hartford. Haynes made one final gesture to avert schism. If the dissenters would remain in First Church, they could have Whiting minister to them according to their own light. Whiting rejected the offer. His primary concerns were the purity of the church and the maintenance of Congregational principles; to remain in a church dominated by Haynes meant compromising both.

February 22, 1670, thirty-one Hartford families joined together to create Second Church Hartford. Ironically, the new church immediately adopted the half-way covenant! At the first meeting thirty-six children of the church owned the covenant, and in the next few weeks six half-way members had children baptized.[1] When the same opportunity had been available in First Church Hartford, they had rejected

[1] Walker, *First Church in Hartford*, pp. 204, 208; "Woodbridge-Baxter Correspondence," p. 578; Edwin P. Parker, *History of the Second Church of Christ in Hartford*, Hartford, 1892, pp. 49-60. The initial membership represented about 20 percent of Hartford's inhabitants; *Wyllys Papers*, p. 191.

it. One conclusion appears inescapable: the half-way covenant had not precipitated the schism in the Hartford church. In his journal Simon Bradstreet identified the crucial issue. "This winter Hartford chh. divided Mr. Whyting and his party, refusing to hold communion with Mr. Haynes and his party bec[ause] of some differences in point of chh government. Mr. Haynes and those with him being lookt upon as Presbyterians."[2] This was the fundamental cleavage. Both factions focused on baptism because it presented a concrete issue, and in the early stages of the debate it had represented a significant difference of opinion. Baptism served its symbolic purpose well, but by 1670 most strict Congregationalists had abandoned their opposition to the enlargement of baptism. Thus when the crisis in Hartford was resolved by separation, Second Church simply discarded the illusory element and adopted the half-way covenant.

In Stratford, as in Hartford, the church suffered from a serious internal division. Although legally Stratford had but one church, for three years two congregations, each with its own minister and its own polity, held separate services in the meetinghouse. This dual establishment proved to be a constant source of irritation, and the bickering between the factions finally forced the General Court to intervene. In the spring of 1669 the Court ordered Israel Chauncy to allow Zechariah Walker and his followers to use the meetinghouse three hours every Sabbath. Six months later the Court recommended reunion of the two congregations; but when attempts at reconciliation

[2] Bradstreet, "Journal," p. 45.

failed, the majority of the church, led by Chauncy, simply forbid Walker's faction to use the building.[3]

The excluded minority, in turn, asserted its independence; and May 1, 1670, twenty Stratford men organized the Second Church. Four days later John Woodbridge, Jr., of Killingworth, Benjamin Woodbridge of Windsor, Joseph Haynes of Hartford, and Samuel Wakeman of Fairfield assisted in the ordination of Zechariah Walker as pastor of the new church. All four ministers participating in the ordination represented a broader church way than Chauncy and the strict Congregationalists. In fact all except Wakeman endorsed the creation of comprehensive parishes. One accurate index to any minister's sentiments about church membership was the clergy who participated in his ordination. Elders rarely crossed party lines for an installation; liberals ordained liberals, and conservatives ordained conservatives.

Walker immediately introduced the half-way covenant in Second Church Stratford and called upon the children of the church to accept their covenant obligations. But he also took the new church beyond the recommendations of the Half-Way Synod. Originally the revisionists' program had provided for the continuation of ecclesiastical discipline and the covenant relationship by stipulating that children of the church might have their offspring baptized upon owning the covenant. Thus half-way members and their children at least descended from regenerate stock. In Stratford's new church this was no longer assured. From the beginning Walker also admitted "stran-

[3] Cothren, *Woodbury*, pp. 128-130.

gers" into church membership without requiring from them any evidence of saving faith. Inhabitants of Stratford who had no previous connection with the church now had an entry, short of full communion, into the church. Between 1670 and 1675 seven men and five women joined the church by virtue of the half-way covenant. After they had "stood propounded" for two weeks, Walker baptized them and they qualified for the same privileges as the children of the church. These new members presented no evidence "concerning the life, & knowledge, & long desires after the enjoym[en]t of ch[ris]t in his ordinances" such as candidates for full communion offered. They were expected only to demonstrate Christian knowledge and a desire to accept the covenant, and to lead civil lives.[4] With this innovation Walker's church came very close to the recommendations made by the Connecticut General Court shortly after the Pitkin petition. Second Church still restricted admissions to the Lord's Supper to visible saints; but persons previously outside the church could join, have themselves and their children baptized, and be accounted members of the church. The Stratford freemen who had condemned Israel Chauncy in 1665 for failing to open the church now had a champion in Walker and an answer to their grievances.

In the spring of 1673 most of the members of Second Church decided to leave Stratford and establish a new town and parish in Woodbury, Connecticut. The migration probably resulted from continued friction

[4] Records of the First Congregational Church in Woodbury, Connecticut, MS, Conn. State Library, *1*, pp. 1-3.

with Chauncy's congregation and from the desire for more land. The new town gave Walker and his congregation the opportunity to keep experimenting with church membership free from the scrutiny of hostile neighbors. In the next thirty years Walker admitted over one hundred persons to the church—virtually all the inhabitants of the town—and many of these joined for the first time as half-way members. By the end of the century, however, half-way membership had almost disappeared from the Woodbury church. Every adult in the church qualified for communion. Decisions regarding admission to full communion were made by the elders after private consultation with the candidate, and the question was no longer put before the congregation for its consideration. In a single generation Zechariah Walker had transformed his church: he eliminated public recitals of the conversion experience; he significantly eased the requirements for admission to communion; and, he made Woodbury into a truly comprehensive parish.[5]

First Church Stratford, from which Walker and his followers had separated, maintained its strict Congregational polity for two decades after the schism. Not until June 1689 did the congregation finally vote "that Bapt: should be extended to the Infants of those qualified according to the 5t prop of synod 62." But Chauncy refused to carry this innovation as far as Walker had his in the early days of Second Church. Half-way membership was only the privilege of those whose parents already shared in

[5] Cothren, *Woodbury*, p. 135.

the church covenant. Inhabitants without a prior church connection could enter the church and have their children baptized only by demonstrating their saving faith; Stratford kept the church covenant "tribal." Nor apparently did Chauncy encourage children of the church to take advantage of half-way membership. Although within two weeks of the vote twenty persons "received the covenant and their children were baptized," relatively few children owned the covenant after this initial flurry. The half-way covenant had no significant effect on Stratford's membership until a mass covenant renewal in 1698.[6] The schism in Stratford and the course pursued by the two churches in the succeeding decades illustrate the degree to which both clergy and laity were divided about the nature of the church.

In Connecticut the most successful advocate of the presbyterial polity which Walker finally adopted in Woodbury was John Woodbridge, Jr., the minister in Killingworth from 1666 to 1679. Woodbridge shared with his entire family an aversion to strict Congregationalism. His father was minister at Newbury, Massachusetts, New England's oldest presbyterial parish; his uncle, Thomas Parker, and distant cousin, James Noyes, had for several decades been major critics of the New England Way; and, his brother Benjamin and brother-in-law Simon Bradstreet both labored in Connecticut parishes to enlarge church membership. To anyone with Woodbridge's convictions, Killingworth offered a challenge. He

[6] Stratford, Connecticut, First Congregational Church Records; 1688-1812, MS, Conn. State Library, *1*, p. 24.

wrote Richard Baxter that at the time of his ordination he had "found above 60 unbaptized persons, men, women, and children, though the whole plantation consist not above 30 householders."[7] This means that in 1666 at least 40 percent of Killingworth's inhabitants had no church connection.[8]

Woodbridge attacked what he considered a deplorable situation by revamping the requirements for admission to full communion and eliminating the traditional public testimony of saving faith. Candidates first came to Woodbridge to "declare their desires"; then the pastor informed the congregation "to the intent that whosoever know them to lye under Scandall and unsuitablenesse for that ordinance would according to rule seeke a reformation of it." If the congregation had no objections, "I Examine them concerning their knowledge and proficiency in the way of life, of the understanding of the Nature of the Sacraments, and the Qualifications of every Communicant." When candidates passed this personal examination, Woodbridge declared "to the church that there is nothing Appearing why they would not partake with us in that holy feast." Thus, although Woodbridge undermined the congregation's role in determining an individual's fitness for communion and assumed the obligation himself, he did not, it would seem, admit persons indiscriminately.

[7] "Woodbridge-Baxter Correspondence," p. 576.

[8] Based on the estimate of 5.7 persons per household in the colonial period; Evarts Greene, *American Population*, New York, 1932, p. xxiii.

Initially, however, Woodbridge encountered opposition to this innovation because the members feared "the infected and Infectious will steale in . . . unlesse every brother be allowed a feeling of his pulse and smelling of his Breath and handling of his necke and hands lest he should prove a smooth supplanter. . . ." It was a habit "so pleasing to Naturall pride" that Woodbridge found it difficult to make his congregation "vomit it up." By 1671 Woodbridge had overcome the scruples, and he reported that "all Christian inhabitants are under the care, Inspection, and Government of the Eldership. . . ."[9]

Although Woodbridge gave Killingworth one of the most comprehensive parishes in Connecticut and set an example for other presbyterialists to emulate, he remained dissatisfied. He wrote Baxter that Killingworth was "little more than the embryo of a presbyterian church." Certainly Killingworth lacked the structured interchurch relation of Presbyterianism, and Woodbridge may have felt the elders still lacked full church power. Even so, his polity was sufficiently radical to earn the disfavor of the neighboring churches in Guilford and Saybrook. ". . . our next neighbours have both refused to joyne with us at the Lords table and also to admit our members occasionally into their Synaxis."[10] Although he was dissatisfied, in five years Woodbridge had realized two of the presbyterialists' goals: he had opened church membership to almost all inhabitants, and he

[9] "Woodbridge-Baxter Correspondence," p. 577.
[10] *loc.cit.*

had transferred most church power from the congregation into the hands of the elders.

Of all the other Connecticut churches only Wethersfield developed a comprehensive parish comparable to Killingworth's in the same period. Although the transformation of Wethersfield into a parish church was achieved during the ministry of Gershom Bulkeley (1667-1677), Bulkeley built his policy upon the foundation laid by his predecessors. Three former ministers of the church had endorsed the half-way covenant, and one, Joseph Haynes, favored a presbyterial polity.[11] By 1667 a majority of the Wethersfield congregation also favored an easier admissions policy, and as Haynes' successor the church chose Bulkeley, who had unsuccessfully attempted to introduce presbyterial polity in the New London church several years earlier. Certainly Wethersfield was familiar with Bulkeley's record in New London, since his innovations had precipitated his resignation.

In Wethersfield Bulkeley found a congregation more sympathetic to his ideas. In four years he brought 350 new members into the church, although the total population of Wethersfield was less than 600. This remarkable increase in membership transformed the Wethersfield church from a select congregation of a minority of the town's inhabitants

[11] Felt, *Ecclesiastical History*, *I*, p. 88. Henry B. Stiles, *The History of Ancient Wethersfield, Connecticut*, New York, 1904, p. 159, asserts that John Russell, Jr., Wethersfield's pastor from 1650 to 1659, was inclined toward presbyterial polity. If so, his views did not extend to church membership, since Russell became a major critic of the half-way covenant and of Stoddardeanism while he was minister in Hadley.

into a true parish church. John Woodbridge wrote: "There are but 2 Townes in the jurisdiction wherein all the Christian Inhabitants are under the care, Inspection, and Government of the Eldership, *vid.* Wethersfield . . . and my own Cure. . . ."[12] Obviously neither Killingworth nor Wethersfield needed the half-way covenant; ministers in both towns had extended baptism and church discipline far beyond the recommendations of the Half-Way Synod.

After Gershom Bulkeley resigned his pastorate in New London, the pulpit there remained vacant for more than two years. New London had had considerable difficulty finding a minister who satisfied its idea of proper polity. From 1657 to 1659 part of the congregation had tried to force Richard Blinman to accept the half-way covenant. Although Blinman successfully resisted, he finally resigned in despair and migrated to Newfoundland. Gershom Bulkeley, Blinman's successor, had posed a different problem for the church: he wanted too many changes in the traditional New England Way. He, too, left New London and found more compatible surroundings. When the church called Simon Bradstreet in 1667, the congregation hoped it had found a moderate who would introduce the half-way covenant without destroying the essence of Congregationalism.

Bradstreet preached in New London for almost three years before his ordination in 1670. Since Gershom Bulkeley and Joseph Haynes participated in the ordination, it seems clear that Bradstreet was not a strict Congregationalist, and that he may have had

[12] "Woodbridge-Baxter Correspondence," p. 576.

broader views of church membership than the congregation had anticipated. At the time of Bradstreet's ordination the church desperately needed rejuvenation. The number of full communicants had fallen to twenty-five, twelve women and thirteen men, and this represented no more than 10 percent of the adult population.

It would appear from the church records that Bradstreet introduced the half-way covenant in the winter of 1670-1671. In February he baptized the grandchild of a communicant, although neither parent had yet joined in full communion. A week later he baptized two adults, Joshua and Elizabeth Hempstead, and the following December, their daughter Elizabeth. Neither Hempstead qualified for communion until a decade after their daughter's baptism.[13] This marked the beginning of a new admission policy for the New London church.[14] Between 1670 and 1673, in the thirteen years he served the church, Bradstreet baptized 264 persons, a large number even for fecund New Englanders.[15] This

[13] New London First Congregational Church Records; 1670-1888, MS, Conn. State Library, *I*, pp. 8-11, 62, 65.

[14] Frances M. Caulkins, *History of New London*, New London, 1895, pp. 193-194, maintains the church used the half-way covenant extensively under Bradstreet; S. Leroy Blake, *Early History of the First Church in New London, Connecticut*, New London, 1897, p. 129, asserts that only children whose parents were in full communion were baptized by the church until the ordination of Saltonstall in 1690.

[15] Caulkins claims 438 baptisms and Blake, 455, but unless part of the church records has been lost since 1897 both figures are excessive. If correct, their estimates would support the conclusion even more strongly.

figure includes an abnormally large number of multiple baptisms, that is, the baptism of several children in a single family at the same time. When many families presented children for baptism, it usually indicated that the church had recently adopted the half-way covenant. With so few persons in full communion, it is unlikely that all of those baptized could have qualified under strict Congregational polity.[16] There is no evidence in the church records that the half-way covenant ever came to a vote, or that Bradstreet required the parents who were not in full communion to own the covenant before their children were baptized.

Bradstreet, like Walker in Stratford, carried his practice beyond the innovations suggested by the Half-Way Synod. Bradstreet accepted unbaptized adults from outside the church as half-way members, baptized them, and received their children into the church (as he had done with the Hempsteads). But he retained the test of faith and repentance for admission to full communion which distinguished New London from the comprehensive parish of John Woodbridge, Jr., in Killingworth.

In his first two years as pastor Bradstreet almost doubled the number of communicants. But the eight men and thirteen women he admitted to full communion represented a relatively small number, considering that there had been no admissions since Bulkeley's resignation in 1666. In the next eleven years Bradstreet added only twenty-three persons to this select circle that could enjoy all the privileges

[16] New London Church Records, *I*, pp. 62-73.

of the church. When Gurdon Saltonstall became pastor of the church in 1690, the communicants numbered only thirty-three—an increase of eight persons in twenty years. Probably at no time in Bradstreet's tenure had the number of communicants exceeded forty-five. The ratio of communicants to population, low when Bradstreet became minister, had dropped even further by 1690. Nonetheless, Bradstreet had altered the relationship of the church to the rest of the community by bringing almost all the inhabitants under the wing of the church through baptism. The half-way membership may have failed to serve as a preparatory stage for entrance into full communion, but its broad application in the hands of Simon Bradstreet subjected many persons to church discipline who would otherwise have remained outside the effective influence of the church.[17]

The Windsor church resolved the problem of church membership less successfully than New London because the congregation was more deeply divided over the the fundamentals of polity. Although the problem had probably existed for years, John Warham's decision to stop using the half-way covenant in 1664 provoked the controversy and split the church into two factions with contrary views of baptism and discipline. Since Warham's move coincided with the congregation's search for an assistant to its aged pastor, the initial conflict centered on the choice of the new minister. When the town voted to call Nathaniel Chauncy, fourth son of Charles Chauncy, President of Harvard, the dissident faction appealed

[17] *ibid.*, *I*, pp. 8-11.

to the General Court for redress, claiming that the church had made a prior commitment to the Reverend Mr. Cheever. After considering the petition, the Court ordered new elections held in Windsor under the supervision of the Court's agent, Henry Wolcott. Of the eligible voters in Windsor (all adult males who paid the minister's rate), 90 percent cast their ballots and once again chose Chauncy, this time by a vote of 86 to 52. Chauncy obviously drew support from the entire community. With only fifty male communicants and these divided on the issue, the large plurality indicated broad support, among communicants and noncommunicants, for Chauncy and the polity he stood for.[18]

The minority, still dissatisfied, requested the Court's permission to call a second minister who would be more suited to its principles. After some consideration, the Court granted "liberty to those inhabitants that are unsatisfied and can not close with Mr. Chauncy, . . . to provide or procure an able orthodox minister . . . and this court leaves the Church at Windsor at liberty for settling Mr. Chauncy and calling him to office." Until the dissenters elected their own minister, however, the Court stipulated that they had to contribute to Chauncy's maintenance.[19] When the dissident faction finally chose Benjamin Woodbridge, it encountered considerable difficulty getting the town to accede to its choice. Once more the minority turned to the General

[18] Stiles, *Windsor*, pp. 198-199; *Wyllys Papers*, pp. 161, 170-171, 191; *Connecticut Records*, 2, pp. 73-74.

[19] Stiles, *Windsor*, pp. 199-200.

Court for aid. Reluctantly, the Court gave Woodbridge permission to preach every second Sabbath and once in the middle of each week on the condition that Chauncy, Warham, and the majority of the church would also give their assent.[20] Windsor was creating a situation similar to that which caused so much difficulty in Stratford—two congregations holding separate services in the same meetinghouse and yet remaining legally a single church.

June 21, 1668, one month after the Court announced its willingness to permit Woodbridge to preach in Windsor, Nathaniel Chauncy reinstituted the half-way covenant. His congregation voted that if persons desiring baptism for their children presented themselves to the elders "and declared to their satisfaction, their knowledge in the principles, and owned the Father's Covenant" then nothing would "be required of them in public, until they presented themselves for full communion."[21] The return to the half-way covenant failed to effect a reconciliation of the two factions. As events in the Hartford church were showing at almost the same time, the roots of church quarrels often lay deeper than the enlargement of baptism.

Despite Chauncy's gesture, dissension continued and relations between the two congregations degenerated further. One Windsor communicant had to appeal to the General Court for relief: Warham and

[20] *Connecticut Records*, 2, pp. 85-86.

[21] "Windsor Church Records," quoted in Stiles, *Windsor*, p. 197.

Chauncy had refused to baptize his child because he supported Woodbridge.[22] Apparently even though Woodbridge had his own congregation within the church, he did not have sufficient autonomy to administer the sacraments to his followers. Thus this settlement, in terms of practical polity, fell far short of what the minority had sought, and this added to the bitterness. In an effort to restore peace the General Court called a council of four ministers to meet at Windsor and recommend a course for settlement. In the interim the Court restricted Woodbridge's preaching privilege to every other Thursday in the meetinghouse.[23] Warham challenged the Court's order, suggesting that it gave the dissenters too much independence; how could they hold separate religious services without the approval of neighboring churches as required by statute.[24]

Personal antipathy and theological differences precluded easy reunion, recommendations of Court and council notwithstanding. In the fall of 1669 Woodbridge and his followers cut their ties to First Church and organized a new church. They did this in spite of warnings from the governor and the assistants that, because this congregation had not been approved by the General Court or the neighboring churches, they "doe at this time desire & advise you not to proceed

[22] George Griswold to General Assembly, October 9, 1668, *Wyllys Papers*, pp. 181-182.

[23] *Connecticut Records*, 2, p. 99.

[24] John Warham to the General Court, October 9, 1668, *Hoadly Memorial; Early Letters and Documents Relating to Connecticut; 1643-1709*, CHS *Collections*, 1932, 24, p. 14.

in your present intended ordination."[25] The only neighboring church which had sanctioned the separation was Gershom Bulkeley's presbyterial parish in Wethersfield. As Bulkeley's support would indicate, presbyterialism versus Congregationalism, not the half-way covenant, provoked Windsor's schism. Simon Bradstreet recorded in his Journal, "My Br[other] Benjamin Woodbridge was ordained minister of the Presbyterian Party (as they are accounted) of Windsor."[26] Apparently Woodbridge's faction suffered no repercussions for defying the magistrates and violating the statute, since they were simply following the recommendation for peace laid down by the General Court several months earlier.

Through the 1670's the two churches continued to snipe at each other, but unlike most towns where schism occurred Windsor finally healed the breach. In 1679 the two churches rejoined and the town agreed to maintain both Chauncy and Woodbridge. When Chauncy resigned to accept a position in Hartford in 1679 and Woodbridge decided to move to Boston in 1681, the way was opened for complete reconciliation.[27] In its search for a minister who would satisfy everyone, one of the candidates Windsor considered was Isaac Foster. John Whiting wrote Increase Mather for more information about Foster, "particularly what his judgment is in respect of church order." Mather replied, "When he joyned

[25] Governor and Assistants to Benjamin Woodbridge and Others, 1669, *Hoadly Memorial*, pp. 14-15.

[26] "Bradstreet's Journal," p. 45.

[27] Stiles, *Windsor*, pp. 207-209, 211-214, 217.

the church in Charlestown [October 28, 1677] he . . . [stated] that he was not satisfyed in that practice of imposing . . . [testimony] respecting the work of grace upon such as they admitted to full communion. . . . To be sure he is as large respecting the subject of Baptisme as the Synod in 62."[28] This answer apparently satisfied Windsor's factions, and the town offered Foster the position. Had Foster come to Windsor, he would probably have retained the half-way covenant and perhaps have eased admission to full communion by eliminating public testimonies. Windsor had finally settled on a course of broad Congregationalism that stopped short of presbyterial innovations. When Foster rejected Windsor's call, the church called Samuel Mather in his place. It seems likely that Mather's views corresponded to Foster's.

The Middletown church escaped the dissension which plagued so many Connecticut churches in these years, partly because it altered its practices to accommodate shifting ecclesiastical currents and partly because the town lacked a forceful presbyterial minority. When the church ordained Nathaniel Collins in 1668, all four ministers who participated were active opponents of the half-way covenant.[29] It seems unlikely that Eleazar Mather would have traveled all the way down the river from Northampton to give his blessing to a minister who endorsed principles he abhorred. At the time of his ordination Collins prob-

[28] Quoted in Walker, *Hartford*, pp. 215-217.

[29] John Whiting, Eleazar Mather, Samuel Hooker, and Nathaniel Chauncy.

ably shared this aversion to the extension of baptism, and for a year he upheld strict Congregational polity. He restricted communion to visible saints and carefully specified in the church records that each child he baptized had at least one parent in full communion.[30] However, in the middle of his second year in Middletown Collins started distinguishing between persons "received as members in full communion" and those admitted to "meer membership . . . and the priviledges Immediately belonging thereunto." Although this distinction indicates a shift in practice, the Middletown church did not formally accept the half-way covenant until January 1670. "The Church Agreed that all the adult children of the church, Males and Females in the state of Innitiation should bee called upon publickly & sollemly to owne the Covenant, not haveing before done it."[31] Not until after this vote were the first children of half-way members presented for baptism.

The response to this innovation was not completely satisfactory and apparently a number of the children of the church refused to participate, either from disinterest or scruples. In 1672 the church set apart a

[30] Collins may have been more charitable in baptism than the synod recommended, but the phrasing of the church records is ambiguous. He baptized several persons "such as were come to years of discretion" and had them "lay hold upon their parents covenant for themselves." Middletown Church Records, MS, Conn. State Library, January 11, 1668/69. The synod held: "They that are come to years of discretion . . . are to covenant by their own personal act." However, "themselves" may mean the children professed personal faith.

[31] Middletown Church Records, p. 70.

fast day "to owne the children of the church," particularly those "whoe have not as yet publickly owned the covenant and been owned by the church explicitly in that way." The congregation hoped that setting apart a special day would "informe them of and acquaint them with, that confession of faith and order, with the awfull covenant bond and them under the Ingagement thereof."[32] Perhaps with special pleading the reluctant children would accept their obligations.

In the few years immediately following the adoption of the half-way covenant, the Middletown church enjoyed a sizable increase in communicants. The total grew from 87 to 120, an increase of 38 percent, without any apparent relaxation of the requirements. Although there is no concrete evidence of any connection between the adoption of the half-way covenant and the increase in full communicants, that the two came so close together suggests a possible relation. It is also very likely that Collins judged the evidence of saving grace with more charity than other strict Congregationalists. From the outset a very large percentage of Middletown's adult population qualified for communion. In 1668 the number of male communicants exceeded the number of freemen in the town, and in the following decade this ratio increased.[33] In light of the large initial membership of the church and the religious malaise that is normally associated with this period, the increase in

[32] *ibid.*, February 28, 1671/72.

[33] *Wyllys Papers*, p. 190; Middletown Church Records, November 4, 1668.

communicants after 1670 seems even more extraordinary.

Collins' departure from strict Congregationalism in 1670 reaffirms the conclusion that the enlargement of baptism no longer generated significant controversy for most ministers and churches, despite the apparent bitterness of the prior decade. By the early 1670's the majority of strict Congregationalists had accepted the half-way covenant or at least tolerated it among their colleagues. It is suggestive that when Collins shifted his position in 1670, three of the four ministers who had participated in his ordination had also submitted to the same innovation. Only Samuel Hooker of Farmington still resisted. But in Middletown, because Collins maintained a high level of full communicants, the church did not depend on the half-way covenant to preserve ecclesiastical discipline and influence.

Although family and ministerial connections often indicated the attitude a minister had toward matters of membership and discipline, they did not always accurately reflect the polity followed by his church. For example, in 1664 the Reverend James Noyes moved to Stonington, Connecticut, from the most completely presbyterial parish in Massachusetts—Newbury; and, Noyes was related to the Woodbridge-Parker-Noyes family, which tried so hard to supplant the traditional Congregational polity of Massachusetts and Connecticut churches. But Noyes labored for ten years in Stonington prior to his ordination without impressing these views upon the inhabitants. When the church was formally gathered in 1674, it followed the practice, traditional in Congregationalism, of starting with a small nucleus of visible saints.[34] In the next five years additions to the original nine "pillars" were few—only eleven women and eight men. By 1689 Noyes had admitted just fifty-two persons to full communion which was less than half the adult population. If Noyes had made any effort to open church membership along the lines followed by his relatives, the church had blocked the bid.[35]

Thomas Minot, one of the earliest settlers of Stonington, wrote in his diary that the church baptized only the children of church members, yet the church records seem to contradict his assertion. Captain James Pendleton had a child baptized in 1675 and another in 1679, although he was not admitted to full communion until November 1680. There is no indication that either Pendleton or his wife had any church connection in Stonington. The only basis he could have had for his children's baptism was his being a covenanted but noncommunicant member of another church. In at least four other instances Noyes baptized children and adults before either parent had a visible connection with the church.[36] However, before 1689 there is no indication that Noyes required

[34] Richard A. Wheeler, *History of the First Congregational Church, Stonington, Connecticut; 1674-1874*, Norwich, 1875, pp. 36, 87; Sidney Minor and George Stanton, eds., *The Diary of Thomas Minot; 1653-1684*, New London, 1899, p. 207.

[35] Wheeler, *Stonington*, pp. 40-41, 189.

[36] *Minot Diary*, p. 208; Wheeler, *Stonington*, pp. 189-194; the appendix of this volume contains all the admissions and baptisms of the Stonington church.

these parents to own the covenant, or that he made any appeal to the children of the church to renew their baptismal covenants. The few exceptions Noyes made to an otherwise strict Congregational polity were done without any formal sanction by the church. The first mention of owning the covenant occurred at a mass renewal in April 1689 when fifty-three persons came forward to affirm their church ties.[37]

After this mass covenant renewal church membership changed radically in Stonington, and by 1696 virtually everyone in town belonged to the church. In his first fifteen years Noyes admitted fifty-two persons to full communion; in the next thirty years he accepted 187. In all, he baptized 1,176 adults and children.[38] It took Noyes twenty-five years to convince his congregation, but he finally transformed the Stonington church into a comprehensive parish.

The polity of the Reverend James Fitch in the Norwick church reflected the changes that were occurring in Connecticut after 1670, and it also indicated that pressures other than presbyterialism could change men's minds. John Davenport had counted Fitch among those "professedly against this new way, both in judgment and practise" in 1666. The Norwich pastor was one of the two conservatives selected by the General Court in 1668 to work out a solution to the colony's ecclesiastical problems, and in the fall of the same year he again represented the conservatives in the peacemaking attempt at Windsor.

[37] Wheeler, *Stonington*, p. 193.
[38] *ibid.*, p. 45.

Fitch modified his strict Congregationalism in the mid-1670's and in 1676 encouraged his Norwich congregation to adopt the half-way covenant.

Concerned by the spiritual condition of his church and the state of affairs in New England, Fitch sought some way to impress on his people their obligations to God. The course he chose was "solemnly to renew our covenant in our church state . . . this is a time when the Providence of God does in a knocking and terrible manner call for it."[39] One of the primary shortcomings of Norwich that Fitch singled out was the church's neglect of the children of the church. The Covenant of Reformation which Norwich adopted committed the church to an elaborate program of discipline and catechizing for the children, thereby insuring proper Christian nurture. The children of the church "when grown up and at their own disposal, . . . should be required to take hold of the Covenant of their Fathers, or at least should use meanes to prepare themselves for it." Any children who neglected this duty were to be admonished, and if they persisted, to be "cut off from the Congregation by the dreadful ordinance of excommunication."[40] Fitch was applying all the suasion and pressure of

[39] Fitch to the Council, March 13, 1676; quoted in Frances Caulkins, *History of Norwich*, Hartford, 1866, p. 123.

[40] *ibid.*, p. 123. Although this quotation can be interpreted as an indication of Fitch's encouraging the unconverted to seek personal faith, my account of Fitch's actions seems more compatible with his phrasing and that of the developing ecclesiology. The emphasis on "require" would be, for a Congregationalist, inappropriate if applied to the covenant of grace but not to the half-way covenant. Although the idea of "excommunication" for non-

the church to keep the children within the fold. The times cried out for an affirmation of the faith, and Fitch adapted his church's polity to achieve it.

First Church New Haven, the bastion from which Davenport castigated the innovators and encouraged the Fitches, first confronted the problem of baptism after Nicholas Street's death in 1674. The domination of ecclesiastical affairs in New Haven by Street and Davenport had precluded any serious consideration of extended baptism as long as either man was active. Street had collaborated with Davenport in the criticism of the Half-Way Synod, and although Davenport's abrupt departure for First Church Boston in 1668 terminated their association and friendship, his opinions about baptism remained unchanged. At Street's death members who disagreed with the restriction of baptism had their first opportunity to discuss the issue openly. For the next eleven years the congregation argued incessantly over baptism. Opinion was so equally divided that the church was unable to find a satisfactory replacement for Street. Although several ministers temporarily supplied the pulpit in that decade, none of them was installed.[41]

The impasse ended with the calling of James Pierpont in 1684 and his ordination in July 1685. With the election of Pierpont the advocates of the half-way covenant had finally gained the upper hand. Although

---

communicants may appear contradictory, no other term existed to express the complete severing of relations between an erring member and the church. The language Fitch used is quite close to that of the Ministerial Assembly of 1657.

[41] Oscar E. Maurer, *A Puritan Church*, New Haven, 1938, pp. 51-52.

no record exists that the church formally adopted the half-way covenant, Pierpont's list of baptisms leaves no doubt that he immediately implemented the innovation. In five years he baptized 400 children, too large a number to be explained except by the half-way covenant.[42] In calling Pierpont the New Haven church rejected the legacy of Davenport and joined the mainstream of Connecticut Congregationalism.

The Fairfield church should also be included among the Connecticut churches which used the half-way covenant prior to 1690. The church adopted the practice sometime during the tenure of Samuel Wakeman (1665-1692), but when and under what conditions remains unknown. Wakeman supported the revisionist faction from the time of his ordination. He sat as one of the liberal ministers on the committee of four in 1668, and he frequently took part in the ordination of liberal ministers throughout the colony. It seems unlikely he would have been called upon so often in the 1660's and 1670's if the issue remained in doubt in his own church. But congregations could be perverse, so one can do little more than speculate about when Fairfield implemented extended baptism. Joseph Webb, when he became pastor following Wakeman's death in 1692, continued using the half-way covenant without any apparent

[42] New Haven, Connecticut, First Church of Christ and Ecclesiastical Society Records; 1639-1926, MS, Conn. State Library, *1*, p. 29; Maurer, *Puritan Church*, pp. 54-55; Leonard Bacon, "Historical Discourse Delivered at Norwich June 23, 1859," *Contributions to the Ecclesiastical History of Connecticut*, New Haven, 1861, p. 29.

opposition. The Fairfield church under Wakeman and Webb seems to have achieved a stable ratio between half-way members and communicants. Although a number of the children of the church renewed their covenants, the church consistently added an even larger number of full communicants.[43]

Against the weight of all these churches which we know enlarged baptism or opened membership to the entire community stands a single church. First Church of Christ in Farmington is the only church which we know did not accept the half-way covenant. Samuel Hooker adhered to the traditional Congregational polity from his ordination in 1661 until his death in 1697. Davenport counted Hooker among the "faithful" in 1666, and he fully justified Davenport's confidence. There is no indication that he ever departed from the principles laid down by his father in *A Survey of the Summe of Church Discipline.* But this might also explain why Farmington never adopted the half-way covenant. Thomas Hooker, although he formally upheld the New England Way, exercised far more charity in recognizing saving faith and thus came closer to the older Puritan standards of professing the true faith and living an upright life than those who sought the "pure church" more strenuously. Perhaps Samuel Hooker preserved the spontaneity and the charity in experiential religion for which his father had been famous. That half the adult inhabitants of Farmington qualified for full communion in 1680 suggests this was the case. Farming-

[43] Frank S. Child, *An Old New England Church*, Fairfield, 1910, pp. 42-43.

ton could maintain the orthodoxy of the first generation because it softened the harshness of the practice which made the half-way covenant necessary.[44]

This chapter has surveyed the baptismal practices of half the Connecticut churches founded prior to 1690. Undoubtedly some other churches for which evidence is no longer available also rejected the half-way covenant and preserved strict Congregational polity. Information is particularly scarce for southern and western Connecticut where we can determine the practices of only four of the thirteen existing churches. These dismal figures prompt a *caveat*. Conclusions drawn from the experience of half the churches in the colony are only tentative. But Connecticut's experience, so far as it can be ascertained, casts new light on the half-way covenant.

Enlarged baptism, whether in the form of the half-way covenant or the comprehensive parish, dominated the churches of Connecticut by 1690. Thirteen of the fourteen churches discussed here significantly eased the requirements for baptism, and the experience of the missing churches probably does not differ appreciably from this average. In the twenty-five years between 1665 and 1690 Connecticut churches abandoned the traditional New England Way and adapted themselves to new institutional demands. If one of the primary purposes of the half-way covenant was to liberalize baptism and extend church

[44] Farmington, Connecticut, First Church of Christ Records; 1652-1938, MS, Conn. State Library, pp. 101-103; *Wyllys Papers*, p. 191.

discipline, the churches in Connecticut achieved that goal. Scores of children in the third and fourth generation who would once have been cut off from the church received the first ordinance and were placed under the watchful eye of the congregation.

The tradition to extended baptism started slowly, however. Despite the concurrence of many ministers and laymen, the churches lagged notably in changing their polity. Only Windsor adopted the half-way covenant after the Ministerial Assembly of 1657, and Warham reversed this decision in 1664. Although the debate over baptism had started dividing congregations, probably not one church in the colony was practicing the half-way covenant in early 1667. The first signs of change appeared the next winter when Hartford implemented the innovation, followed shortly by Windsor's reinstitution of the half-way covenant. The decisive years were 1670-1671 when seven more churches altered their practice to accommodate part of the community formerly excluded from baptism. Of the churches whose adoption of the half-way covenant we can date, 70 percent made the change by the end of 1671. Two more accepted the principle in the middle of the decade, and the last two in the 1680's.

Several factors contributed to the delay in implementing the recommendations of the Ministerial Assembly and the Half-Way Synod. The General Court's involvement in ecclesiastical affairs created new confusion. While it searched for a decisive answer to the questions of baptism and membership, the Court advised mutual forbearance among the various factions. Although the debates continued, some churches may have temporized until official policy was determined. The removal of this hindrance in the spring of 1669 with the announcement of the Court's policy of "toleration" gave the churches a relatively free hand. In addition, ministers in some of the churches had to educate the members about the innovation. Until a congregation understood the half-way covenant and the necessity of altering traditional polity, there was little chance that it would accede to the innovation. The minister's endorsement of the principle was not enough; he had to convince a majority of the congregation to follow his advice and vote for the measure. Unlike Massachusetts, in the first decade of the debate (1660-1669) ministers and congregations in Connecticut appear almost equally divided in their attitude toward the enlargement of baptism. In some churches a majority of the members pulled a reluctant minister toward change in baptism. Others reversed the situation and the minister led while the congregation procrastinated. In still others, the pastor and a majority of the church agreed in principle, but a sizable minority refused to concede the issue. This relative balance of forces resulted in a number of schisms and the creation of several new churches. Only one Massachusetts church resorted to schism to resolve a debate over baptism, and this started a political battle which lasted two years. Although the pressure of an increasing population gave added impetus, the Connecticut General Court was primarily responsible for the erection of second churches in Hartford, Windsor, and Stratford.

Its decision in 1669 had virtually sanctioned schism.

If the division of opinion was so nearly equal between 1660 and 1669, why did extended baptism achieve such rapid acceptance in the next two years? Why did the division not continue to be reflected in the polity of the churches? The answer lies in the growth of the presbyterial party in the colony and the change in focus this caused. The central issue after 1669 was not whether baptism would be enlarged, but how much. Initially the debate over the half-way covenant obscured the more fundamental conflict between Congregationalists and presbyterialists. The General Court in 1664 and again in 1669 demonstrated an extremely tolerant attitude toward a more inclusive admissions policy. The recognition and tacit approval it gave to religious diversity emboldened the presbyterial faction. Led by the Woodbridges and Bulkeley, supported by Haynes, Walker, Noyes, and a large number of laymen, this party threatened to undermine the Congregational establishment. In response to the emergence of a presbyterial party the Congregationalists pulled together; the half-way covenant paled before the larger threat. Congregational ministers who had once recoiled in horror from this practice now acceded to the innovation, or at least tolerated it among their colleagues.

By 1690 the baptismal practices of the churches in Connecticut were as varied as the ministers and people who shaped them. In this diversity we can, however, discern four major groups. First and smallest were the churches which maintained strict Congregational polity and rejected enlargement of baptism in any form. Only Farmington and perhaps Branford fit in this category. The second category of churches stayed close to the traditional patterns of the New England Way but accepted the half-way covenant as an orthodox adaptation. Stratford and Second Church Hartford apparently incorporated owning the covenant into their polity, but they did not encourage members to take advantage of it. Neither church averaged more than two covenant ownings per year before 1695. Norwich, Middletown, and New Haven used the half-way covenant as the synod had originally envisioned it. They requested children of the church to own the covenant when they came of age and encouraged half-way membership. However, they did not extend this privilege to those outside the church, nor did they ease the qualifications for communion.

Those churches which ventured beyond the half-way covenant form the third group. First Church Hartford, the New London church, and Second Church Windsor permitted children of the church to have their children baptized, and they also extended this privilege, in varying degrees, to inhabitants of the town who had no church connection. Woodbury and Stonington followed the same principles and carried the practice so far that they eventually brought the entire community under the watch and care of the church. In all these churches which exceeded the recommendations of the Half-Way Synod the innovations came in several stages: first the half-way covenant; then the admission of strangers; finally, in some cases, the reaching out to encompass the whole town. Up to 1690 the churches in all three of these categories retained the essential element of regenerate membership for admission to communion. Although some of the ministers might have wished to eliminate it, the sentiments of the congregation restrained them.

The final group departed the furthest from the New England Way. The presbyterial parishes of Killingworth and Wethersfield, joined in the 1690's by Woodbury and Stonington, rejected all semblance of restricted membership. They made the sacraments available to all godly, moral men. In the presbyterial parish the half-way covenant was irrelevant; it represented a half-hearted, insufficient attempt to extend church discipline and membership. Wethersfield and Killingworth passed beyond it very early. For Woodbury and Stonington, however, the half-way covenant bridged the gap between traditional practice and the minister's ideal of the church. The half-way covenant could lead to the destruction of the New England Way, but it did not have to.

These four categories do not reveal any apparent geographical, economic, or demographic patterns. The largest towns in the colony—New Haven, Hartford, Windsor, and Wethersfield—differed appreciably in their practices, and the small towns exhibit equal diversity. Economic circumstances apparently made no difference in the response of the churches. Commercially oriented river towns and rural agricultural communities divided in equal proportions into the various categories. Similarly, no geographical pattern emerges; in each of the three counties for which we have a reasonable sample (Hartford, Fairfield, and New London) the diversity is apparent. More information about New Haven County might reveal a slightly higher proportion of "orthodox" churches than elsewhere; thirty years of John Davenport must have had an impact.

In only one instance does the suggestion of a pattern appear. Three of the most isolated communities in the colony—Woodbury, Killingworth, and Stonington—ended the century with comprehensive parishes. Although it would be dangerous to attribute too much to this phenomenon, it does suggest that the traditional identification of religious liberalization with mercantile, urban interests is of questionable validity.

The Connecticut experience defies simple socioeconomic categorization. The response of each church was shaped by local circumstances—personalities, jealousies, tensions—within the framework of a changing ecclesiology. The Ministerial Assembly and the Half-Way Synod had reinterpreted the meaning of the covenant, but individual congregations and ministers applied it to fit their own theology and locale.

The attitude of the General Court and the existence of a strong presbyterial faction added dimensions to the debate over the half-way covenant in Connecticut that made implementation of extended baptism relatively easy. In Massachusetts neither element was present. Clerical division came from within orthodox Congregationalism, and the General Court reflected the general antipathy of the laity toward religious innovation. When Massachusetts churches finally resolved the issue after 1675, their solution was remarkably similar to Connecticut's.

FIVE

Trials of Orthodoxy: Massachusetts Churches and the Half-Way Covenant: 1662-1670

THE Half-Way Synod concluded the first chapter of the struggle to extend baptism in Massachusetts churches and opened a second one which proved equally frustrating to the revisionist clergy. Assemblies, synods, and courts recommended, but in the nuclear polity of Congregationalism the final resolution of all questions lay with the individual churches. Without the support of a majority in the churches the half-way covenant was little closer to realization after the synod than before. Unfortunately for the revisionists the laity in Massachusetts had substantial reservations about extending baptism.

If the Massachusetts Clergy had held all the authority that historians frequently attribute to them, the half-way covenant would have received general acceptance before the synod met. But the revisionists made very slow progress prior to 1662. When the synod convened, only five of the thirty-four churches in the colony had accepted the half-way covenant in principle, and two of these had never used it. In the decade following the synod nine more churches accepted the principle: in one, not a single person owned the covenant and in two others, only a small fraction of those eligible took advantage of the opportunity. The traditional picture of seventeenth-century Massachusetts—a conservative clergy restraining the liberal impulses of the laity—seriously distorts reality. The ministers favored liberalization of church membership through the half-way covenant. But, as contemporary accounts frequently pointed out, they confronted a laity hostile to religious innovation. ". . . in very many of the churches a number of brethren were so stiffly and fiercely set the other way, that the pastors did forbear to extend their practice."[1] John Woodbridge, Jr., phrased it more graphically: "Many of the Ministers would launch out further but . . . the Churches are such a heavy stone at the ministers leggs that they cannot fly their owne Course."[2] Even when ministers successfully enlisted a majority of their congregation in support of the half-way covenant, they often deferred its implementation "for fear of making a breach in their respective churches."[3]

Why did church members resist the half-way covenant? It is quite probable that the people had learned their lessons too well. For two generations ministers had taught them that the New England Way perfectly imitated the Biblical model for Christian churches, and the limitation of membership to visible

[1] Mather, *Magnalia*, 2, Bk. 5, p. 266.

[2] "Woodbridge-Baxter Correspondence," p. 574.

[3] William Hubbard, *A General History of New England from the Discovery to 1680*, Boston, 1840, p. 570.

saints was an integral part of that way. The laity now balked at the idea that children of the church retained their membership and passed on the covenant relation to their children without a regenerative experience.[4] To compound this problem a vocal minority of the clergy insisted on telling the laity just how far the innovation departed from original purity. Thus encouraged, church members confronted their ministers with vigorous arguments against the half-way covenant. In the clerical dissenters the laity saw proof that the issue remained unresolved. Undoubtedly the cry "innovation" frightened many persons, but pride surely contributed its mite to the opposition of many full communicants; having themselves attained a difficult goal, many must have resented any cheapening of the church covenant. The minister's quandary was how to overcome this conservatism and hostility without splitting his congregation.

The Dorchester church of Richard Mather illustrates the tenacity with which the laity clung to a familiar orthodoxy. But Mather never allowed his congregation to rest comfortably in its opposition to the half-way covenant. Almost every year he found some pretext for introducing the issue and bringing it to debate. He read and reread the propositions of the synod to the members; he preached on the church's responsibility toward the children of the church; he made the church vote on the question every time he found a parent who was willing to own the covenant so as to have his child baptized. If

[4] Perry Miller, "Solomon Stoddard, 1643-1729," *Harvard Theological Review*, 1941, *34*, p. 290.

the congregation gave ground, he took full advantage of it. The unwillingness of the members to compromise what they considered "first principles" led them into strange paths. When Mather presented the case for one woman's admission as a half-way member, "she being a member of this Church by her parents Covenant," the congregation sought an alternative solution. ". . . after much adjetation the Issue was that Mr. Mather should speake with Mrs. Taylor to see if she would join in full communion with the Church & soe come to lords Supp[er] alsoe." This, of course, would have qualified her children for baptism and solved the impasse. To accept the half-way covenant was unorthodox, but the members considered easing the path into full communion a palatable solution. Mrs. Taylor felt otherwise. "She did not Judge her self as yet fitt for the Lords Supp & therfore durst not adventure ther uppon but yet did desier baptizme for her Children. . . ." Reluctantly the church refused.[5] Had she been less scrupulous, had she wanted baptism for her children above all, Mrs. Taylor could easily have taken advantage of the alternative course offered by the congregation.

Those who mark the half-way covenant as certain proof of decline might well consider this second dimension of "religious scrupulosity." In Mrs. Taylor it appeared as the unwillingness to enter full communion because she considered herself unfit, although she qualified by all external signs and her unwillingness meant leaving her children unbaptized. More frequently scrupulosity appeared in the reluctance

[5] *Dorchester Church Records*, October 24, 1668, p. 55.

of persons to utilize the half-way covenant even when it became available to them. If we can assume that most persons wanted church membership for themselves or for their children, what restrained them? Why did ministers have to plead with the children of the church to own the covenant, and why did churches have to threaten admonition or excommunication to those who refused? Had the concept of testified regenerate membership as the only proper entry into the church become so ingrained in their minds that parents preferred to leave their children unbaptized rather than use a questionable means?

This pattern of reluctance appeared in Charlestown and was repeated in a number of Massachusetts churches. Both of Charlestown's ministers, Thomas Shepard, Jr., and Zechariah Symmes, were active advocates of the new polity and defenders of the synod's recommendations. Symmes had, with three other ministers, presented the propositions to the General Court, and Shepard had published his father's manuscript defending extended baptism. In January 1663, four months after the synod adjourned, Charlestown's elders read the preface to the propositions to their congregation and reported that the principles were "generally well approved." At a second church meeting four weeks later they invited members of the church to raise any objections they might have to all or part of the synod's recommendations. More than three-fourths of those present participated in the discussion that followed and then acknowledged their approval "to the whole book." The members requested "that the will of God therein might be attended; & upon a *vote silentiary* propounded, it was so carried, nemine contradicente. . . ." [6]

Although the church had unanimously accepted the principle of the half-way covenant, implementation did not automatically follow. Twenty-two months later the half-way covenant remained unused in Charlestown. Once more Symmes and Shepard carried the question to a church meeting. ". . . in order to the effectual practice [of the innovation] . . . it was propounded to vote whether the brethren were satisfyed soe far forth as that there might be a proceeding to the practice thereof. . . ." Once again the congregation had the opportunity to raise objections, but the members remained silent and voted to practice the half-way covenant.[7]

The first children of the Charlestown church owned the covenant in July 1665, and it appeared that the church had made the transition to extended baptism with comparative ease. However the initial implementation was only superficial. In the next ten years only nine persons owned the covenant, while in the same years ninety persons joined in full communion.[8] Adoption and implementation of the half-way covenant had left church membership in Charlestown virtually unaffected, despite both ministers' advocacy of the practice. The members recognized the validity of the principle as explained by the elders, but they refused to use it within their own families.

[6] *Records of the First Church in Charlestown, Massachusetts; 1632-1789*, Boston, 1880, p. ii.

[7] *ibid.*, pp. iii-iv.

[8] See Appendix, Graphs 7-8.

John Eliot had experienced a very similar set of events in his Roxbury church a half-decade earlier. Although the members adopted the half-way covenant in 1658, only twelve persons took advantage of it in ten years.[9] Even Third Church Boston, established by Davenport's opponents in 1669 to preserve the half-way principles,[10] used the practice sparingly in its early years. Although one would expect immediate and full implementation of the innovation where the majority of the congregation had risked so much in defense of the idea, in five years a total of ten children of the church accepted half-way status. In all three of these churches effective implementation of the half-way covenant came only when the conditions in Massachusetts had drastically altered. Although the half-way covenant was incorporated into the polity of each, the children of the church seemed most hesitant to accept it.

In several instances a church's conversion to the half-way covenant proved so superficial that it later reversed its position and rejected the innovation. The Dorchester church changed thusly within weeks in 1655; John Warham returned his Windsor church to the older system after using the half-way covenant only six years. The undercurrent of lay resistance would emerge when the prospects for overturning the innovation appeared good. This happened in First Church Boston after the deaths of John Norton and John Wilson. The congregation decided to fill the vacancy with an avowed critic of extended bap-

[9] See Appendix, Graphs 5-6.

[10] See Chap. VI, pp. 156-165.

tism. First Church had favored the adoption of the half-way covenant in 1661 but had never used it, and the election of John Davenport in 1667 insured that it would not be used in the foreseeable future. The members had given ground to Wilson and Norton, but they took the first opportunity to change the church's direction by selecting a minister hostile to the innovation.

Lay opposition to extended baptism, although clearly a powerful restraint in the majority of churches, did not dominate every congregation. Part of the complexity of measuring the response to the half-way covenant derives from the independent structure of Congregationalism. Each church responded to local issues and local traditions, as well as to the general ecclesiastical situation in the colony, when it confronted the synod's proposals. In some parishes this meant rejection, or at best limited use, of the half-way covenant. In a few churches members accepted the innovation with few reservations and made it an effective part of their polity.

In 1669 John Brock's Reading congregation adopted the half-way covenant without any apparent opposition, but Brock had spent seven years guiding the church toward that decision. Although Brock had once baptized the child of a half-way member of the Ipswich church who was living in Reading, he did not extend the same privilege to members of his own congregation until the church had voted on the principle. After educating the members regarding their responsibility to the children of the church and overcoming their scruples, he could finally report in 1669:

"The minds of the Brethren [were] fixed as to the children's duty to owne the covenant inorder to their childrens Baptism."[11] At a church meeting the congregation accepted three propositions which incorporated the heart of the synod's recommendations into Reading's polity.

Immediately after this vote the members prepared a list of all the mature children of the church "that according to their number a place of meeting for their awakening might be appoynted." Those affected were brought together and "instructed referring to the beauty of owning the Covenant & exhorted, comforted & charged as the case of any of them required. . . ." If anyone desired to own the covenant after he had given the matter serious consideration, he had "liberty to come to the Elder to be examined." If he satisfied Brock and no one raised objections to his moral life, he could then proceed to own the covenant and have his children baptized. Although Reading was only a small town, thirty children of the church owned the covenant in the first year, and the church averaged seven new half-way members annually for the next six years.[12]

Several other churches apparently made the transition to the half-way covenant in this decade without serious problems. The Beverly church, created from the part of Salem which lay across the Bass River, adopted the half-way covenant at the time of its or-

[11] Church Records of the Old Town of Reading, Massachusetts, Reading Public Library, p. 9; "Ester Dix an Adult member of the Church of Christ in Ipswich She owning the covenant, had her children Baptized. . . ."

[12] *ibid.*, pp. 9-10.

ganization in 1667. Beverly encountered no problem because fifty former members of the Salem church formed the nucleus of its membership, and in their old parish the half-way covenant had been used for almost two years.[13] However, the church records do not reveal how extensively Beverly used the half-way covenant. The Dedham church probably began using the innovation in October 1663. At least this is suggested by the change in style of John Allin's entries in the church records. Until then the pastor had simply written "admitted" when someone joined the church, but after 1663 he specified admission "to full communion." One of his entries suggests the difference in status: "Samuell Gay was received to full communion in this church & his wife to be a member of it. . . ." In the remainder of his records, Allin carefully distinguished between those "admitted to membership" and those "received to full communion."[14]

Samuel Whiting successfully introduced the half-way covenant in the Lynn church about 1665, but his congregation restricted the innovation to those members still subject to its discipline. In Massachusetts it was quite common for church members to retain membership in their original church even though they moved to a new town. In Lynn when these persons returned to own the covenant and have their children baptized, the congregation refused to accept

[13] "Records of the First Church in Beverly, Massachusetts; 1667-1772," *Historical Collections* of the Essex Institute, 1899, 35, pp. 8-10.

[14] "Dedham Church Records," Don G. Hill, ed., *A Memorial Volume*, Dedham, 1888, p. 36.

them, claiming that they were no longer "under the Watch of our Church." Whiting, who had no objections to baptizing their children, overcame the impasse by sending them to Peter Hobart in Hingham.[15] This created an anomalous situation in which Lynn church members who lived in Boston had their children baptized in Hingham. A similar incident in Roxbury in 1665 indicates that the Reverend Edmund Browne's Sudbury congregation had adopted the half-way convenant shortly after the synod adjourned. Roxbury church members, who themselves had accepted the half-way covenant, refused to allow the baptism of a child whose mother had owned the covenant in Sudbury but was living in Roxbury at the time. Like Whiting, the elders of the Roxbury church had no objection to the baptism, but were forced to send the woman to Hingham to have her child baptized.[16] Hobart was one of the few ministers who accepted a parent's desire to have his child baptized as sufficient grounds for administering the sacrament and who was free to practice what he believed.[17]

Two other churches not only accepted the principles laid down by the Half-Way Synod, but introduced liberal innovations of their own. Both Salem and Northampton discarded parts of the traditional New

[15] Samuel Whiting, Sr., to Brother Hubbard [Hobart], August 6, 1667, "Extracts from the papers of Noah Hobart," quoted in Ezra Stiles, Itineraries; 1760-1794, MS, Yale University, 3, p. 248.

[16] Edw. Denison & Thomas Weld to Peter Hobart, October 27, 1665, "Papers of Noah Hobart," Stiles, Itineraries, 3, p. 237.

[17] Stiles, Itineraries, 2, p. 394.

England Way to broaden church membership even further. Salem had made some progress in defining the status of the children of the church in 1661, and two years after the synod John Higginson felt he had gathered enough support to risk pushing through the half-way measures. He called a church meeting, read the propositions, and promised to give the members a "short writing as a help for them." Not long after he preached a sermon on Acts 3:25: "you are the children of the Covent. wch God made with your Fathers whence he delivered this Doctrine that children born of Parents in Covenant, they are children of the Covenant & continue so to be untill they be discovenanted in a way of God." When he finished, four children of the church stood up and announced their desire to own the covenant; each requested baptism for his children and defended their right to it on the basis of the sermon. Higginson "professed his willingness & readines to baptize these or any other Children of the Covenant amongst us." He saw this as his obligation, but he also wanted the peaceful assent of his congregation. "One of the great sinnes of the Countrey," he told the members, was "that so many of the children of the Covenant were unbaptized, that he would not that the sinne would lye any longer at his dore."

Higginson reminded the congregation of past debates on this matter; had he thought they would not accept their responsibility toward the children, he would never have accepted the ministry of the Salem church. The pastor frankly admitted his dilemma. On one side stood the "children of the Covenant claiming baptism for their children wch he knew not how to deny." One the other side were "some brethren that were otherwise minded." Higginson placed his prestige on the line: he would not wait any longer; he must "have liberty to act." Although he had hoped for unanimity, it could not be. God and time would have to heal the differences.

Confronted with his ultimatum, the church gave way. After lively debate the congregation voted to accept the fifth proposition of the synod and only two members dissented. July 30, 1665, after undergoing examination by the pastor, the first four members of the Salem church owned the covenant and had their children baptized.[18]

Salem paused only momentarily at the half-way covenant before stepping into more controversial innovations. Sometime in the next four months Bartholomew Gidney, one of the four who had owned the covenant in July, addressed the congregation. He requested admission to the Lord's Supper, "saying he had submitted unto Exam of the Pastor, & publickly professed his Faith & owning of the Coven[an]t [and] he saw not that anything was required of him. . . ." Several members, including Higginson, defended the appeal, and the congregation finally voted to admit Gidney. "Though with respect unto others it was left unto further consideration."[19]

Gidney's prominence in the community might explain the church's willingness to make an exception to the normal procedure. As the son of a Salem select-

[18] Salem Church Records, *1*, pp. 233-235.
[19] *ibid.*, *1*, p. 236.

man and a rising member of Salem's mercantile community, he was clearly marked for success. He owned a wharf and a shipyard, and over the next four decades filled countless public offices: selectman in 1668; deputy in the 1670's; and a councillor under Governor Joseph Dudley, Governor Edmund Andros, the provisional government, and Governor William Phipps. In addition, he commanded the Essex South Regiment and served as a member of the Court of Oyer and Terminer.[20]

The exception made for Gidney opened the doors to other less prominent persons. In December 1665 when the church admitted Gidney to full communion, the other three men who had owned the covenant in July stood with him again. This became the normal procedure in the Salem church; an individual owned the covenant one week and, if no one raised objections to his request, he qualified for full communion within the month. Testified regenerate membership, familiar to a generation of Salem church members, was eliminated for those already in covenant, and the church reverted to an earlier New England practice. This shift may have reflected Salem's Separatist heritage. Although officially Nonseparating Congregationalist, Salem had frequently endorsed Separatist views. John Higginson's father had filled the teaching office in the first years when Salem searched for a viable polity, and the lessons learned in those early years never completely disappeared.[21] The three tests the

[20] James D. Phillips, *Salem in the Seventeenth Century*, Cambridge, 1933, pp. 358, 361, 386.

[21] Morgan, *Visible Saints*, pp. 74-75.

church imposed after 1665—civil life, confession of faith, and assent to the covenant—were the same ones John Higginson had met in 1630 when at the age of fifteen he entered full communion.[22] The ecclesiastical line ran straight and unbroken.

The combination of the half-way covenant and easier access to full communion effected a major change in Salem's church membership. Baptisms particularly showed a marked increase. In the previous decade (1655-1664) Salem ministers had baptized 156 persons, an average of fifteen per year. In the twelve years following the adoption of the half-way covenant, Higginson initiated 433, or more than thirty-six annually. In the last six months of 1665 alone, he baptized twenty-eight. Obviously the introduction of the half-way covenant fulfilled a demand in the church; a significant number of parents wanted baptism for their children and took advantage of the new opportunity to realize it.

Logically the same pattern should emerge for admissions to full communion, but the church records do not support this assumption. In the five years prior to Higginson's arrival Salem admitted only twelve new communicants. Between 1661 and 1665 (Higginson's first five years) the number tripled, averaging seven annually. In the twelve months after Gidney's successful bid for membership, the number admitted leaped to twenty-four. Apparently the number of persons willing to avail themselves of this easier access to communion was limited because the

[22] Nathaniel Morton, *New England's Memorial*, Boston, 1855, p. 101.

following year only nine joined, and the average for the next five years dropped to six. Possibly the decline reflected the disinterest of many, but in an era when political rights and higher prestige accrued to church members, a more reasonable explanation is that relatively few church members dared step so far beyond accepted orthodoxy. The synod had categorically denied that owning the covenant qualified an individual for full communion. If this explanation is valid, it illustrates once again that a church could accept in principle what a majority of the congregation refused to utilize. There is additional evidence to support this theory in the practice of the Beverly church. Although gathered from Salem stock, this church never deviated from conversion as the basis for full communion.

Northampton, like Salem, carried the half-way covenant beyond the synod's recommendations. This parish also reversed the traditional pattern of Massachusetts churches: the congregation demanded adoption of the half-way covenant, and the minister resisted the innovation. Eleazar Mather, Northampton's pastor since the founding of the church in 1661, had joined Davenport and Chauncy in opposition in 1662 and never overcame his scruples against the new ways. For six years Mather kept his church in line, but in 1668 the congregation rebelled and defied the young pastor.

December 29, 1668, the church "haveing perused the result of the late Synod . . . seriously weighed, Considered and discussed what it held forth——— [illegible] therin as their mind and Counsell of God . . . we see not cause by any light from Gods word to withold our Consent & approbation . . ."[23] The members approved six propositions to guide implementation of the principles. In most respects they conformed to the statements of other churches. However, the fifth proposition spelled out, with a clarity and fullness unusual in church records, those who qualified for the church covenant and on what grounds. It was here that Northampton introduced its own innovation:

> 5. It is voted and agreed by this Church, that such amongst us being setled inhabitants that give us ground to hope in charity ther may be some good thing in them towards the Lord, tho but in the lowest degree, understanding, and beleeving the Doctrine of faith, Publickly, seriously, and freely Professing their assent therunto, not Scandelous in life, sollemnly takeing hold of the Covenant, wherin they give upp themselves and their children to the Lord and his Church, subjecting themselves with feare and humblenesse of mind to the Government of Christ therin, sincerely engaging to rest contented with that share and prtion of priviledges belonging to them that art only in a state of Education in Christ house . . . and not essay the breaking in upon the priviledges of Lords Supper and votting, untill they shall bee judged upon due Examination to hold forth such an experimentall Worke of faith . . . such persons thus

[23] Northampton, First Church of Christ, Church Records, 1661-1924, microfilm, Forbes Library, Northampton, *22*, p. *6*.

> qualifyed upon their desire, . . . may themselves be entertyned into a state of membership, and have their Children Baptized and entered. . . . Allsoe the Adult Children hitherto unbaptized of Confederate Beleevers without themselves comeing upp to foresaid qualifications may bee accepted members and themselves baptized.[24]

Mather discovered to his horror that the parish wanted not only the half-way covenant, but that it intended to open church membership to all godly inhabitants. Although the requirements appear stringent, nothing lay beyond the compass of "civil men." Honest life and good intentions could qualify anyone in Northampton for partial membership in the church. Not everyone agreed with the decision, but the majority offered to "beare with differing apprehensions of fellow brethren. . . ."[25]

Apparently low levels of church membership had not driven Northampton to this solution since church affiliation was high. By 1669 Mather had admitted seventy-one persons to the Lord's Supper. Three out of every five adults in town qualified for communion, and three out of every four inhabitants had some church connection.[26] There was no membership crisis in Northampton, and these figures would have re-

[24] *ibid.*, pp. 7-8; although unusual in 1669, this decision appears frequently in parishes after 1676 and merits attention.

[25] *ibid.*, p. 7.

[26] See James R. Trumbull, *History of Northampton*, Northampton, 1898, pp. 1, 107, 203 for church membership and population figures; the number of adults is based on Evarts Greene's estimate of 5.7 persons per family and assumes two adults per family.

flected creditably on any minister in the province. Since religious decline (if that is measured in membership) did not cause the shift, perhaps it was a new sense of the covenant and the relationship of the church to the community that motivated the church members. The church was in the process of transition from a narrower, sectarian conception of its mission to a broader, territorial view. Northampton refused to keep its doors closed to honest, religious men. Few other Massachusetts churches saw the issue in the same terms until the end of the following decade.

Ironically, Eleazar Mather and his father, although diametrically opposed during and after the synod, shared a similar fate. Dorchester frustrated Richard Mather for fifteen years and Eleazar, ministering to a congregation drawn almost exclusively from his father's parish, lived to see his church repudiate the principles he had defended for six years. Congregations then, as now, could prove a contrary lot.

In 1669 everything appeared propitious for enlarging Northampton's church membership. The new confession of faith and the new church covenant had been prepared when Eleazar Mather snatched his final victory from the revisionists. He died on July 24, 1669, before a single person could own the covenant. Any innovations in Northampton's church membership would have to wait for the ordination of a new minister.

Although Northampton and Salem carried the recommendations of the synod the farthest beyond orthodoxy, these innovations were not the remarkable aspect of the decade after 1662. More notable was the small number of churches using the half-way covenant and the hesitance of the laity to accept the idea. Endorsement of the ministers notwithstanding, most churches still adhered to the traditional New England Way. By 1670 the recommendations of the Half-Way Synod had had no significant impact on church membership in Massachusetts. They had, however, formulated a new orthodoxy with the potential to broaden church membership once lay resistance was dissipated.

The debates which followed the synod undoubtedly bolstered lay resistance to the half-way covenant, but one feels the laity were vaguely uncomfortable in their dissent. They sensed that the innovation was wrong, but the near unanimity of the clergy to whom they looked for leadership perplexed them. John Davenport took this sullen resistance, welded it into a single voice, and disrupted the ecclesiastical and political life of Massachusetts. Davenport's Boston career raised lay dissent to its highest level and his death robbed it of its vitality.

SIX

John Davenport and the Politics of the Half-Way Covenant

THE arrival in 1664 of the King's commissioners in Massachusetts temporarily silenced debate over the half-way covenant. Congregationalists put aside their differences to resist the threat to church and commonwealth, but they did not forget the half-way covenant. When the crisis had passed, the laity's hostility to the clergy's innovations still lay just beneath the surface, but John Davenport changed the quiescent hostility into open defiance. In 1667 Davenport thrust himself back into the center of controversy by accepting a call from First Church Boston. From New England's most prestigious pulpit, he rallied the synod's opponents and galvanized the laity. Within two years of his ordination Davenport had disrupted Massachusetts politics, alienated the clergy, and split First Church.

What John Wilson and John Norton had for years labored to create in First Church, Davenport destroyed in months. Wilson and Norton had eased some of the synod's recommendations into First Church's polity. Although no one had owned the covenant, the church had extended discipline and had tentatively approved the half-way principle. Despite the opposition of some prominent members, they had preserved peace in the church. But the death of Norton in 1664 and of Wilson in 1667 robbed the church of its moderate leadership. Wilson's deathbed warning to the elders that "neglect of baptizing the children of the church" would provoke God's wrath against New England made little impression.[1]

When the congregation met several weeks after Wilson's death to choose a successor, it revealed how superficial its conversion to the half-way covenant had been. Despite the protests from some members, the church voted to call John Davenport to become pastor and dispatched three messengers to New Haven bearing letters of invitation.[2] Most members had resisted implementation of the half-way covenant while Wilson and Norton lived, and at the first opportunity they set the church back on an "orthodox" course. By calling a minister who had attacked extended baptism for two decades, First Church defied the Massachusetts ministers and the innovation they advocated.

First Church's invitation coincided perfectly with Davenport's ambitions. By 1667 Connecticut had completely absorbed New Haven Colony, and Davenport's vision of a holy commonwealth had vanished. Connecticut's broad franchise and the General Court's receptiveness to religious innovation already threatened New Haven. In Boston, in the center of Congregationalism, Davenport recognized an opportunity

[1] Morton, *New England's Memorial*, p. 211.

[2] *Boston First Church Records*, *1*, p. 62.

to turn the tide of apostasy and restore the churches to purity. Two years earlier Davenport had written John Leverett, a member of First Church and a critic of the half-way covenant, expressing his "zeal for preserving Christs interests in your parts (though in N.H.C. it is miserably lost) and my unfeigned love to your colonie and my fervent desire of the wellfare of the churches." God would surely protect us, Davenport wrote, "If N.E. would returne to the first waies of reformation here begun . . . from which the compas of the last synods conclusions seems to be varied by some degrees towards the antartique."[3] The two men continued to correspond, and it is not surprising that Leverett considered Davenport an ideal successor to Wilson.

Davenport's answer to First Church displayed his eagerness: ". . . be assured of my strong inclynation to obey this call. . . . I hope to be with you this winter."[4] But despite Davenport's prodding, New Haven refused to dismiss him, and he was forced to change his plans. He now hoped to spend the winter and spring in Boston as a trial "for to find out the minde of God" and then to return to New Haven for a final decision.[5]

While Davenport made plans and cajoled his congregation, a crisis had arisen in First Church. Serious opposition developed to the choice of Davenport as

[3] John Davenport to John Leverett, June 24, 1665, Calder, *Letters of John Davenport*, pp. 252, 248-249.

[4] John Davenport to First Church, October 8, 1667, *Letters*, p. 269.

[5] *ibid.* (October 28, 1667), pp. 271-272.

pastor, and the church verged on schism. The crux of the conflict was Davenport's attitude toward the half-way covenant. Although the majority of the congregation endorsed his views, those who dissented thought the church "lay under an awfull ingagement to maintaine *the travelling truth relating to duty unto the children of the church* . . . it having bin a received and professed truth by the body of our Church."[6] Although the majority refused to reconsider, the New Haven church was deeply disturbed when it received reports "of the strong opposition of above 40 Brethren" in First Church to the calling of Davenport.[7] When New Haven wrote to Boston that it saw no cause "to resigne our Reverend Pastour to yourselves," it cited the lack of unanimity in First Church as a major reason.[8] Davenport lingered in New Haven through the winter and early spring, unable to get his dismissal, and First Church was left without a minister. As the Davenport affair dragged on inconclusively, bitterness increased, and the majority blamed the dissenters for prejudicing New Haven against First Church.

Davenport finally arrived in Boston in May 1668,

[6] "Third Church Narrative," 1691, quoted in Hamilton Hill, *History of the Old South Church Boston*, Cambridge, 1890, *I*, p. 17. This narrative is an account of the First Church schism written by members of Third Church twenty years later and includes all the major documents relating to that event. It is reproduced in its entirety in Hill.

[7] John Davenport to First Church, October 28, 1667, *Letters*, p. 271.

[8] First Church New Haven to First Church Boston, October 28, 1667, *Letters*, p. 271.

and a large crowd turned out in heavy rains to welcome him.[9] Although Davenport had left with the understanding that his stay was only temporary, he never again set foot in New Haven. John Davenport knew his mind; he had made his decision eight months earlier when the first letter arrived from Boston. With Davenport in Boston, the dissenters' hopes faded. The harder they tried to find ways to stop the ordination, the more abuse the majority heaped upon them. Church meetings broke up in disorder. Some members suggested that the dissenters get out and let the church practice what it wanted; others demanded that the elders censure the dissenters for defaming the church.[10] Twice Davenport met with his opponents, but they found no basis for reconciliation. In mid-July Davenport himself added to the bitterness between factions by using the lecture day prayers as a forum to condemn the dissenters. He knew not, he said, whether they acted "from errour in judgement, or . . . designe, [but] . . . it is evident Satan hath a great hand in it."[11] His charges did little to placate his opponents.

In late July both factions agreed to call upon a church council for advice. After listening to the arguments of both sides, the council recommended that First Church permit the dissenters to separate and erect a new church without censure. Boston needed another church for its growing population, and this action would restore peace while serving

[9] Hull, *Diary*, pp. 226-227; Felt, *Ecclesiastical History*, 2, p. 427.

[10] "Third Church Narrative," p. 25.

[11] *ibid.*, p. 24.

God's interests.[12] Two days later twenty-nine dissenters, including two deacons, petitioned the ruling elder for their dismissal from First Church. In the next church meeting, while the dissenters were absent at the request of the congregation, the remaining members unanimously rejected the petition on the grounds that any separation was premature since Davenport had not yet received his release from New Haven. And while the dissenters and their wives sat next door at the home of Captain Davis waiting for an answer, the church meeting unanimously renewed Davenport's call.[13]

November 1, 1668, Elder James Penn read the long awaited letter from New Haven: "we doe dismiss unto your holy fellowship Mr. Jo: Davenport." The church immediately admitted Davenport, who was sitting in the congregation, to full communion[14] and gave him an authoritative call to become pastor. The dissenters objected to no avail. Then Davenport rose and addressed the congregation; he accepted the call, and told the members that "the dissenters cheif reason of non complyance therein was his Crown." That "Crown" symbolized his defiance of the Half-Way Synod.[15]

The dissenters had a single objective now—separation—and would accept nothing less. When the church offered a compromise in late November, they

[12] *Dorchester Church Records*, p. 54; *Roxbury Church Records*, p. 207; "Third Church Narrative," pp. 25-26.

[13] "Third Church Narrative," p. 27.

[14] *Boston First Church Records*, *1*, p. 62.

[15] "Third Church Narrative," pp. 36-37.

rejected it. James Allin[16] asked them "if at least one of teaching officers will owne the Church seed, exercise Church watch and discipline to them according to the late Synod," would they submit to Davenport's ordination? Although this would have continued the practices established under Wilson and Norton, it still stopped short of the half-way covenant. The dissenters saw within their grasp the opportunity to implement the synod's entire program; half a loaf had no appeal.[17]

On December 9, 1668, First Church ordained John Davenport pastor and James Allin teacher. With Davenport in control the dissenters' situation became untenable. Davenport knew only one solution to the crisis—unconditional submission by the dissenters. When they refused to accept his terms, Davenport devised a stratagem to trap the dissenters. First Church would celebrate the Lord's Supper. If the dissenters participated, Davenport told the congregation, it would signify their acceptance of the church officers. If they abstained, the dissenters knew they risked censure for scorning the sacraments. On the appointed Sabbath, the dissenters attended church, but left when the sacrament was presented. Davenport had his issue, and in mid-February the church expelled two deacons from office "for setting there hands with other brethren to desire their dismission." The First Church fight was attracting so much atten-

[16] First Church called Allin to become teacher at the same time the initial overture was made to Davenport. Although no one opposed Allin, the church delayed his ordination until he had an older colleague to guide him; *ibid.*, p. 17.

[17] *ibid.*, p. 38.

tion in Boston that over 500 persons attended the church meeting at which the two deacons were ousted.[18]

When the dissenters renewed their appeal for separation at the end of March, the church again unanimously denied the request.[19] Their plea for a new church council met a similar fate. "A Councill tends to overthrow the Congregationall way," the church claimed. "There was no releife for a greived . . . Brethren in a church unless the Church will releive them." First Church threatened the dissenters with censure if they did not stop seeking their dismission and the calling of a council.[20] Confronted by this ultimatum, the dissenters took the only step possible: they defied First Church and called the council themselves.

Plans were made for a council of all the churches in eastern Massachusetts. John Allen of Dedham and John Eliot of Roxbury wrote several ministers telling them it was "high time for the Elders to interpose."[21] First Church refused to take part, claiming it was not "an orderly Councill" and "wee cannot meet and act with you in matters that concerne this Ch[urch]."[22] Despite the lack of cooperation from First Church, twenty-seven messengers representing fifteen churches met in Boston, and after three days of

[18] *ibid.*, pp. 40-49; *Boston First Church Records*, *1*, p. 62.

[19] *Boston First Church Records*, *1*, p. 62.

[20] "Third Church Narrative," pp. 52-53.

[21] *ibid.*, pp. 53-55.

[22] John Davenport and James Penn to the Council of Neighboring Churches, April 13, 1669, *Letters*, pp. 279-280.

consultation reaffirmed the decision reached the previous August. "The Dissenting Brethren might seasonably make use of their Xtian libertie unto a regular coalition in another church body."[23] When the dissenters presented this decision to First Church, the congregation denied the council's authority and refused to hear the report. It then censured the dissenters and barred them from communion.[24] Davenport could hardly view with equanimity the prospect of a new church dedicated to principles he had come to Boston to eradicate. All his past endorsements of the healing benefits of church councils were forgotten.[25] It depended on whose ox was getting gored.

The dissenters ignored the censure and asserted their independence. They asked five churches to send messengers to participate in the gathering of the new church on May 12 in Charlestown. They petitioned the magistrates for permission to proceed with the organization and received letters of approval from seven of the twelve. The conservatives tried several tactics to obstruct these plans. Davenport, Allin, and Penn went to Charlestown and presented their case against the dissenters, but the assembly remained unmoved. Later in the day, a letter arrived from the

[23] *Roxbury Church Records*, p. 207; Hull, *Diary*, p. 229; *Dorchester Church Records*, p. 58; "Third Church Narrative," pp. 57-72.

[24] "Third Church Narrative," pp. 74, 76.

[25] In 1658 Davenport had advised Wethersfield to accept the Hartford dissenters because a council had recommended it and failure to do so would overpunish the godly; John Davenport to Wethersfield Church, February 1658, *Letters*, pp. 114-119. He amplified this position in *Another Essay*, p. 8.

governor and five magistrates asking those present to delay the proceeding until an investigation could be made. Formation of a new church was contrary to the "order of the Gospel," they wrote, since the dissenters still belonged to First Church Boston and lay under censure there.[26] Despite these warnings, the messengers gave their assent, and twenty-nine men signed the covenant of the Third Church Boston.[27]

Davenport struck back by appealing directly to the laity. He asked them to ignore the reports they heard; First Church was fighting for congregational autonomy, and it deserved sympathy not condemnation.[28] Davenport's supreme opportunity came only a week after the gathering of Third Church, and it indicates the broad support he had already gained among the laymen. Invited by the General Court to preach the election sermon, Davenport attacked the gathering of Third Church and condemned the half-way covenant. This sermon was the opening shot of a political battle that engulfed the colony for two years.

Davenport's portrayal of First Church as the injured party suffered a rude setback in mid-June. Nicholas Street, in Boston to wind up affairs with Davenport, discovered that the elders of First Church had completely misrepresented the letter sent by the

[26] "Third Church Narrative," pp. 77-79; Governor Bellingham and two of the magistrates who signed this letter belonged to First Church.

[27] *Roxbury Church Records*, p. 208.

[28] John Davenport to Church at Roxbury, May 16, 1669, *Letters*, pp. 281-282; a similar letter was read the same day to the Salem church.

New Haven church. They had, in fact, forged a more satisfactory letter, complete with Street's signature, that gave Davenport a full dismissal from New Haven and liberty to settle in Boston. Within a few days Street's charge against the elders became the gossip of Boston. Even some of Davenport's staunchest supporters found the action of the elders inexcusable. Anthony Stoddard and John Leverett claimed that the church had been shamed by the elders and that New Haven had certainly been wronged. Davenport hotly denied any wrongdoing and rebuked his ruling elder for suggesting that First Church had acted improperly.[29] Davenport maintained that the elders had "perceived that the preface to the dismission was altogether superfluous, yet such as might cause difference." So they extracted the sense of the letter to prevent "dishonour to the Church of Newhaven and disturbance to this Church."[30] Davenport then presented First Church with an ultimatum. If they refused to acknowledge the extraction as legitimate, he would resign. Without ever seeing the original letter, the members of First Church bowed to his demands and voted that the elders had dealt honestly and fairly with the congregation. To keep John Davenport they would overlook the contradictions and the admitted forgery of Street's signature.

Although First Church might condone the behavior of its elders, the ministers of the colony demanded satisfaction. Seventeen ministers met in Bos-

[29] "Third Church Narrative," pp. 81-82.

[30] John Davenport to First Church, June 29, 1669, *Letters*, pp. 283-284.

ton and publicly condemned the three elders of First Church for "the great and publique scandall of unfaithfulnes and falsehood committed . . . to the great dishonour of God, the scandall of our profession, the reproach of New England and of the Elders in particular." They requested the elders to make "a suteable manifestation of their repentance, to the recovering of the name of God."[31] But neither Davenport nor First Church were ready to do penance. When the Dedham church asked about the letter, First Church answered, "wee understood and still doe" that the letter "was a plenary desmission." The church stood solidly behind its elders, and in October it once again voted its approval of the elders' extraction.[32]

Although the letter incident certainly helped its cause, Third Church discovered that secession had been only the beginning of its troubles. The Davenport faction still obstructed the church at every turn. In May 1669 Boston granted Third Church land on which to erect a meetinghouse, but the congregation decided the site lay too far from the center of town and voted instead to build on a plot adjoining the common and donated by John Norton's widow. Work was begun on the foundation in early July, but Bellingham and two magistrates ordered it stopped on the grounds that it was "contrary to what hath bin the practise and orderly custome" of Boston "which is to the greife and offence of many sober and

31 "Third Church Narrative," pp. 84-87.

32 *Boston First Church Records*, *1*, pp. 5-6, 63.

discreet Persons." When the builder and several workmen ignored the constable's orders, they were seized, brought before the governor, and imprisoned. Until Third Church received permission from Boston to build on Mary Norton's lot, it violated colonial law.[33]

The governor's harassment only temporarily hindered Third Church, since four of Boston's seven selectmen and the moderator of the town meeting belonged to the new church.[34] When members of First Church tried to proscribe the selectmen's power to sanction erection of a new meetinghouse without the town's approval, the town meeting decisively defeated their motion. July 26, 1669, the selectmen approved the Norton site and gave Third Church permission to build.[35]

By early December Third Church had completed construction and was making plans for the ordination of Thomas Thacher as pastor. They invited sixteen

[33] "Third Church Narrative," pp. 140-141; the law in question was the statute passed March 3, 1636. ". . . this Court doeth not, nor will hereafter, approve of any such companyes of men as shall henceforth joyne in any pretended way of church fellowshipp, without they shall first acquainte the magistrates, & elders of the greater parte of the churches in this jurisdiction, with their intentions, & have their approbation herein." Apparently this was interpreted to require also the permission of the town itself. *Massachusetts Records*, *I*, p. 168.

[34] The First Church schism apparently had no effect on Boston elections. The same selectmen served in 1668 and 1669; in 1670 the only change was the replacement of one Third Church member by another. In the same period, the town consistently elected members of First Church to the General Court.

[35] Hill, *Old South Church*, *I*, p. 128; "Third Church Narrative," p. 142.

churches to send messengers and only First Church refused. "Wee Cannot but wonder . . . in callinge your Combination a regular Church Constitution. . . . And that you dare entitle the favor of god, to that which is onely the fruitt of your owne wills," First Church answered. "Wee Judge it our duty to declare our dissatisfaction in your proceedinge . . . as an act highly displeasinge to God and Dangerous to the wellfare of Civill and Church government." The day of the ordination First Church sent four prominent laymen to dissuade the messengers from giving the right hand of fellowship, but they failed. Despite heavy snow, four churches sent messengers, and they carried out the ordination. Even Davenport's old ally Charles Chauncy attended and prayed for God's blessing.[36]

Although the ministers won the Third Church battle, the victory proved almost pyrrhic. Their defense of schism and their attacks on Davenport had alienated the laity, and as the battle shifted from churches to politics the ministers found themselves at a severe disadvantage. John Davenport's election sermon had made Third Church and the half-way covenant political issues, and after 1669 they dominated Massachusetts politics.

The half-way covenant had never been entirely free from politics. Although Massachusetts separated the functions of church and state, the two were intimately related, and anything that affected religion ultimately

[36] "Third Church Narrative," pp. 156-163.

had political ramifications. Religion and politics were too deeply interwoven at the center of men's daily lives to remain distinct.

Initially the General Court appeared sympathetic to the Half-Way Synod. Although it had not enforced the propositions and had permitted the anti-synodists to publish, the Court had commended the innovation to the churches. The election sermon, that annual union of politics and religion, probably reveals the prevailing sentiments of the deputies. Since they chose the preacher, they exercised some control over the views presented. After 1662 four of the five ministers invited to preach the election sermon had endorsed the half-way covenant.[37] Prior to 1670 these sermons were the only occasions when the half-way covenant became truly political.

John Higginson defended the synod before the General Court in 1663, but he also attempted to restore peace among the clergy. "Our CAUSE is not barely a *Reformation*, but a PROGRESS in *Reformation*. . . . A conceit of having already attained *Perfect Reformation* should be far from us." But since men perceived things differently, "it is our Duty to forbear One another in Love."[38] Jonathan Mitchel, author of the synod's propositions, used stronger language four years later. "To leave the *Children* of non-scandalous Orthodox Christians *Unbaptized*, will

[37] John Higginson (1663), Richard Mather (1664), Thomas Cobbett (1666), and Jonathan Mitchel (1667); the lone dissenting voice was John Russell (1665).

[38] John Higginson, *The Cause of God and His People in New-England*, Cambridge, 1663, pp. 8-9; election sermon, May 27, 1663.

. . . be one day found a thing displeasing unto Jesus Christ." But Mitchel warned the people not to become too lax in baptism; that too, subverted "the *Rules of Scripture*." The churches should seek all means to achieve uniformity, "even in lesser matters," but if differences remained, "*Agree* not to *Disagree* about them."[39] Mitchel's defense of the synod and plea for unity fell on deaf ears.

Shortly after Mitchel's sermon the deputies reversed their attitude toward the half-way covenant. With the First Church fight and the arrival of Davenport, the deputies adopted an anti-synodical position and invited ministers hostile to the half-way covenant to preach the election sermons.[40] The first of these, William Stoughton's *New Englands True Interest*, attacked the synod as moderately as Higginson had defended it five years earlier. "Covenanting holy Parents, they are a *holy Root* unto their Seed, and the Lord may well expect that the *Branches* should be answerable unto the Root."[41] It remained for John Davenport to create a political crisis out of the election sermon.

Just one week after the First Church dissenters seceded and established their church against the advice of the governor and five magistrates, Davenport

[39] Jonathan Mitchel, *Nehemiah on the Wall in Troublesome Times*, Cambridge, 1671, pp. 28-30; election sermon, May 15, 1667.

[40] William Stoughton (1668), John Davenport (1669), and John Oxenbridge (1671); in these four years, Samuel Danforth (1670) was the only defender of the synod.

[41] William Stoughton, *New Englands True Interest Not to Lie*, Cambridge, 1670, p. 9; election sermon, April 29, 1668.

preached to the General Court. The schism became the focus of Davenport's attack and the basis of his charge to the General Court. "Rule in the fear of God . . . protecting the Churches that are orderly gathered, and walk according to Gospel-Rules, from the violence and injuries of their opposers." God would have a sad reckoning for any rulers who failed this obligation, Davenport warned. The Court should take particular care not to impose on the churches "Mens Opinions, especially when they . . . prevailed in an hour of Temptation, though consented to by the major part of a Topical Synod." Take heed of church councils "which under a pretence of helping the Church with their Light, bereave them of their Power, binding them to rest in their decisions." If the Court sanctioned any departure from the original purity of the churches, Davenport warned them that God would "remove the golden Candlesticks, and the burning shining Lights in them." Davenport left no doubt in anyone's mind that he considered himself one of the "shining Lights." Davenport's message was clear: New England had to return to its original purity, restore the independence of churches, and reject ill-considered innovations.[42]

The response to the sermon revealed the increasing cleavage within the colony. The deputies voted to thank Davenport and requested that the colony print the sermon at public expense. A majority of the assistants rejected both motions. The sermon had offended "the Revd Elders of other churches" and

[42] John Davenport, *A Sermon Preached at the Election of the Governor*, 1670, pp. 12-15; election sermon, May 19, 1669.

had slandered Third Church. Approval of such partisan comments, the assistants maintained, was "altogether unseasonable." The deputies, in turn, rejected the assistants' remonstrance, and there the matter rested for the moment. Davenport had the thanks and the support of half the General Court.[43]

Although the upper house had rebuked Davenport for his intemperate sermon, the First Church schism had seriously divided its own ranks. A majority of the assistants favored the Third Church cause and in alliance with the clergy acted as its benefactor and protector. Lt. Governor Francis Willoughby and seven others had sanctioned the dissenters' secession from First Church and had approved erection of a new meetinghouse once the congregation had complied with the colony's laws. But Governor Bellingham and the other five assistants, who considered the clergy's interference in First Church affairs indefensible, used all the power at their disposal to impede Third Church and keep it on the defensive. The majority consistently outvoted this faction; and since the assistants ran the day-to-day affairs of the colony between sessions of the General Court, the upper house cast the mantle of its protection over Third Church in the stormy summer of 1669.

The deputies played a minor role in those events; their adjournment in June had cut short any direct influence they might have exerted to check the assistants. But certainly the attitude the deputies had displayed toward Davenport's sermon encouraged

[43] Massachusetts Archives; Ecclesiastical, *10*, 7.

the assistants who opposed Third Church. When the new church made plans for Thacher's ordination, Leverett begged for delay until the General Court reconvened and could consider the entire question. This stalling tactic more than likely reflected Leverett's confidence that the deputies would sustain Davenport and First Church if the issue could be kept in abeyance.

The repercussion of the First Church schism and Davenport's election sermon touched every person in Massachusetts. Not since the antinomian crisis of 1637 had an ecclesiastical controversy attracted so much attention. Davenport used this interest to strengthen his own position. He skillfully manipulated the issues to gain lay support by shifting the focus of the debate from the half-way covenant to congregational autonomy. In Davenport's propaganda, the villain became the council which had intruded upon the internal affairs of First Church. The laymen responded to Davenport's call with enthusiasm. Opponents of the half-way covenant had found a focal point for their hostility in the First Church schism, and now, by defending Congregationalism with Davenport, they clothed their opposition with a legitimacy they had lacked before. But Davenport's alarms also appealed to many other laymen who had no special antipathy to the extension of baptism and who joined Davenport's ranks because he championed the independence of churches against outside meddling. With these combined forces Davenport hoped to strike the final blow against innovations.

Although Davenport planted and nurtured the

seeds of discontent in Massachusetts, he did not live to see them bear fruit. On March 13, 1670, he suffered a stroke and was dead three days later. He had fulfilled his own prophecy; God had taken away the foremost of the "shining Lights." First Church, as a measure of its affection and respect, interred Davenport in the same tomb with its beloved John Cotton.[44] Davenport's death in no way eased strife in the colony; in fact, it goaded opponents of Third Church. The loss of Davenport capped eight years of frustration for the laity, and when the General Court met in May, the accumulated bitterness burst the traditional restraints. The deputies rebelled against the clergy.

In the election sermon of 1670 Samuel Danforth placed the onus for the discord on the laity. God had directed the hearts of the ministers "for the good of the people; but many times the people are straitned in their own bowels, and cannot receive such a large portion, as the Lord hath provided for them." Danforth was hardly impartial; he had participated in both councils that had sanctioned Third Church, and he had censured Davenport for the forgery.[45] Danforth's sermon may have contained wise counsel, but it hardly corresponded with the mood of the deputies.

Two days after the sermon the deputies found the means to strike back at the clergy. The immediate occasion of the dispute was a petition to the General

[44] "Third Church Narrative," p. 165.

[45] Samuel Danforth, *A Brief Recognition of New Englands Errand Into the Wilderness*, Cambridge, 1671, p. 15; election sermon, May 11, 1670.

Court from the freemen of Hadley drafted by Rev. John Russell, a close friend of Governor Bellingham. The petition revealed how deeply Davenport's ideas had permeated even the western part of the province. The petitioners asked the Court "whether the rods of God upon our churches and land have not this speaking voice to us that there should be some publike and solemn enquiry what it is that hath provoked the Lord against us?"[46] The deputies accepted the proposal without hesitation and appointed a five-man committee to determine the causes of God's displeasure. The magistrates selected Thomas Danforth to consult with the committee on their behalf.[47]

It took less than two weeks to complete the report, and the deputies approved it without reservation. It resembled the jeremiads with which they were all familiar, but it included several particulars which struck to the heart of the controversy. Among the causes of God's wrath it listed:

> 2. Woeful declining from our primitive and foundation work.
> 3. Innovation threatening the ruin of our foundations, and the extirpation of those old principles of the congregational way laid by so many of the Lord's worthies who are now at rest.

Peter Tilton, deacon of the Hadley church, prepared the report. Danforth sent his own report to both houses which, although otherwise similar, deleted the sections quoted above and substituted as a cause

[46] Massachusetts Archives; Ecclesiastical, *10*, 286.
[47] Hill, *Old South Church*, *1*, p. 97.

"the boldness found in many to rise up against the Lord's faithful ministers."[48]

When the magistrates requested amplification of the charges, the deputies transmitted a second report even more controversial than the first. Here the deputies laid the blame for New England's woeful situation squarely on the clergy. In bitterness and anticlericalism this report was unequalled in seventeenth-century Massachusetts. The lower house accused the ministers of:

> declension from the primitive foundation worke, innovation in doctrine & worship, opinion & practise, & invasion of the rights, liberties, & priviledges of churches . . . to the utter devastation of these churches, turning the pleasant gardens of Christ into a wildernesse, . . . these are the leven, the corrupting gangreens, the infecting spreading plague . . . which hath provoked divine wrath.

The deputies cited as an example the gathering of Third Church; the participation of the elders and churches in that proceeding was "irregular, illegal, & disorderly."[49] Although the magistrates conceded that many things in the first report "must be acknowledged," they dissented from the crux of the deputies' case, "not owning or knowing of any Elders or Churches amongst us that can be so characterized without Calumny and Slaunder."[50]

48 *ibid.*, *1*, pp. 97-99.
49 *Massachusetts Records*, *4*, Part 2, p. 490.
50 Hill, *Old South Church*, *1*, p. 99.

The magistrates then resorted to an old tactic that had served them well since the first days of the colony; they asked the clergy to consider the crisis and recommend a solution to the next session of the Court, even though in this instance the ministers were the aggrieved party. The deputies accepted this resolution on one condition; the ministers must also consider the "perticular evills of persons standing in publick capassitie, in Cases wherein they . . . concerne themselves unnecessarilye, which may occasion publick Calamitye." Massachusetts law prohibited gathering a church without approval from the elders and magistrates. "When some magistrates appeare and declare Openlye against the [establishment of a church] as Irregular, That others that are absent shall abett or Incourage the same" threatened the liberty of every church to rule itself.[51] In an effort to reduce tension, the General Court set June 16 as a day of humiliation for the entire colony, so that all might consider the general decline of religious affairs.

The "calumnies," which the deputies had heaped upon them, stirred the clergy to unprecedented political activity. Such manifest anti-clericalism threatened their prestige and leadership in the community; indeed, it endangered the whole fabric of the New England Way. Through the winter and spring of 1671 the ministers campaigned to elect deputies sympathetic to the clergy. (One historian has called the election in 1671 "the first organized campaign in America to elect an entire ticket.")[52] The only issue

[51] *ibid.*, *1*, pp. 100-101.

[52] Miller, *Colony to Province*, p. 108.

was, "Are you for or against Third Church?" What tactics the clergy employed we shall never know, but at the end of May they won a smashing victory.

The election upset the traditional pattern of Massachusetts politics. In the past the membership of the lower house had changed very gradually, but in 1671 sixteen deputies lost their seats; for every three deputies reelected, four new representatives assumed seats in the house. Thirteen towns changed their representation entirely. The size of the new General Court reflected the intensity of the clergy's campaign; in 1671 the house was almost one-third larger than the previous year. Eight towns that had failed to send representatives in 1670 elected deputies, and five more towns increased their representation from one to two men. Another indication of the clergy's success was the election of five members of Third Church as representatives of outlying towns; in 1670 not one member of Third Church had sat in the house. The altered balance of power became apparent as soon as the deputies organized for the new session. Thomas Savage of Third Church displaced Thomas Clarke of First Church as speaker of the house, a position Clarke had held the two previous years. Although the ministers had achieved a decisive victory, they had not completely eliminated the Davenport faction. Ten members of the Davenport faction were reelected and seven new opponents of Third Church joined them in the house.[53]

[53] *Massachusetts Records*, 4, Part 2, pp. 448-449, 484-488. Miller overestimated the clergy's victory when he claimed "fourteen Deputies (all opponents of the Third Church) were defeated,

The election had almost no effect on the magistrates. Leverett replaced Willoughby, who had died, as lieutenant governor, and William Stoughton filled the vacancy Leverett had created. Seven of the twelve magistrates still favored Third Church, but now both the governor and lieutenant governor belonged to First Church.

One of the ironies of the election was that the old house had chosen John Oxenbridge, Davenport's successor in First Church, to preach the election sermon. Undoubtedly Oxenbridge prepared his sermon with different election results in mind, but he never faltered in his message. "Take heed," he told the assembled freemen, "least ye bare false witness for or against any whome you chuse or refuse . . . nothing can undo this Country but unwariness and unfaithfulness, but mis-making or mis-acting of Freemen." But Oxenbridge addressed most of his warnings to the General Court. "Minde faithfully . . . your liberties . . . [or] other men will be your masters." "Have any of you a thirst and longing to make any change in Church or Common-wealth, . . . let me intreat you . . . forbear your own desires." Ecclesiastical matters could not be ignored because "your civil and your religious liberties are so coupled here, that if one be lost the other cannot be kept; . . . when you are so sheepish to be bound, your fleece will be shorn." Oxenbridge feared that the interference of

---

nineteen (all 'safe') were reelected, and thirteen new names were chosen (all amenable)."; *Colony to Province*, p. 108. Of the twenty-one deputies reelected only eleven were "safe"; of the twenty-eight new men, only three-fourths were "amenable."

magistrates and ministers in the affairs of First Church had set a dangerous precedent; "the major part of a Church must issue their matters." Oxenbridge recognized that behind all the strife lay the half-way covenant, and he condemned the innovation. "Ye can never really love either by outward fleshly circumcision alone, when ye are only custom born." "If a degenerate and spurious Generation will not stand by the intendents of their faithful Ancestors, . . . the Lord, he will ruine them."[54] But the clergy had done its work well; the General Court turned a deaf ear to Oxenbridge's "warning and warming."

When the General Court convened, seventeen ministers presented a petition answering the charges levelled the previous year. They maintained that the ministers had never departed "from the safe & sober principles of the congregationall way laid in the first foundation of these churches." Of the charges of innovation and apostasy they proclaimed their total innocence. The whole affair, the ministers said, "would wee haue borne & buried in silence, . . . had wee binn only privately & personally concerned therein, or had it issued only as an abortive motion, without any abiding effect or influence upon the spiritts of men." But the reports of the deputies had increased and made more credible "the loud cry & clamour" circulating in the colony.

The petition undertook a point by point refutation of the reports. The deputies had insinuated the

[54] John Oxenbridge, *New Englands Freemen Warned and Warmed to be Free Indeed*, Cambridge, 1673, pp. 18, 21-22, 27, 32-33, 42-43; election sermon, May 31, 1671.

charges on the entire ministry "without proofe by any one instance, of those hethrodox & corrupt principles." And from this presumption the lower house had concluded "woeful declension"; yet, in fact, the ministers felt that God still owned the churches as true to their "primitive constitution." The deputies themselves had undermined the true nature of Congregational churches "by denying the membership of church children, when adult, as not having either materiall nor formall cause of church membershipp." The entire report had resulted "from a present, personal, & passionate concerne in the interest of a party . . . to scandelize the pretious church of Christ." The ministers placed their petition before the General Court, "humbly wayting upon you for redresse."[55]

They did not wait long. Within four days of the election the deputies recanted. By a two-thirds majority the house passed a complete retraction of the charges against the ministers and Third Church. But the deputies prefaced it with an assertion of their prerogatives. "The acts of this honoured Court, being the supreme authority, are not liable to quaestion by any, & that free debates are the indubitable right of the said Court." However, acts occasionally passed in "an hower of temptation" and must be, "upon mature deliberation, rectified." The deputies ordered that the reports of the house be "accounted uselesse." The Court knew "no just cause of those scandelizing reflections . . . either in refference to the new church

[55] *Massachusetts Records*, 4, Part 2, pp. 489-493.

of Boston or otherwise and . . . must judge them innocent, and unduly calumniated."[56]

Seventeen deputies remained defiant to the end; they refused to humble themselves to the clergy and demanded that their negative votes be recorded. Three of the dissenting votes came from the remaining members of the committee that had drafted the original report of the deputies in 1670. Five other deputies voted against retraction even though their own ministers had signed the petition to the General Court. The final vote of the deputies followed town lines. Of the thirty-seven towns represented in the General Court, nine voted solidly against retraction; twenty-five towns supported the motion without a dissenting vote; and only three towns had one deputy on each side.[57] June 4, 1671, the ministers won their victory. The deputies absolved them of any guilt, and the political crisis was over.

The submission of the deputies ended open resistance to the half-way covenant. The laity, chastened by their anti-clerical outburst, retreated from politics to the churches. Although their hostility to the innovation occasionally reappeared within individual congregations, the opposition was sporadic and localized after 1671. Davenport's death had robbed the laity of leadership, and no one of sufficient stature remained to take up his mantle. Perhaps even Davenport would have had trouble sustaining the attack after 1671. The clergy's triumph in the elections suggests that the laity had recoiled from what they had

[56] *ibid.*, *4*, Part 2, pp. 493-494.

[57] Massachusetts Archives; Ecclesiastical, *10*, 201.

wrought and had tried to make amends. The rebellion of 1670 had drained their bitterness, and the half-way covenant ceased to be a major issue in Massachusetts.

The ministers neither forgave nor forgot the abusive language of the deputies' reports. At every opportunity they impressed upon the freemen the lessons to be learned from the events of 1670-1671. Massachusetts had gone to the brink, and only God's favor had preserved it from destruction. Religion is "best established when there is an concurrence of Magistracy and Ministry together to promote the true worship of God," proclaimed Thomas Shepard, Jr., in the election sermon of 1672. The danger to New England lay in the growing contempt of magistrates and ministers. One of God's gifts was "blessing the order of Councils, and Synods"; rigid independence betrayed the "practice of our first leaders." Shepard had especially harsh words for those who opposed the Half-Way Synod: "Foxes full of subtility and mischief, that would else have destroyed his Vineyard, and that by plucking off its buds and tender grapes." Only "by a more thorough, conscientious, religious, effectual care for the Rising Generation," Shepard warned, could New England recover its religious mission.[58]

Urian Oakes denounced the clergy's critics even more bluntly the following year. He called them "merchants of lies" whose attacks on the ministers

[58] Thomas Shepard, Jr., *Eye Salve*, Cambridge, 1673, pp. 1, 13, 15, 22-24, 43; election sermon, May 15, 1672.

demonstrated their "disaffected and embittered Spirit." Every disaster that struck New England they blamed on "the Defection and Apostacy of their Ministers." It was too bad, Oakes lamented, that these men were not "better enformed and affected, or less considerable in the Common wealth." Although Oakes admitted that the ministers should avoid interfering in politics, a threat to religion and society demanded that they assert their leadership. "Accusers of our Civil and Ecclesiastical Rulers," Oakes announced, thought they were better "rid of such Leaders in Church and Common wealth." If left unchecked, these men who "gloried in their *Rebellion* against the Authority of Christ in his Churches" would destroy Massachusetts. Oakes feared that the dissension had already gone too far. "God alone in some more than ordinary way of working" could restore peace. "It must be some sharp affliction, some smarting rod, or sore tryal." Two years later King Philip's War amply fulfilled Oakes' forebodings.

Oakes saw another threat in the divisive quarrels; they endangered Puritan control of the colony. Internal dissension, he warned, opened the "way of those that will make no difference between Synodists and Anti-synodists." The political crisis had attracted persons who had no interest in the ecclesiastical principles involved. But they recognized an opportunity to increase their own freedom. Certainly some artisans and merchants in Boston chafed under the economic and political restrictions of the Puritan state and welcomed any movement which offered relief. In the antinomian controversy the merchants of Boston had allied themselves with Anne Hutchinson, not out of sympathy for her mysticism, but because she challeged the existing power structure that limited their opportunities. The role of these "civil men" was not as obvious in 1670 as it had been in 1637, but they must have rejoiced in the quarrels. As Oakes characterized them: "it is all the Religion some men have, to *villifie*, and *traduce*, and lower the *reputation* and Authority of Ministers of Christ."[59] In 1684 when the Massachusetts charter was revoked, it was this faction that assumed power. But in the dissension of 1670-1671 they gained very little. As the issues which had precipitated the crisis faded, Congregationalists closed their ranks and forgot their differences.

By the early 1670's not one of the dissenting brethren of 1662 remained to rally opponents of the half-way covenant. Death had cut a swath through the anti-synodical faction. Eleazar Mather died in 1669; Davenport in 1670; Chauncy in 1672; and Street in 1674. Mayo retired from Second Church Boston in 1673 and settled quietly in Barnstable. Increase Mather, the one man who might have assumed Davenport's leadership, had changed sides in 1671 and now championed the half-way covenant. Although *First Principles* was not published until 1675, Mather dated this recantation May 1, 1671, a month before the deputies made their submission to the

[59] Urian Oakes, *New England Pleaded With*, Cambridge, 1673, pp. 8-9, 24-26, 35-37, 40-41, 47, 58; election sermon, May 7, 1673.

clergy. In *First Principles* Mather compiled every shred of evidence available to prove that the founding generation had favored the principle of extended baptism. For Mather it marked the culmination of a change of heart that had been in progress for three years. Although Mather credited his conversion to Jonathan Mitchel, the death of Richard Mather in 1669, the incident of the forged letters from New Haven, and the anti-clericalism of 1670 helped convince him of his error.[60] As a convert to extended baptism, Mather spoke to the people with more authority than most of his colleagues.

Even from beyond the grave one opponent of the half-way covenant attempted to fight the innovation. When Governor Bellingham died in 1672, he left his entire estate at Winnisimmet "to be an annual encouragement to some godly ministers . . . faithful to those principles in church discipline which are owned and practiced in the First Church in Boston." To insure that no one misinterpreted his instructions he appointed three confirmed opponents of the half-way covenant as his trustees: Anthony Stoddard, John Russell, and James Allin. After the will was made public, some persons in Boston hinted darkly that Allin had tampered with Bellingham's will just as he had with the New Haven letters four years earlier. Although unsubstantiated, the charge illus-

[60] Kenneth Murdock clearly misinterpreted Mather's position in 1668, when he claimed that "Mather, by his opposition to the rebellious faction [in First Church], gave prompt notice of his change from his views of 1662"; *Increase Mather*, Cambridge, 1925, pp. 87-88. Had Mather changed his mind by 1668, he would have supported the dissenters in First Church.

trates the unfortunate legacy of the First Church schism. Ultimately the courts frustrated Bellingham's effort; his son contested the will and it remained in litigation until after the American Revolution.[61]

Death had also taken its toll of the men who had defended the synod's propositions in 1662. Richard Mather and Jonathan Mitchel died in 1669 in the midst of the First Church fight, and John Allen died in 1671. The loss of the principal actors in the post-synodical debate symbolized the end of one era and the opening of a new one in which the half-way covenant became part of Massachusetts orthodoxy.

[61] Felt, *Ecclesiastical History*, 2, p. 501; Hill, *Old South Church*, 1, p. 190.

SEVEN

The New Orthodoxy: 1676-1692

THE recantation of the deputies in 1671 ended overt, organized resistance to the half-way principles, but it brought the ministers no closer to general acceptance of the synod's recommendations. Lay opposition retreated from courthouse to meeting-house, but defeat had robbed its vitality. For the next five years the issue seemed suspended. Only one additional church is known to have adopted the half-way covenant in this period. Had the religious environment in Massachusetts remained stable, full implementation of the half-way covenant would have come very slowly indeed. But in 1675 the colony stood on the brink of a traumatic social upheaval. In the decade and a half of crisis which began with King Philip's War and ended with the Witch Trials, Church after church adopted and utilized the half-way measures until by 1692 probably not more than one church in five still followed the older practice. The half-way covenant no longer generated controversy; in fact, the propositions of the Half-Way Synod represented a moderate position. A large number of churches, as they confronted a radically altered social and religious context, introduced innovations which broadened church membership beyond anything envisioned in 1662. After 1676 the half-way covenant became part of the new orthodoxy.

In 1675 God's judgment fell on New England. A generation of ministers had warned the people what would happen if they turned their faces from God and dishonored His churches and servants. But no one could have prophesied the horror of King Philip's War. The Indians, quiet since 1637, broke loose with unequalled vengeance. Terror stalked the fields and fresh scalps adorned the belts of savages. Half the towns in Plymouth and Massachusetts experienced Indian raids, and at least ten towns were abandoned as the frontier settlements collapsed. Women and children perished by the score and others lived to wish they had. The war decimated the militia and left the colonies reeling. No sooner had this scourge passed than new signs of God's wrath appeared: two great fires in Boston; a smallpox epidemic; an outbreak of the fever; and threats to Puritan political control.

A people reared on the Old Testament and the history of Israel saw the message clearly; God was warning and chastising His chosen people. New England would have to discover its errors and return to the paths of godliness; the people must reform or perish. With the support of other ministers, Increase Mather took the lead and in May 1679 proposed that the General Court call a synod.[1] The Court approved the motion without hesitation and ordered the synod to consider the "revisall of the platforme of disci-

[1] Walker, *Creeds and Platforms*, pp. 412-415.

pline . . . and what else may appeare necessary for the preventing [of] schismes, haeresies, prophanes, & [for] the establishments of the churches in faith & order. . . ."[2] The Reforming Synod met, but despite its incantations conditions in Massachusetts continued to degenerate. The 1680's proved disastrous to the standing order. The political confusion which followed the revocation of the Massachusetts charter in 1684 culminated in the Andros regime. The Dominion of New England threatened every element of stability in the colony; land tenure, self-government, Congregationalism, all appeared marked for major revision. The destruction of the Puritan state, for a half-century the bulwark of Congregational orthodoxy, challenged the churches to redefine their role. The broad implementation of the half-way covenant that occurred between 1676 and 1692 can only be understood in the context of crisis.

Once more the Dorchester church illustrates the general temper of the churches. Rev. Josiah Flynt filled the Dorchester pulpit after Richard Mather's death in 1669, but he had no more success than his predecessor in introducing the half-way covenant. A majority of the congregation still refused to consider the innovation, and a vocal few demanded punctilious observation of the rules.[3] But in the aftermath of King Philip's War opinions changed, and Flynt

[2] *Massachusetts Records*, 5, p. 215.

[3] In the case of Susanna Kingsley, April 7, 1672, some of the members opposed the baptism of this infant because her mother had died in childbirth and therefore was no longer a member in full communion; *Dorchester Church Records*, p. 179.

took advantage of the shift to introduce the half-way covenant. As Dorchester searched for the causes of God's displeasure, it found the reason in its own backsliding. In a meeting at Flynt's house in the late winter of 1677, the congregation decided that an explicit covenant renewal might reform the evils into which it had fallen and firmly impress the covenant obligations on the entire church. One evil stood out: "our defects and neglects of duty toward the Children of the Covenant, humbly & from or harts acknowlidging & bewailing or sin heerin, beseeching & waiting upon god in or lord Jesus for pardon & healling. . . ." The members then prepared a list containing the names of all children in the church over sixteen that they might be called upon to own the covenant and submit to the government of the church.[4]

March 5, the day appointed, Flynt charged the children to take their profession to heart and act sincerely. In baptism they had received the means of grace and had given themselves to the Lord, and now they should manifest those blessings in their lives.[5] Following Flynt's sermon fifty-two children of the church stood and owned the covenant. Some whose names appeared on the list abstained, requesting more "time to Consider of it." In the next three weeks nineteen more assented, and by the end of the year the total reached 106.[6] Once Dorchester had decided on its course, it reached out to bring a large percentage of the children into half-way membership.

[4] *ibid.*, pp. 18-20. [5] *ibid.*, pp. 17-18. [6] *ibid.*, p. 74.

In Dorchester the introduction of the half-way covenant coincided with a mass covenant renewal as part of an overall program of reformation. Without the crisis it is doubtful that the church would have accepted the innovation.

Several other churches also adopted all or part of the synod's proposals in 1677. Quincy extended church discipline to include the children of the covenant who had reached maturity, and the relatively large number of adults subsequently received into the church indicates that it used the half-way covenant, although concrete evidence is lacking.[7] According to John Cotton, Jr., at least one Plymouth church adopted the proposals. He wrote his brother-in-law Increase Mather that Thomas Thornton of Yarmouth "hath begun & practiced the Synods 5th Prop: in baptising sundry. There are 5 or 6 dissenting brethren. Your booke of the 1st principles . . . I wish 20 of them. in Yarmouth they might be of great use, to establish the unsettled."[8] Cotton never mentioned where he intended to use the extra fifteen copies, but it may well have been within his own Plymouth congregation.

Among the new churches gathered in the colony after 1675 it became fairly common to use the half-way covenant from the start. Often these churches received the majority of their members from a single older town, and the inhabitants transplanted polity

[7] Charles F. Adams, *History of Braintree*, Cambridge, 1891, pp. 151, 145.

[8] John Cotton, Jr., to Increase Mather, August 26, 1677, *Mather Papers*, p. 247.

along with household goods. When the half-way covenant had been used in the old church, it usually became part of the new. In other cases the younger generation, who tended to dominate the newer settlements, would cast off the conservative traditions in the new churches. The town of Westfield, slowly settled in the 1660's by the expansion of Northampton and Springfield, chose as its first pastor a young Harvard graduate Moses Fiske, who had been one of the first persons in the entire colony to become a half-way member. Westfield's first permanent minister, Edward Taylor, came to the town in 1671 and served for eight years before the formal gathering of a church. From Taylor's baptismal records and his sermons it seems apparent that within two years of his ordination the church was using the half-way covenant. A remarkable increase in baptisms in 1680 probably marks the initiation of the practice.[9] Taylor freely baptized children whose parents had owned the covenant in other churches, and in 1683 he recorded that Mary Gun "entered under the church watch and had her children baptized."[10] Implementation of the half-way covenant in Westfield was perfectly natural, since both Northampton and Spring-

[9] "Publick Records of the Church of Christ at Westfield . . . Baptisms," typed transcription, Westfield Atheneum, pp. 1-4. December 5, 1680, Taylor baptized thirty persons, yet in 1679 the total was nineteen, and in the rest of 1680, only twenty-five. See also Michael Colacurcio, "God's Determination Touching Half-Way Membership," *American Literature*, 1967, *39*, pp. 298-314.

[10] "Publick Records, Westfield," pp. 4-5.

field which provided the majority of the settlers had used the innovation for several years.

The Milton church, gathered in April 1678, followed a similar pattern. The majority of the congregation had belonged to the Dorchester church and was familiar with the half-way covenant. The pastor, Peter Thacher, had learned the virtues of the half-way covenant from his father, the first minister of Third Church Boston. When the congregation voted whether to practice extended baptism in August 1681, "all but 3 voted in favor, none against." Four weeks later Thacher initiated the practice by baptizing the six children of Goodwife Fenno.[11]

The Bradford Church also chose the son of a revisionist minister as its pastor. Twenty years before his own ordination Zechariah Symmes, Jr., had watched his father introduce the half-way covenant in the Charlestown church. Within two months of his ordination in December 1681 the younger Symmes had his congregation considering the church's responsibility toward the children of the church. Symmes calculated that Bradford had at least 110 baptized adults who were no longer subject to church discipline, could not present their children for baptism, and had no immediate connection with the church. Because they had not experienced saving faith, they had lost the church tie they had known as children. After some discussion among the members the Bradford congregation directed Symmes to consult pri-

[11] "Peter Thacher's Journal," Albert Teele, ed., *History of Milton*, Boston, 1888, p. 645; Milton Church Records, MS, Milton Public Library, pp. 3, 201.

vately with the children of the church over sixteen "concerning their knoledge and good intentions" and remind them of their covenant obligations. Those over twenty he was to call to own the covenant, and, if they refused, the elders were to admonish them. This decision carried unanimously, and in the summer of 1683 Bradford received its first half-way members.[12] In 1692 the church reconsidered its policy and ruled it would no longer extend baptism unconditionally. If possible, parents should join in full communion, or the church should at least test their fitness for this ordinance. If the parents still proved unqualified, they could take the alternative course of owning the covenant.[13] Apparently too many half-way members rested comfortably in their status or scrupled at presenting themselves, and Bradford hoped to rouse them to seek full membership.

In Marblehead, as in Bradford and Milton, adoption of the half-way covenant came shortly after the establishment of the church. Although it was one of the older towns, Marblehead had remained churchless longer than any other town in the colony, and it probably deserved the irreligious reputation that its fishermen had earned for it. Solicitous neighbors had made several abortive attempts to gather a church, but their efforts were unsuccessful until settlers from Salem changed the character of the town. In 1684 Marblehead chose Samuel Cheever, son of New England's famous schoolmaster, as its first pas-

[12] "Bradford Church Records," *Articles of Faith and Covenant . . . First Church . . . Bradford*, Haverhill, 1886, pp. 11, 39.

[13] *ibid.*, pp. 40-41.

tor. Two weeks after his ordination the members gave Cheever an unusual measure of freedom: "the Pastour should have free liberty . . . [in] the administration of the said ordinances [baptism and communion] without any interruption and disturbance." To insure that Cheever understood the congregation's sentiments, however, the members laid down certain guidelines: children of the church had the right to have their children baptized without qualifying for full communion. The half-way covenant had to be part of Cheever's "free liberty,"[14]

Even some of the older parishes that had resisted the half-way covenant for years finally succumbed to the innovation in the last decade of the century. The Rowley church, after ignoring the synod's recommendations for almost three decades, voted in 1690 to adopt the half-way covenant. But Rev. Edward Payson never recorded how the change was accomplished or how many persons it affected.[15]

The decisions of the little Rowley church meant very little to the colony, but what the Mathers did in Boston's Second Church attracted the attention of everyone. Increase Mather dominated the ecclesiastical scene in his generation, and his son and assistant, Cotton, held the same preeminence in the next generation. Despite the publication of Increase Mather's *First Principles* in 1675 and Cotton Mather's endorsement of the half-way covenant, the congregation of Second Church lagged in accepting

[14] First Book Containing the Records of the First Congregational Church, MS, First Church Marblehead, pp. 1-2.

[15] *Early Records of Rowley; First Record of the First Church*, Salem, 1889, p. 16.

the synod's proposals. For more than twenty years the only church in Boston which used the half-way covenant was Third Church. First Church, of course, made it a point of principle to uphold the orthodoxy of John Davenport, the Second Church simply ignored the principles its ministers preached. In 1693, primarily through the efforts of Cotton Mather, Second Church reversed its stand and committed the church to the half-way covenant. Prior to this only communicants and their minor children were subject to church discipline. Once adult, the children of church members passed into limbo if they failed to have a regenerative experience. They were baptized but isolated. Although strict, this policy had not adversely affected Second Church's membership. Between 1673 and 1685, allegedly a period of marked declension of religion, the number of full communicants rose nearly 50 percent.[16]

The experience of the Mathers in Second Church clearly demonstrates that not all lay resistance had disappeared in 1671. Even when a majority of the congregation finally supported the introduction of the half-way covenant, the opposition of a few prominent men weighed heavily as a counterbalance. To accomplish the desired change in policy, Cotton Mather resorted to the most artful tactics of pressure and persuasion. In his diary Mather describes his guile in gaining freedom to baptize "such as were Instructed and Orthodox in the Christian Religion"

[16] Boston Second Church Records, MS, Massachusetts Historical Society, Book 1½, p. 9; Cotton Mather, *Diary of Cotton Mather; 1681–1708*, MHS *Collections*, 1911, *67*, pp. 108, 161.

without jeopardizing his own position or risking an open confrontation with his opponents:

> My method for it was this. Having first, in a Sermon, at a Church-Meeting, declared my own Perswasion about this Matter, I permitted no public *Disputation* to follow upon it; but I employed fitt Hands, to carry an *Instrument*, containing my *Sentiments* and *Purposes*, unto the Brethren of the Church; who generally *signed*, a Desire and address unto myself, thereto annexed that I would act accordingly. As for the few *Brethren*, who were disaffected unto my Presceedings, I carried it so peaceably, and obligingly, and yett resolutely towards them, that they patiently lett mee take my way. . . .[17]

Altogether Mather's "fitt Hands" obtained seventy-five signatures on this petition, including those of three magistrates, and Mather claimed he might have had ten more names for the asking. Although Mather accomplished all this in the winter of 1691-1692, he refrained from implementing the practice or bringing it to a church vote, despite the obviously overwhelming support of the members. Even one member who had refused to sign the petition "told mee hee thought I sinn'd by Delaying to proceed unto the practice of my proposals."

The reason for the delay, Mather explained to John Richards, was that "I have been loth to go against the sense of *but Two* very Good men, whom I value at so high a rate; and of These, Dearest Sir,

[17] Mather, *Diary*, pp. 161-162.

You are the cheef."[18] Several months earlier Mather had written Richards of his desire to liberalize baptism, but apparently he had not convinced Richards. One by one he now answered Richards' objections. Unregenerate persons should not be baptized, Mather agreed, "but then I also think that a person so Qualify'd, as has been described, . . . should not be pronounced Unregenerate." The reasons they had not come to full communion were their "Doubts and Fears." Beside, full communion required not just grace but growth in grace from those initiated in baptism. ". . . wee may justly expect more positive Attainments, for the one, then for the other." Where would the innovations end, Richards had asked. Mather claimed the petition took care of that; he had so carefully circumscribed the minister's power that, if a later pastor "not bee so concerned for purity of Administrations," he would find the petition "an Everlasting Clog."

Mather also appealed to Richards on the basis of their friendship and the dire circumstances of the colony. "For my part I shall not bee able to hold up my Head, before the whole Christian World, untill I do more than I have done in this regard." Finally, in a point gauged to touch Richards, who at that moment sat as a judge in the witch trials, Mather wrote:

[18] Cotton Mather to John Richards, December 14, 1962, *Mather Papers*, pp. 398, 400; Richards was a wealthy merchant, a major of the Artillery Company, a former deputy, a judge of the Supreme Court, and had married well twice, once to John Winthrop, Jr.'s daughter. *ibid.*, p. 494.

> I have seen that the Divels have been Baptising so many of our miserable Neighbours, in that horrible Witchcraft . . . I cannot be well at Ease, until the Nursery of Initiated Beleevers . . . bee duely Watered, with Baptism . . . I would mark, as many as I should, that the Destroying Angels may have less claim unto them.[19]

Mather's arguments must have carried the day. January 15, 1693, the first of the children of the church renewed her covenant and had her child baptized.[20] So many persons took advantage of the new opportunity for baptism that Mather reported his "charge of . . . *ecclesiastical Watch*, was exceedingly increased."[21]

The Richards incident is doubly illustrative: it shows that some members still objected to changes in polity that threatened the purity of the ordinances, even late in the century; and it demonstrates how a single influential man could hinder a minister and the majority of a congregation. Cotton Mather had to plead with Richards: "almost all men living would say, I ought. Lett my Major then say it." Until he said it, Mather refused to extend baptism. The entire episode reflects the tenuous position of the clergy as ecclesiastical leaders and sources of religious authority.

Although it took the members of Second Church thirty years to overcome their scruples, once the decision was made they apparently used the half-

[19] *ibid.*, pp. 397-401.

[20] Chandler Robbins, *History of the Second Church*, Boston, 1852, p. 36.

[21] Mather, *Diary*, p. 162.

way covenant without reservation. But in several churches adoption of the half-way covenant met with far less success, and lay resistance reappeared within a short period. After a prolonged struggle over the innovation, Dorchester's implementation of the half-way covenant in 1677 appeared to be an overwhelming success. Yet the conversion to the new practice was only temporary. Many children of the church refused to own the covenant, and in 1679 the church called them "to give an acc[oun]t or answer for their obstinancy. . . ." This plea bore little fruit and in 1688 the church begged the children to take advantage of their covenant right.[22] Between 1677 and 1679, 114 persons owned the covenant; in the next decade the total dropped to twenty-one. Yet in that same decade almost three times as many persons joined in full communion. The excitement of the covenant of reformation and the anxiety caused by King Philip's War had created an artificial situation in Dorchester, during which the basic hostility of the congregation to the half-way covenant was overcome. Once this crest passed, the old attitudes reappeared. Although the congregation never retracted its decision, the children stopped using the half-way covenant in meaningful numbers.

Milton, formerly part of Dorchester, followed a similar course, although the reasons for it may have differed. Thacher introduced the half-way covenant with almost no opposition in 1681, yet few members took advantage of it. In a decade only ten persons

[22] *Dorchester Church Records*, pp. 79, 98.

owned the covenant, but six times that number joined in full communion. Half-way members never overwhelmed the communicants in the Milton church because few persons bothered to take hold of the covenant. The children of the church preferred to gain admission and qualify their children in the traditional manner.[23] When the church had paused to pray for "converting grace for the rising generation" at the time it adopted the half-way covenant, the Lord must have listened. Either that or Thacher measured saving faith with a charity that kept few persons from the Lord's Supper. Milton had little need for the half-way covenant when so many people qualified for communion.

Salisbury, founded in 1687, had trouble accepting even a limited variation of the half-way covenant. The members reluctantly granted James Allen's request "that they would not interupt me . . . in baptizing grandchildren." For four years Allen kept records of full communicants, regular baptisms, and grandchildren baptized; then he abruptly stopped making entries in the last column in 1692. In five years he had baptized only eleven grandchildren of communicants. Grace could skip one generation in the Salisbury church before the covenant relation was terminated. In Salisbury's system the parents remained uninvolved; they neither owned the covenant nor pledged themselves to the church. Grandchildren received baptism in their grandparents' right, and baptism still came through a visibly regenerate pro-

[23] Milton Church Records, pp. 3, 22, 150, 200, 241.

genitor. Not until 1737 did Salisbury ease its requirements and allow children of the church to own the covenant to qualify their children for baptism."[24]

In the parishes discussed above the half-way covenant failed to take deep root and become an integral part of the polity of the churches. In part at least, this failure reflected the continuing hesitancy of the members; after accepting the innovation, they backed away from it. In several other churches the resistance of the laity prevented even a temporary lapse. These churches joined Salisbury and First Church Boston in retaining the old ways and refusing to submit to the new orthodoxy.

Most of the churches in Plymouth Colony had followed the example of Massachusetts churches and had adopted testified regenerate membership by the middle of the century. Once adopted, the Old Colony congregations seemed less willing to modify their polity and incorporate the half-way covenant. The Barnstable church limited baptism to communicants and their minor children throughout the seventeenth century. The only exception was made for a youth judged mentally incompetent "and not of any maturity to act for hims:" Barnstable changed its strict polity in 1715 when the church voted to "admit their children when they have any to Baptism themselves to all ordinances If they be intelligent & sound In the faith not scandalous in Life."[25] The church never

[24] "Records of the First Church at Salisbury," *Historical Collections* of the Essex Institute; 1879-80, *16*, p. 40; *17*, pp. 8, 36.

[25] Diary of Rev. John Lothrop from 1634 to 1653, MS, copy by Ezra Stiles, 1769, New England Historic and Genealogical

used the half-way covenant; it passed from limited membership to open admission without any intermediate step.

The Plymouth church also completed the century without altering its qualifications for membership, despite John Cotton's advocacy of the half-way covenant. In 1676 all the children of the church were brought together, and the elders asked if they "did owne their interest in the covenant of their fathers" and would "stirre up themselves . . . for obtaining the good & blessings of that covenant." A week later the entire church renewed its covenant, but the children received no new privileges in return for their assent. Cotton probably hoped the extra copies of *First Principles* he requested from Mather in 1678 would help convert his congregation to the half-way covenant; if he ever received them, they had no appreciable effect. In 1693 when the church considered the innovation, "some spake for it, some said it was an indifferent thing, but generally the bretheren seemed not free to admit of it, but to continue the practice in that matter as formerly." Finally, in 1726, thirty years after Cotton's death, Plymouth accepted the half-way practices.[26]

In Topsfield the pastor, Joseph Capen, was probably responsible for the failure of the church to accept the half-way covenant, although he may well

---

Society, Boston, p. 4; "Records of the West Parish of Barnstable, Massachusetts; 1668-1807" (photostatic copy, Yale University), March 23, 1683/84, February 9, 1715.

[26] *Plymouth Church Records; 1620-1859*, CSM *Publications*, 1920, 22, pp. 149-152, 172, 231.

have reflected the view of the majority of his congregation. Capen kept the church records from 1684 to 1725 and after each person admitted he carefully noted, "full communion." But Capen apparently outlived the conservative segment of his congregation; immediately after his death in 1725 the church voted to permit the children of the church to own the covenant and have their children baptized.[27]

The Reverend John Russell's Hadley congregation probably joined the five churches above in refusing to adopt the propositions of the Half-Way Synod. Russell's petition to the General Court in 1670 had brought the political battle over the half-way covenant to a head, and in recognition of his defense of strict Congregationalism Governor Bellingham made Russell a trustee of his estate. In a letter to Increase Mather in 1681 Russell reaffirmed his aversion to the half-way covenant.[28] So far as we know the church followed the pastor's leadership on this issue.

No visible pattern emerges from these six dissenting parishes that explains why they chose their course. They represent three of the five Massachusetts counties and two of the three Plymouth counties. They include the principal church in the major commercial center of New England, a river town in the Connecticut Valley, and small to medium sized agricultural towns. Their geographical dispersion is obvious. In some of the towns the pastor led the

[27] "Records of the Topsfield Church," *Historical Collections* of Topsfield Historical Society, 1909, *14*, pp. 6, 11.

[28] John Russell to Increase Mather, March 28, 1681, *Mather Papers*, pp. 82-84.

resistance to the half-way covenant; in others, the laity provided the leadership; in still others, the ministers and members worked in unison. The only element these towns held in common was their antipathy to the half-way principles.

In the 1690's Cotton Mather described the variety of baptismal practices in the Massachusetts churches:

> . . . some of our churches yet baptise the children of none but their communicants, and extend their church-watch to none but the persons of their communicants, and tho' some of the churches go a step further, and extend their church-watch to the children of their communicants, but . . . will not baptise the offspring of these, . . . nevertheless, the most of the ministers in the countrey, have obtained of their churches, not only to forbear all expressions of dissatisfaction at the baptism of such as the synod had declared the subjects of it, but to concur with them, when their votes are upon occasion demanded. . . .[29]

The survey of Massachusetts and Plymouth churches undertaken in the preceding chapters confirms Mather's basic outline, but it also gives a much clearer picture of the relative strength of each group and the variety of ways in which churches applied the half-way covenant.

The conversion of Second Church Boston in 1693 brought to twenty-three the number of churches that had adopted the half-way principles. If the informa-

[29] *Magnalia,* 2, Bk. 5, p. 267.

tion gathered from thirty churches constitutes an accurate sample, then we should be able to gauge the total response to the propositions of the Half-Way Synod. Three of every four churches for which we have direct or inferential evidence regarding baptismal practices used the half-way covenant by the early 1690's. Although we know very little about the practices of another twenty-five churches, except that the ministers of five of them publicly endorsed the half-way principles at one time or another, the ratio of adoptions should be very similar. In only two areas does this ratio deviate from three out of four. In Suffolk County where the largest amount of data is available, churches using the half-way covenant outnumbered conservative parishes seven to one. Conversely, in Plymouth Colony, where information is available for only three of the twelve churches, only one used the half-way covenant, although this may have resulted from a more charitable admissions policy that made the half-way covenant less attractive and less necessary.[30] It seems fairly certain that, with the exception of the Old Colony, by the time the new charter was received in 1692, a large majority of the churches in the new royal colony of Massachusetts had accommodated their polity to conform to the propositions of the synod.

In this transition to the modified polity the date 1675 appears to have been crucial. Although thirteen churches adopted the half-way covenant prior to 1670, in 60 percent of them effective implementation came

[30] George D. Langdon, *Pilgrim Colony: A History of New Plymouth; 1620-1691*, New Haven, 1966, pp. 129-133.

only after the outbreak of King Philip's War. It seems quite likely that this shift in the attitude of church members was a direct response to the tragic events they saw around them. But this descriptive survey of Massachusetts churches fails to suggest the real impact of the half-way covenant on church membership and institutional structure, even though it reveals the breadth of implementation. What the half-way covenant meant to the churches that adopted it becomes apparent only with close internal analysis.

EIGHT

Their Separate Ways: Four Churches and the Half-Way Covenant

THE half-way covenant helped to sunder the established orthodoxy and uniformity of Congregationalism; given shape and content by autonomous congregations, it became the basis for a bewildering variety of individual polities. To know that three-fourths of the Massachusetts churches practiced the half-way covenant gives only a general impression of what was happening to the churches in the second half of the seventeenth century. The broad lines are distinct; the finer ones are lost. One way to see a clearer picture is through the close scrutiny of several churches as they lived with the half-way covenant. Ideally every church should receive this examination, but the inadequacy of existing records makes such a study impossible. The four churches selected here for extensive internal analysis—Roxbury, Charlestown, Third Church Boston, and Dorchester—while their experiences are not universally applicable, suggest more clearly the meaning of the half-way covenant.

Basically, the questions to be answered are simple. How many persons owned the covenant and did the half-way members constitute a majority of the members? Was it customary for children of the church to own the covenant, and if so, at what age? How many children of the church later became communicants? And, was the half-way covenant a way station or the final religious commitment? Once answered, a more important question arises: are there any consistent patterns that permit generalization, or is the experience of each church idiosyncratic?

Of the four churches selected, Roxbury adopted the half-way covenant first. The year after the Ministerial Assembly the members accepted the principle and in 1660 began its practice. But the members still entertained some doubts about the wisdom of their course and discouraged many from owning the covenant. By 1664 only three women had taken the step, and the total for the decade reached only twenty. On at least four occasions prior to 1669 the Roxbury congregation refused to allow individuals to own the covenant, and the elders were forced to send them to Rev. Peter Hobart in Hingham to obtain baptism for their children. On the first of these occasions the objection was raised that the woman had owned the covenant in another church. But in the fall of 1668, when the trouble in First Church Boston was coming to a head, Roxbury denied three requests from its own members. The elders wrote to Hobart again: "here is another young man namely John Loving who is a child of our Church, and desireth to have that ordinance administered to his Child, he had thought to have obtained it here the last Lords day and Water prepared but an uncomfortable agitation there was amongst us and thereby it was prevented. We desire you would be pleased to let him have his Desire."[1] It is not known how many others, rejected by the congregation as unfit to become half-way members, did not choose to make the trip to Hingham. Clearly not everyone who satisfied the requirements of the ministers met with approval from the congregation. The Roxbury members had set standards of their own that limited the use of the half-way covenant.

Despite these restrictions the number of persons owning the covenant gradually increased after 1664. From twenty in the first decade the total rose to 113 in the 1670's and 191 in the 1680's. As the number owning the covenant increased, the age of the new half-way members steadily decreased until it was apparent that owning the covenant had become a normative religious act for the children of the church. Girls in their mid-teens and boys at about twenty were expected to renew their bond with the church as evidence of their religious commitment and as another step in preparation for full membership. The children did not take this step instead of entering communion but as part of what was hoped would be progress toward that goal. By the 1680's the effective use of the half-way covenant was obvious; two out of every three persons entering full communion had owned the covenant earlier. Two decades earlier less than 10 percent had owned the covenant before becoming communicants.[2] As Roxbury became accustomed to the half-way covenant, the initial rigor disappeared, and the members came to expect the

[1] Stiles, Itineraries, 3, pp. 237-238, 248. [2] Appendix, Table 1.

children of the church to accept, at least temporarily, half-way membership.

The flow of children into half-way membership was not smooth, however, and the fluctuations tended to be very sharp. Even in the last decade, when the half-way covenant was fully integrated into Roxbury's polity, the number of new half-way members ranged in any given year from zero to eighty-five. As Graph 1 indicates, there were four periods when unusually large numbers of children joined as half-way members. The first peak occurred in the midst of King Philip's War, and the total for 1675 doubled that of any previous year. The second peak came the year after the Reforming Synod and may have been a response to an increased consciousness on the part of the church of its obligations toward the children of the church. In 1684-1685 the church received a truly extraordinary number of half-way members; this increase may reflect the anxiety that followed the revocation of the Massachusetts charter in 1684. The final peak coincides with the most arbitrary period of Sir Edmund Andros' regime. It is quite probable that in each of these four periods of unusual activity by the children of the church, the external realities and dangers were combined with particularly effective preaching to bring about a revival of religion. These periodic revivals, whatever their cause, helped to keep the children in the church. By breaking the deadening routine of religion, the revivals brought back into the fold, in a way that custom alone could not, many children who stood at the periphery in their relations with the church.

GRAPH 1. ROXBURY

ENTERED THE CHURCH 1665-1690

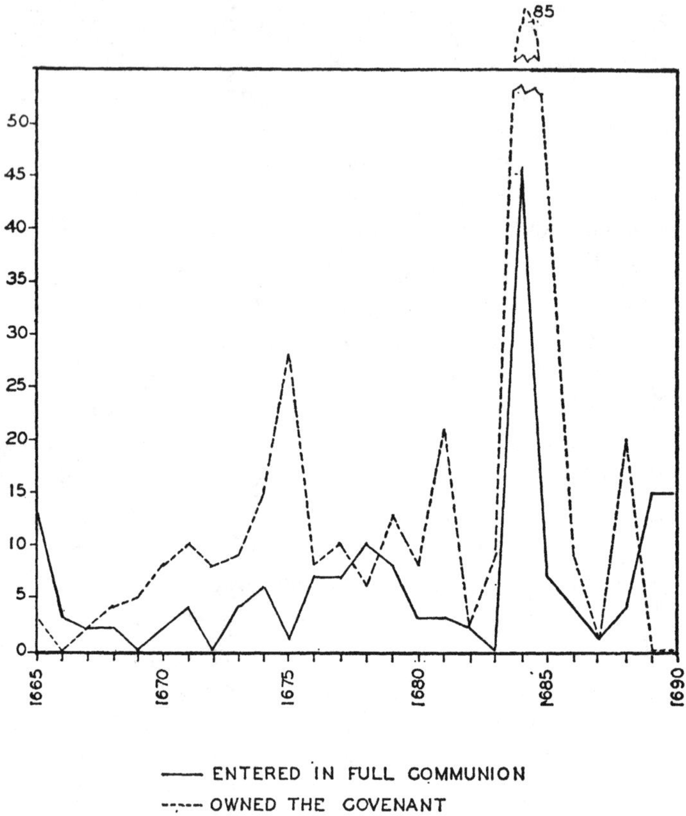

Historians from Cotton Mather to Perry Miller have assumed that the half-way covenant was introduced in response to a decrease in full communicants, and that as the century wore on this decline became more marked, until those in the half-way status constituted a majority of the church. Roxbury only partially conforms to this stereotype. The average number of new communicants that Roxbury added started dropping shortly after the founding of the church, but the decline was not constant throughout the remainder of the century. The table below illustrates the cycle of church membership in Roxbury and suggests a different picture from that normally drawn.

AVERAGE ANNUAL INCREMENT OF COMMUNICANTS[3]

1640-1649	*1650-1659*	*1660-1669*	*1670-1679*	*1680-1689*
7.8	4.8	4.4	5.1	9.1

The flow of communicants into the Roxbury church forms an almost perfect U-curve over the half-century. The lowest point occurred between 1660 and 1669; and in the final decade, the years normally associated with precipitous decline, the average number of new communicants exceeded that of any period since 1635. The number of communicants in proportion to the total population had been dropping steadily in Roxbury until the 1670's, when church membership began to increase. Between 1680 and 1689 the number of new communicants was increasing at the same rate as the adult population of the town.[4] Rather than religious decline, the Roxbury church seems to have found new vitality in the 1680's.

[3] *Roxbury Church Records*, pp. 74-88.

[4] This estimate is based on the approximate adult population in 1690 and 1765, and takes into account the death rate and the increase in population. These calculations suggest that Roxbury gained about nine adults per year in the 1690's.

Roxbury does appear to substantiate the allegation that half-way members inevitably became the fatter end of the wallet. The total number who owned the covenant far exceeds the number admitted to full communion,[5] but the apparent ratio of two to one is deceptive. Ninety-two of those who owned the covenant joined in full communion before 1690. This means that only slightly more than half of all the new members in the Roxbury church in these three decades retained half-way membership, and even this figure may well be too high. The scarcity of marriage records makes it quite probable that many women have been counted twice, once under their maiden name when they owned the covenant and again under their married name when they entered communion.[6] Between 1660 and 1690 the half-way members never achieved a numerical superiority in the church.

However, the revival of 1684-1685 shifted the balance between full communicants and half-way members, and the latter became an increasingly large proportion of the church. As owning the covenant became more routine for the children of the church, the percentage that made the transition from half-way membership to full communion decreased steadily. The broader the compass of half-way membership, the more the church drew in the less religiously inclined. If this trend had continued after

[5] Appendix, Table 1.

[6] *ibid.*; the statistical table tends to support this conclusion. In every other instance the women outnumbered the men by at least 50 percent; yet in #18 the percentages are quite close.

1690, half-way members would have eventually outnumbered the full communicants.

The adoption of the half-way covenant clearly served the church's interests. The number of persons who desired full membership had not declined with the innovation; and by bringing in a very large number of half-way members, the church had enormously increased the number of persons on which it could bring to bear its disciplinary and moral force. The church was not yet a voice crying in the wilderness; in fact, the church probably ministered to a higher proportion of the people in 1690 than at any other time in its history.

One other aspect of Roxbury's membership merits attention: the preponderance of women. The women of the church had a consistently higher level of participation both as half-way members and as full communicants. This trend began in 1640 and became more marked between 1660 and 1676, but the men began to redress the imbalance after 1676.

PERCENTAGE OF NEW COMMUNICANTS—MALE

1640-1660	*1660-1669*	*1670-1676*	*1677-1679*	*1680-1689*
41%	36%	19%	40%	46%

PERCENTAGE OF NEW HALF-WAY MEMBERS—MALE

1660-1669	*1670-1676*	*1677-1689*
30%	29%	41%

The tendency to leave religion to women is normal in a relatively stable society. The increase in the religious activity of the men between 1677 and 1689 may have resulted from the increased instability of the province. The revocation of the charter and its attendant political disruption, the threat of economic dislocation, and the social disorientation undoubtedly increased anxiety, and men may have turned to religion for solace and security.[7]

Charlestown was the second of the four churches to adopt the half-way covenant. Although both Charlestown and Roxbury depended primarily on agriculture and enjoyed proximity to Boston's markets and urban environment, Charlestown differed perceptibly from Roxbury. Charlestown had a population half again as large as Roxbury and was evidently far wealthier.[8] If mercantile activity and general prosperity affect the quality of religious activity, as several historians have suggested, Charlestown's experience with the half-way covenant should reflect this pattern.

Charlestown took twelve years to overcome its initial reluctance toward the half-way covenant. Despite the congregation's approval of the principle, the endorsement of Symmes and Shepard, and the involvement of Charlestown in the formation of Third Church Boston, very few members exercised their right to renew the covenant. Between 1663 and 1676 only thirteen children of the church accepted half-way membership. In 1677 the number almost doubled, but quickly dropped again as only three persons owned the covenant between 1678 and 1680. Twice in the 1680's the number jumped to new

[7] Appendix, Graphs 5-6.

[8] Charlestown's levy for the Indian war in 1676 was £180; Roxbury's was £30; *Massachusetts Records*, 5, pp. 55-56.

peaks only to fall immediately to nominal levels. Owning the covenant never became, as it had in Roxbury, a traditional responsibility for the children of the church. The number who availed themselves of the half-way covenant, although increasing between 1680 and 1689, remained low. Two factors indicate that use of the half-way covenant was haphazard rather than customary: the very few persons who owned the covenant prior to their admission to full communion, and the virtually constant ages of those who owned the covenant over the three decades.[9] The sporadic peaks illustrated in Graph 2 suggest that owning the covenant generally coincided with "harvest" of new communicants. Perhaps in these revivals some children, considering themselves unfit for the Lord's Supper, used the half-way covenant to draw closer to the church. When the religious excitement passed, so did owning the covenant.

One of the primary functions advocates of the half-way covenant envisioned for their innovation was that the continued discipline and teaching of the church would prepare children for full membership. In Charlestown the preparatory role failed to materialize. Few children chose this path to full communion; they waited instead for the regenerative experience. Eighty-nine percent of the new communicants were admitted without first taking hold of the covenant in the decade between 1680 and 1689. Equally significant, for more than three-fourths of those who owned the covenant it marked the final religious commitment. Even when the half-way mem-

[9] Appendix, Table 2.

GRAPH 2. CHARLESTOWN
ENTERED THE CHURCH 1665-1690

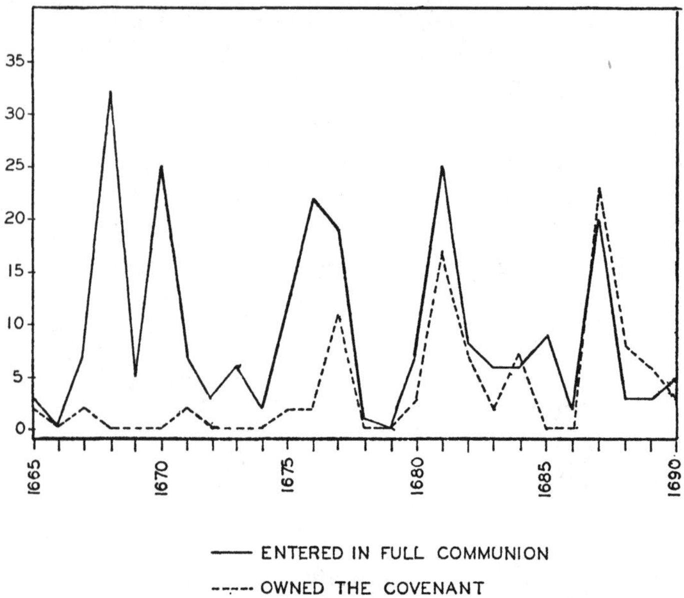

bers went on to join in full communion, they took considerably longer to make this step than their peers who omitted the half-way covenant.

Despite the failure of the half-way members to make the transition from covenant to communion, they never became the larger part of the Charlestown church. At every point between 1665 and 1690 full communicants formed a clear majority of the total congregation. Two and one-half times as many persons entered communion as owned the covenant, and only twice in twenty-five years did the number owning the covenant in a single year exceed the new communicants.

Charlestown, like Roxbury, does not conform to the generalizations about declining church membership as the century progressed. The average annual increment of new communicants was higher between 1670 and 1689 than in any other decade since 1640. Despite the addition of thirty-two communicants in 1668, the annual average for that decade was less than five new communicants. For the next two decades that annual average figure almost doubled. Although the nine new communicants per year that the church added in this period certainly did not keep pace with the increase in Charlestown's adult population,[10] it improved the ratio of communicants to population significantly. Taken in conjunction with the half-way covenant, the increase in communicants meant that Charlestown probably had a higher number of inhabitants with church connection in 1690 than at any other time since the middle of the century.

In Charlestown, as in Roxbury, religious participation centered increasingly on the women, and this phenomenon dated back to the first decade of the church's existence. As the years passed the number of women in the church became increasingly disproportionate, and only in rare years did the new male members outnumber the women. The percentage of men among the new communicants is revealing: in 1632-1649 they represented 43 percent of the increment; in 1650-1669 this figure dropped to 35 per-

[10] Charlestown's increase should have been 50 percent higher than Roxbury's or at least thirteen new adults per year.

cent; and in 1670-1689, to 33 percent. The same pattern holds for owning the covenant. By the final decade three of every four new half-way members were women.[11] The numerical superiority of the women in owning the covenant appears quite reasonable, for by taking this step, they qualified their children for baptism and the attendant parochial obligations of the church. The women, as centers of family life, responded more readily to this opportunity than the men. Although the ratio of men to women improved in the years after 1680, the increase was not significant.[12] Women proved superior in almost every external measure of religious life. They entered communion and owned the covenant in greater numbers, and they did so at an earlier age. The church played as important a part in the lives of the women late in the century as it had earlier.

In the short run, introduction of the half-way covenant in Charlestown did not accelerate religious decline. The church may have adopted it in response to the apparent decline in new communicants, but it had little effect on membership until the last quarter of the century. Most people avoided it. If religiously inclined, they apparently preferred to attain membership through relation of the regenerative experience, a practice Charlestown retained beyond 1690. The second and third generations maintained the meticulous religious principles of the founders in unusual numbers and applied them just as scrupulously.

[11] Appendix, Graphs 7-8.

[12] It increased from 30 to 36 percent for communicants and from 25 to 28 percent for half-way members.

Short cuts and the easy way had little appeal in Charlestown. If Massachusetts had been "secular," as it has often been portrayed, the church should have been filled with half-way members. Easier terms would have acted as a lure to secular men, since prestige still accrued to church members. The few half-way memberships, however, suggest that in Charlestown, at least, time had not seriously undermined the religious tradition, although there certainly were inhabitants to whom church membership must have meant very little.

Perhaps more than any other church in Massachusetts, Third Church Boston had a vested interest in the half-way covenant, since that issue above all else had provoked the schism in First Church.[13] From the beginning Third Church was committed to the principle that was its raison d'etre. Since we most frequently associate religious decline with the urban mercantile environment of Boston, and since Third Church alone deviated from the "old orthodoxy" in Boston, more knowledge of the men who led the separation and signed the church covenant in May 1669 may provide a further key to understanding the half-way covenant.

The dissenters who formed Third Church included some of the most prominent men in Massachusetts, and as a group they were distinguished by two characteristics—above average economic status and frequent public service. Of the twenty-eight founders we know the vocations of fifteen. The eight skilled artisans

[13] *ante.*, pp. 156-165.

included an apothecary, a bookseller, a silversmith, a feltmaker, a butcher, a shipmaster, a tailor, a brewer, and a mason-builder. At least two of these artisans carried on sufficient trade to warrant our including them with five other dissenters who derived their income principally as merchants. Thus at a minimum half the original members had achieved economic status and were closely involved in the growing cosmopolitan atmosphere of Boston. It is doubtful that either First Church or Second Church equalled the ratio of well-to-do men that founded Third Church. As a concomitant of their economic status these men filled a number of offices, both in Boston and in the province. Two served as selectmen, seven sat as deputies in the General Court, others held the offices of Secretary, Treasurer, and Mintmaster of the colony, and one had acted as speaker of the house. In addition twelve belonged to the Artillery Company (half as officers), three had served as deacons of First Church, and more than half were of the first generation of Massachusetts settlers. Together they constituted a formidable array of talent, wealth, and prestige.[14]

In its first six years the growth of Third Church was extraordinary. When the wives finally transferred their membership from First Church to Third Church in 1674, the number of full communicants rose to 153. Third Church already had 25 percent more communicants than Increase Mather's Second Church.[15]

[14] Hill, *Old South Church*, *I*, pp. 113-119.

[15] *Boston Second Church Records*, Book 1½, p. 9; December 15, 1673, Mather listed forty-two men and seventy-nine women in full communion.

Only two-fifths of these communicants joined from First Church; the remainder came from a variety of sources—members of Second Church who found the

GRAPH 3. BOSTON THIRD CHURCH
ENTERED THE CHURCH 1669-1690

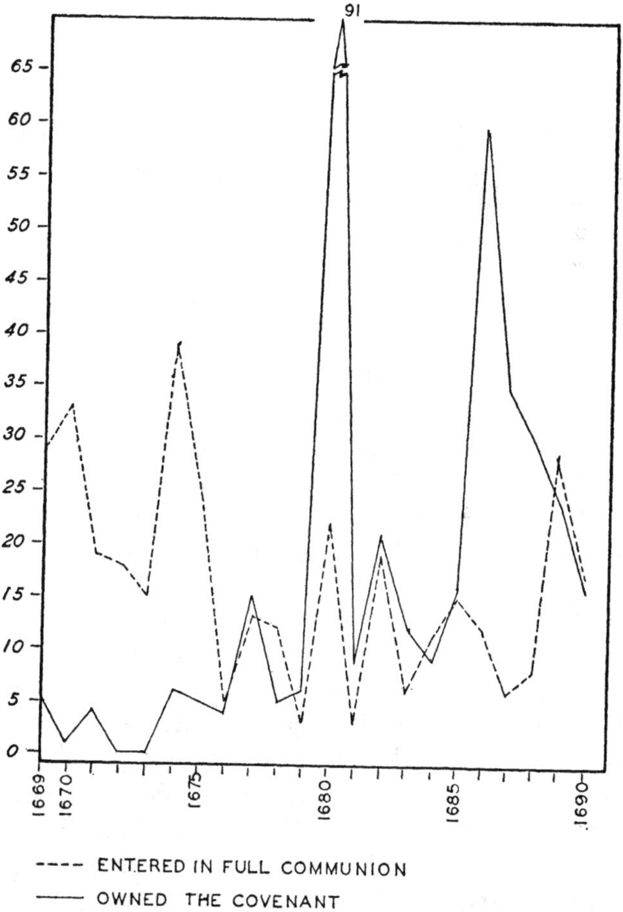

new church more convenient, new converts, and recent settlers in Boston. Yet it is doubtful that the church grew so rapidly because of the half-way covenant. In the same half dozen years only fifteen children owned the covenant, a surprisingly low number for a church founded primarily to perpetuate the membership of the children of the church. Since everyone was a new member, theoretically there were no children of the church except newly baptized infants. What happened to the children over sixteen who followed their parents? Did they remain subject to the discipline of their former church? They could have owned the covenant and taken their place in Third Church, yet they did not. Once again we confront a reluctance to use the innovation in the first few years, more remarkable in Third Church because of its outspoken advocacy of the half-way covenant.

The practice gained acceptance slowly in the second half of the decade when the number owning the covenant doubled. All hesitancy disappeared in 1680 when ninety-one children of the church accepted half-way membership following a series of revival sermons by Samuel Willard. Although the church never again brought in that many children in a single year, the relatively high levels during the period of the Andros regime significantly increased the total of half-way members. Normally the children of the church accepted their new role not when they reached the age of discretion but at about the time their first child arrived and thus could be qualified for baptism.

Increasingly half-way membership became a permanent status in Third Church. The more children owning the covenant, the fewer of them who went on into full communion. Three out of five who owned the covenant in 1669 later qualified for communion; only 30 percent who owned the covenant between 1670 and 1679 made the transition; by the final decade fewer than 22 percent entered communion. Of those who were able to meet the test, a few entered communion within months after they owned the covenant, but the median period was eight years. One woman waited thirty-eight years, one man thirty-seven. The preparatory benefits of the half-way covenant in Third Church[16] were very limited indeed.

The trends that were becoming visible in the 1690's boded ill for Third Church. By 1690 the number of half-way members probably equalled the number of full communicants and within the next few years should have achieved a sizable majority. As the percentage that went from covenant to communion decreased, the smaller number entering communion without first owning the covenant compounded the trouble. The children of the church were unable to sustain the high number of communicants attained in the first decade. Without constant accessions to the church from outside, the half-way members had to predominate.

The plight of the church becomes more obvious when one considers the decline in new communicants. In the decade of 1670-1679 the church had averaged fifteen new communicants per year (excluding those who entered from First Church). Between 1680 and

[16] Appendix, Table 3.

1689, a decade when Boston's population increased 55 percent, new communicants in Third Church dropped 20 percent.[17] Third Church not only failed to convert its own, it failed to attract its share of the new inhabitants of Boston. Several members tried to persuade Samuel Willard to ease the rigors of testified regenerate membership, and at a meeting in Samuel Sewall's home they made known their "desire to come into the Church without making any Relation at all; or having Mr. Willard report the substance of what they said to him." Two weeks later the church members considered the proposal and voted in the negative. The most they would do to ease the requirements was to permit "that Persons may be taken in, the Church only being present, and not the Congregation." Benjamin Davis and Nathaniel Oliver, the two men who initiated the appeal, apparently found the solution satisfactory, because two weeks later they were admitted to full communion after giving their personal relations, although Sewall found their testimony unremarkable.[18] Had the innovation been accepted, it might have attenuated the rigors of experiential religion and made it easier for "civil" men to reach the Lord's Table. But Third Church would not sacrifice its ideals to bolster its lagging membership. Only in baptism was Third Church relatively open. Edward Randolph remarked that Willard "is a mod-

[17] Carl Bridenbaugh, *Cities in the Wilderness*, New York, 1964, p. 6.

[18] *Diary of Samuel Sewall*, MHS *Collections*, 45, 1878, pp. 92, 94-95.

erate man and baptizeth those who are refused by other churches, for which he is hated."[19]

The inclination to leave religion to the women is as evident in Third Church as in Charlestown and Roxbury. Twice as many men as women owned the covenant from 1669 to 1675 when participation was very low, but only once in the next fifteen years did the number of men again exceed that of women. Among communicants the preponderance of women appeared almost from the beginning. Between 1669 and 1675 the women admitted outnumbered the men more than two to one. Although the men reduced this ratio to five to three in the next decade, the cumulative effect remained the same. Even given this disparity in numbers, the women were more likely to own the covenant. More than half the women who entered communion had first owned the covenant; among men only four in ten took this preliminary step. In all likelihood, the women's sense of responsibility for the religious welfare of their children (baptism and discipline) explains the difference.

The half-way covenant may not have accelerated the decline in Boston's Third Church, but it certainly did nothing to retard it. Ironically the church did better when many persons still considered it to be an illegal gathering operating in violation of the statute of 1636. The hardest times came after its reconciliation with First Church and its full acceptance as an equal with the other churches in the colony.

[19] *Hutchinson Papers*, 2, pp. 273-274.

Of the four churches analyzed here, Dorchester was the only one to resist the half-way covenant and the last one to adopt the practice. After years of frustration the congregation finally acquiesced in 1677 and within weeks of the vote called on the children to renew their baptismal covenants. Success was immediate. One hundred and fourteen, or one of every six persons in Dorchester, owned the covenant in 1677. Unlike other churches Dorchester, once it had made the decision, put the innovation to use.

Superficially the figures for 1677 appear to demonstrate the advantages of the half-way covenant; baptisms for that year tripled the annual average of the preceding six years. But only twelve of the sixty-six children baptized were the children of half-way members; the parents of the rest were in full communion. The sharp rise in communicants, which followed the mass covenant renewal, caused the increase in baptisms; the parents of half the children baptized had entered full communion in 1677. The puzzling question is why more half-way members did not present their children. At least half those who owned the covenant had reached an age where one would expect them to have children.[20] Is it possible that reservations toward the half-way covenant ran so deep that even when members accepted the half-way status—at the urging of the church—they refused to believe that this status qualified their children for baptism? If so, how ironic that declining membership might have been caused not by a falling away from God, but by children of the church punctiliously

[20] Appendix, Table 4.

adhering to testified regenerate membership. There is the possible alternative that neither parents nor children cared about joining the church. However this seems less plausible; once the children of the church had accepted half-way membership, there was little reason to keep their own children from baptism except for religious scruples.

The 114 half-way members added in 1677 represent an impressive achievement. One would assume that this figure included virtually every eligible person in the parish, but the total is deceptive. In 1676 Dorchester had prepared a list of all the children between eight and twenty-two whom the elders were to catechize. Of the eighty-eight boys whose names appeared, forty-two never owned the covenant; of the eighty-five girls, fifty-three failed to take advantage of the opportunity. Despite pressure from the church more than half the children of the catechism list remained aloof; death, migration, and marriage undoubtedly removed some of them, but the number is still high.

Implementation of the half-way covenant had little permanent effect on Dorchester. In the four years after 1677 not a single person owned the covenant, and the total for 1682-1690 reached only twenty-one. Even if the renewal of 1677 had brought in every child over twelve (which it did not), the number after 1680 was remarkably low—far below the number of children who came of age in Dorchester. The half-way covenant simply never became an integral part of Dorchester's polity. Twenty-five years later Dorchester duplicated the call to the children of the

GRAPH 4. DORCHESTER
ENTERED THE CHURCH 1677-1690

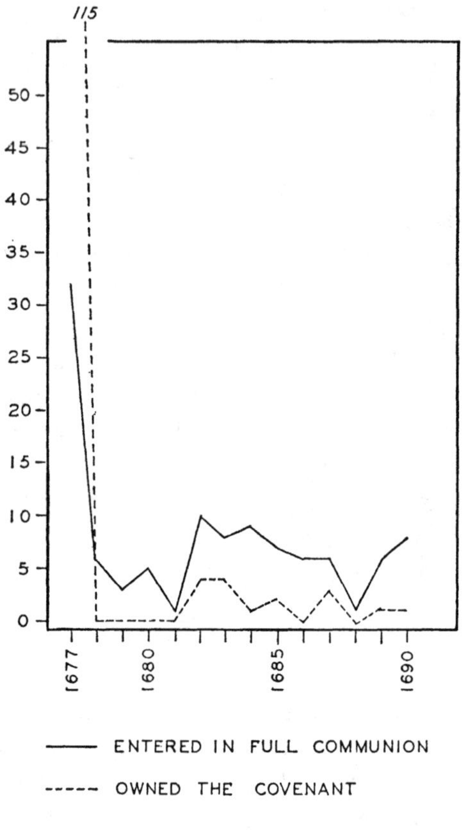

church and reaped another large harvest. This procedure might work for each generation, but it hardly provided a smooth or routine flow of children into the church.[21]

[21] *Dorchester Church Records*, p. 120.

The adoption of the half-way covenant was followed by a sizable increase in Dorchester's communicants. Between 1677 and 1690 the average rose to 7.6 per year. One cannot attribute this increase solely to the introduction of the half-way covenant. Rather, both the number of new communicants and the original use of the covenant are signs of a general revival of religion in Dorchester. For some individuals owning the covenant may have helped prepare them for the Lord's Supper, for which they would not have qualified otherwise, but the lapsed time between owning the covenant and entering full communion indicates that this did not apply to many people.[22] Only one-third of the new communicants of 1677-1689 had owned the covenant; the majority entered in the traditional way without any preparatory step.

The full communicants never lost their numerical superiority in the church. Between 1677 and 1690, 135 children owned the covenant, and thirty-two of these joined in full communion before 1690. In the same period the church added 106 new communicants. Half-way members came closest to domination in 1677, but continually lost ground after that.

Was Dorchester in a period of religious decline? The covenant of reformation to which the congregation assented in 1677 indicates it was, but can this jeremiad be taken at face value? One of the few tangible measures of decline is the number of full communicants, and the membership statistics in Dorchester reveal that the church was in a weaker posi-

[22] Appendix, Table 4.

tion between 1650 and 1677 than at any other time in the century.

Average Annual Increment of New Communicants

1640-1649	*1650-1659*	*1660-1669*	*1670-1676*	*1677-1689*
4.5	4.2	3.7	4.0	7.5

The average of new communicants for 1677-1689 was double the average for 1660-1676. In absolute terms the Dorchester church grew, and the ratio of communicants to adult inhabitants improved, although it did not keep pace with the increasing population.

Once more the key date is 1677. The mass covenant renewal, the introduction of the half-way covenant, and a sudden surge in new communicants (the highest level since the church was gathered in 1636) coincided in that year. It seems hard to escape the conclusion that Dorchester responded to the period of crisis with an outpouring of religious fervor. In Dorchester the men appear to have been more affected by these circumstances than the women. Men represented 38 percent of all communicants in 1660-1669, 45 percent in 1670-1679, and 49 percent in 1680-1689. Surprisingly the men constituted the majority (56 percent) of the half-way members and the majority (56 percent) of the half-way members who later joined in full communion (although they generally took longer to make the transition). After 1677 the religious participation of Dorchester's men more than matched the women's.

The half-way covenant contributed nothing to decline in Dorchester because the children of the church rarely relied on it. After 1677 owning the covenant affected a very small portion of the congregation. In Dorchester the regenerative experience remained the traditional entry into the privileges of the church.

The preceding analysis of each congregation provides individual answers to the questions posed initially and increases our understanding of the ways in which the half-way covenant functioned. When the four churches are brought together is there any apparent pattern, or were they captives of congregational autonomy responding uniquely to their dilemmas? Obviously neither polarity—consistency or uniqueness—describes the response of the churches to the half-way covenant and the religious environment of the last third of the century.

One element which appears in all the churches is the reluctance to fully accept the half-way covenant. In Roxbury, Charlestown, and Third Church this hesitancy was exhibited only after the congregation had voted to accept the innovation in principle. When the pastors attempted to implement the decision, the response of the congregation was nominal. Church members accepted the principle out of respect for the minister, or because they understood that some change in polity was necessary, but they showed great reluctance to apply the half-way covenant within their own families. The Dorchester congregation reflected its misgivings about the innovation by waiting an additional decade before accepting the synod's recommendations. It is striking, however, that practical acceptance of the principle came at almost the same time in all four churches: 1675 for one, 1677 for two, and 1680 for the other. This acceptance occurred despite the widely separated dates when the churches voted to accept the principle. It was not simply a matter of waiting a few years until the reservations disappeared; it took an external force to convince the churches that they had seriously neglected their obligations. The events from King Philip's War to the Reforming Synod, filled as they were with all the signs of God's hand set against New England, would seem to have provided the critical push. The implementation of the half-way covenant may have occurred partially to satisfy their own insecurity and partially to mollify a vengeful God.

Once effective utilization of the half-way covenant took place, the churches diverged noticeably in their use of the covenant. In only two of the churches did it become the custom for the children of the church to renew their covenants. By the last decade Roxbury had incorporated the measure as a standard part of a child's religious obligations. Normally by the time a child reached his late teens he had appeared before the congregation and reaffirmed the baptismal covenant. Third Church also applied the innovation to the majority of the children, but here renewal usually took place when the child was in his early twenties. Since the men who owned the covenant were generally older than the women, one suspects that owning the covenant generally coincided with marriage or the arrival of the first child. In Charlestown a reasonably large number of children availed themselves of the half-way covenant in the 1680's, but the church never made owning the covenant a normal part of religious life. The children used the covenant sporadically, in sudden spurts followed by rapid declines, and the high points normally coincided with periods of general revival. Dorchester stood at the opposite end from the first two churches. After 1677 almost no one in the church took advantage of the half-way covenant. Apparently the soul-searching in 1677 momentarily deflected the general opposition to the innovation and, when the religious peak passed, the hostility to the half-way covenant reappeared virtually unabated.

The ratio of full communicants to half-way members is almost directly proportional to whether the individual church incorporated the half-way covenant as a standard element in its polity. Thus in Third Church the half-way members almost exactly equalled the number of communicants by 1690. If the trend that had prevailed in the previous decade continued, the half-way members probably became the major part of the church within a few years. Roxbury was not far behind Third Church in this process. Although the ratio of new members in both categories was closer here, the half-way members were increasing faster than communicants. As the backlog of older communicants died off, the half-way members would appear to have achieved numerical superiority early in the next century, unless the church successfully reversed the trend established in the 1670's. In the two churches in which owning the covenant never became the custom, the communicants always made up the largest part of the church. Charlestown children used the covenant more than those in Dorchester and so the ratio of communicants to half-way members was closer. But Charlestown consistently drew more full members than half-way members, and this pattern showed no signs of changing by 1690. In Dorchester the half-way members drew close to the communicants only once. After 1677 the ratio of communicants to half-way members constantly increased. The half-way members were unlikely to become a majority so long as no one owned the covenant.

One cannot automatically assume that owning the covenant, when it became the custom of the church, insured that half-way members would become the majority. Two other factors are directly involved: half-way members who later joined in full communion, and converts outside of the half-way covenant. If the number in either category was high, obviously the ratio of half-way members to communicants would be lower.

Despite the variations among these churches in their implementation of the half-way covenant, they had a remarkably similar experience with the innovation as a source of new communicants. The table below gives the percentage of half-way members who later joined the church in full communion.

	Roxbury	*Charles-town*	*Third Church*	*Dor-chester*
1670's	46%	41%	33%	39%
1680's	25%	30%	25%	24%

In the last decade the percentage is almost the same for all four churches. Although deaths, marriages, and migration probably make these percentages lower than they actually should be, it is clear the half-way covenant represented the terminal commitment for most children who took advantage of it. If these percentages held for any length of time, it meant each church had to attract three communicants who had not taken hold of the covenant for every member who improved his half-way status. If a church failed to do this, the half-way members inevitably became the greater part of the church. The percentage of new communicants who entered without owning the covenant in the 1680's clarifies what was happening to the ratio of communicants to half-way members in each of the four churches.[23]

Percentage of New Communicants Who Had Not Owned the Covenant: 1680-1690

Roxbury	*Charles-town*	*Third Church*	*Dor-chester*
37%	88%	62.5%	63%

These tables suggest the relative balance between the two categories of membership, but they do not indicate how effectively the church fulfilled the religious needs of the community. Communicants might outnumber half-way members four to one, but if only a handful of persons are involved, the church is hardly a success. How successful were the churches in at-

[23] This table includes everyone who owned the covenant in those decades and at any time later joined in full communion. Therefore the correlation between the two tables is not exact.

tracting communicants? In the three churches for which we have long run membership figures the statistics are enlightening. The churches were more successful in the decades from 1670 to 1689 than they had been in the middle of the century.

AVERAGE ANNUAL INCREMENT OF COMMUNICANTS

	Roxbury	*Charlestown*	*Dorchester*
1660-1669	4.4	4.7	3.7
1670-1679	5.1	9.7	6.9
1680-1689	9.1	9.0	5.7
Increase of 1670-1689 over 1660-1669:	61%	100%	70%

These percentages certainly contradict the assumption that church membership kept declining as the century wore on. In fact there was a remarkable upturn in communicants. That these increases frequently coincided with the crucial years after 1675 supports the hypothesis that the new religiosity was an effect of social disorientation and insecurity. Each one of these churches had a better ratio of communicants to population in 1690 than it had had twenty years earlier. Those churches that also effectively used the half-way covenant further broadened the system of church discipline and moral inculcation in the communities.

The statistics above also may explain cogently why in 1662 the ministers reached their decision to accept the half-way covenant as part of orthodox Congregationalism. What appeared reasonable in 1647 had become a necessity by the 1660's. Faced with a declining rate of new communicants, they saw in the half-way covenant a way to continue the institutional life of the church without compromising testified regenerate membership. In a way their decision appears justified; the increase in communicants coincides in most cases with the implementation of the half-way covenant. Although owning the covenant did not operate as a preparation for full communion, its introduction may have excited some members to search themselves for signs of grace, which ultimately brought them to full communion. It seems probable that implementation of the half-way covenant and the increase in communicants both came as a result of external factors.

The quantitative impact of the half-way covenant on these four churches is obvious from the material presented here. Assessing the qualitative effect of the half-way covenant presents a far more difficult task. One can never resolve the basic quandary: did the half-way covenant help or impede the religious development of the individual? Undoubtedly it helped some individuals who would never have come into any meaningful relationship with the church without the opportunity to own the covenant. Although as half-way members they could not vote or take communion, they received the watch and care of the church and kept their children within the fold. They participated to the limits of their ability and derived real benefits from their bond to the church. The low percentage of persons who entered communion after owning the covenant seems to support this interpretation. But quite probably the half-way covenant had the reverse effect on some of the children of the church. That is, they took hold of the covenant as the easiest way to maintain their relations with the church. Had the half-way covenant not existed as an alternative, many of those who comfortably rested in their half-way status might have been forced to prepare themselves for the Lord's Supper rather than see their children and themselves cut off from the church. Since human motivations are complex and often contrary, men undoubtedly took advantage of the half-way covenant for a variety of reasons. In most cases they probably could not have explained their actions themselves; for us to explain three centuries later is impossible. However, the recurrent themes of reluctance and scrupulosity suggest that the third generation of New Englanders was no less religious than the first and that its conception of true religion corresponded remarkably with that of its forebears. Only the forms had changed.

The world of Cotton Mather was not the world of John Winthrop. Neither society nor religion is static. As Massachusetts changed, the churches changed; and the men who worshipped in the churches adapted their ideas and their institutions to fit the world they faced. They not only made the half-way covenant part of a new orthodoxy, they sought ways to buttress themselves against the disasters that threatened their world by redefining the relationship of the church to the community. The half-way covenant was both an end and a beginning.

NINE

The Continuing Search: 1675-1692

REVEREND John Russell started the new year of 1681 with a letter to Increase Mather in Boston. It was not a joyful letter of greeting but a lamentation for New England. "The Lord hath been aloud alarming all of us," he wrote; portentous signs, the death of faithful Christians, blazing comets, and Indians plotting, gave him pause. He was sure in his own mind that defilement of the sacraments and pollution of the churches lay at the root of New England's trials. Across the river from his Hadley parish Russell saw at firsthand "our good Brother Stoddard" encouraging the unprepared to come to communion and baptism. All decline flowed from a single source, the half-way covenant. "I do every day sorrowfully increase in satisfaction, that the doctrine of those propositions in the Synod 62 doth tend in the end of the worke (how good soever the end of the workers was) to shake & undermine the fundamentall doctrine & practise of the Congregationall way, viz. that visible Saints are only matter of a ch[urch] of Ch[ris]t."[1] Was Russell merely the last weak echo of John Davenport, or had the half-way covenant, devised originally to preserve the purity of the visible

[1] March 28, 1681, *Mather Papers*, pp. 82-84.

church, destroyed the foundations and opened the doors to a host of corrupting innovations?

When Cotton Mather described the practice of the half-way covenant in Massachusetts, he told only half the story and neglected the more interesting account of his own generation's continuing search for a viable polity. In a variety of ways, sometimes together and sometimes independently, the churches created innovations in church membership and in the process destroyed all but the barest semblance of Congregational uniformity. In all of these innovations Increase and Cotton Mather became involved, at one point encouraging, at another deprecating. Out of this continuing process of innovation the half-way covenant finally emerged as a moderate position.

The churches had adopted the recommendations of the synod in response to a specific need; too few children of the church demonstrated saving grace. The synod had done its best to insure the preservation of pure churches: faith and repentance alone could qualify an individual for the Lord's Supper; only church seed should own the covenant; and voting in church affairs ought to be restricted to communicants. But Congregational autonomy gave the churches a relatively free hand to solve their own problems. When the half-way covenant proved inadequate to the tasks they faced, the churches formulated new answers, alone or in concert. Some churches used the half-way covenant as a point of departure for further innovation; others discarded it as an obsolete remnant.

One of the most common and the most acceptable

of the innovations was the mass covenant renewal. James Fitch of Norwich, Connecticut, has received credit for this innovation, although he cited the precedent set by Samuel Stone in Hartford shortly after Hooker's death. In March 1675, Fitch, with the approval of his congregation, called upon the entire church to reaffirm the original church covenant. The children of the church were asked to own the covenant made for them in baptism or at least to prepare themselves for it; if they refused, the church threatened them with admonition. As part of the solemn ceremony Fitch prepared a covenant of reformation. The entire congregation was required to stand and renew its pledge to God's church and vow to eliminate the evils which beset church and country.[2]

Plagued by a multitude of trials, churches accepted Fitch's idea with unseemly haste. Mass covenant renewals could serve the interest of the churches in at least two ways: they promised to lessen the evils which provoked God's wrath, and they reached the children of the church who had shown little inclination to come into full communion. Even the magistrates recognized the potential of this practice. In the midst of King Philip's War the Plymouth General Court appointed a day of humiliation and "added thereto a solemne motion to all our ch[urch]es to renew a covenant engagement to God for Reformation of all provoking evills."[3] Into the traditional fast day was incorporated a practice designed to impress in-

[2] Caulkins, *Norwich*, p. 123.

[3] *Plymouth Church Records*, *1*, p. 148.

delibly on the entire parish the seriousness of the occasion.

The Plymouth church, taking the Court's advice, set out to reform its ways. First the congregation prepared a new church covenant and heard the pastor list the various manifestations of its religious decline. Twelve days later all the children of the church appeared before the elders, acknowledged their covenant relation, and promised "to stirre up themselves." July 18 the entire congregation gathered for a day of humiliation to complete the work of renewal. The pastor spent the morning praying and preaching to the assembled members. The afternoon Cotton divided into two parts. First the elder read to the full communicants the covenant of reformation, and when he finished, they stood and consented to the document. Next the pastor directed his remarks to the children of the church. In this second and separate covenant of reformation the children admitted that they had "violated the holy covenant . . . made with us in our parents . . . in that wee have not hearkned to the voice of the Lord Jesus Christ . . . wee are, though descended of a noble vine, yet become the degenerate plant of a strange vine unto God." Then the children stood "to manifest their consent thereunto."[4]

In these separate covenants Plymouth made a clear distinction between the communicants and the mature children of the church. Unlike Norwich, Plymouth did not introduce the half-way covenant as part of the mass covenant renewal. Although the children owned

[4] *ibid.*, *1*, pp. 148-152.

their "interest in the covenant," they did not acquire any additional rights in the church.[5]

The rest of the churches in Plymouth Colony also responded favorably to the Court's request, and "all the ch[urch]es did in solemne manner . . . renew their covenant with God. . . ." Few people in the colony doubted that God had heard their solemn supplications. Within a month Philip was slain and "his Head was brought into Plymouth in great triumph." The sudden reversal of fortunes impressed "us to be careful to pay our vowes made to the most High in the days of distre[ss]."[6] Who could question the efficacy of mass covenant renewals with evidence like that? Call on God, ask His forgiveness, promise to cherish Him, and He would make the sun shine on New England.

The practice rapidly spread to Massachusetts churches, and in 1677 Dorchester, spurred by Increase Mather, initiated the half-way covenant as part of its covenant of reformation. The procedure closely resembled Plymouth's. First the church voted to renew the covenant; meetings with the children followed; and the process culminated with the entire congregation confessing its faults and pledging to hew closer to God's word. Increase Mather, now the champion of mass covenant renewals, gave the practice a central position in the *Necessity for Reformation.* "What is to be done that these Evils may be Reformed," the Reforming Synod asked. "Solemn and explicit renewal of the Covenant is a Scripture

[5] Ante, p. 201.
[6] *Plymouth Church Records, 1*, pp. 152-153.

Expedient for Reformation." It puts "an awe of God upon the Consciences of men when so obliged" to stand and recommit themselves to His service. Even among "Legalists and Hypocrites" solemn covenant renewals "enforce them unto an outward Reformation, and that doth divert temporal Judgements." If every congregation took this course the "Clouds of wrath hanging over these Churches" would disappear, and New England's people would once again experience "the prescence of God with them. . . ."[7]

Boston's churches felt the impact of the synod's plan for reformation immediately. In March 1680 between the sessions of the synod Increase Mather led Second Church in a covenant renewal. Although the sermon he preached on that occasion received wide circulation and helped spread the principle of covenant renewals, Mather was unsuccessful in introducing the half-way covenant as part of the covenant of reformation in his own church. At almost the same time Samuel Willard preached a series of sermons on reformation in Third Church that brought about the first broad use of the half-way covenant in his congregation, even though his church had accepted the principle eleven years earlier. In June Third Church followed the example of Second Church and undertook a mass covenant renewal.[8]

Most churches accepted the advice of the Reforming Synod and proceeded with covenant renewals, although Cotton Mather reported that "there were

[7] *Necessity for Reformation*, Walker, *Creeds and Platforms*, pp. 435-436.

[8] *ibid.*, p. 418.

some churches, who from I know not what objections . . . [except] the imaginery danger of innovations, would not comply. . . ."[9] Except for these punctilious few, mass covenant renewals became a routine part of New England Congregationalism at the end of the century.

Events in New England in the decade after King Philip's War belie the traditional identification of the half-way covenant with declension and the covenant renewals with revitalized piety. The zeal for revival of religion, expressed in the covenant renewals, was associated with adoption and implementation of the half-way covenant, not with opposition to it. Both innovations reflected the sense of declension that plagued the churches and were introduced to reverse this trend. Mass covenant renewals had no integral relation to the half-way covenant, but the possibility of connecting the two was obvious. Covenant renewals, by focusing the attention of the congregation on the evils of the times and the need for reformation, often encouraged churches to adopt the half-way covenant. They frequently singled out neglect of the children of the church as one of the major evils of the day and then remedied it by applying the half-way principles. In parishes where the half-way covenant was already in use, the covenant renewal invariably included the children of the church. The sermons and excitement connected with the renewal often awakened the children to take advantage of an opportunity they had previously

[9] *Magnalia*, 2, Bk. 5, p. 282.

ignored. Covenant renewal could transform the half-way covenant into a meaningful part of the church's polity and make it part of the general revival. The half-way covenant, like the covenant renewal, was a tool by which the zealous Puritans rejuvenated Congregationalism.

In some ways the covenant renewals built on the foundation laid by the half-way practices. The idea that the children of the church, although not yet visibly regenerate, could pledge to lead godly, honest lives was a basic tenet of the Half-Way Synod. Both the half-way covenant and the mass covenant renewal demanded of the children of the church an explicit avowal of their intention to prepare themselves for full communion. However in owning the covenant and acquiring half-way status, the children of the church usually made a voluntary commitment; the new practice tended to eliminate voluntarism. Mass covenant renewals transformed an individual decision into a community rite. So long as ministers restricted participation in covenant renewals to members of the church, the innovation had a limited effect on membership or the nature of the church covenant. But after 1690 the clergy increasingly courted inhabitants of the town who had no church connection and invited them to share in the renewals. Participation in the covenant renewal then qualified the inhabitants for half-way membership. When this occurred, the church covenant, once restricted to the visible saint and his children, took on an entirely new dimension.

A precedent for this broadening of the covenant came from the way in which a number of churches applied the half-way covenant. Several churches, after a few years' experience with the half-way covenant, attempted to enlarge the scope of the synod's fifth proposition by reaching out for inhabitants who did not meet the synod's qualifications. Not that this idea was new; Thomas Allen had recommended in 1642 a policy which would have qualified the children of all godly parents for baptism and church discipline. But Allen's successor in Charlestown, Zechariah Symmes, did not put this policy into practice until 1677. On the first occasion Symmes baptized a girl whose father had died without renewing the covenant. After this, however, Charlestown accepted persons without any previous church connection, baptized them and their children, and received them into the covenant.[10] Thereafter the church kept triple-entry books; one column for full communicants, a second for children of the church received as half-way members in their parents' right, and the third for those admitted to the church in half-way status from the outside. This innovation in Charlestown coincided with the first really extensive use of the half-way covenant by the children of the church.

Salem adopted a very similar course in 1678. When baptisms started declining toward the end of the 1670's, despite Salem's liberality, John Higginson appealed to his congregation for more latitude in baptism that he might bring into the church inhabitants without covenant relation. This did not mean "the Baptizing of the Children of all promiscuously,"

[10] *Charlestown Church Records*, p. 41.

Higginson promised; he would continue to exclude the scandalous and the ignorant. In the debate which followed:

> many of the chief of the Brethren did express themselves as concurring in judgmt. with the Pastor & Teacher & that they thought they should not onely have liberty but countenance & Encouragemt in their way & work though some others of the Brethren that were otherwise minded did Express their Scruples fears & doubts, they would not oppose but suffer the Elders to Act peacably in this matter.[11]

Baptisms in Salem increased immediately, although not to the level one might expect in a town of that size (between 1677 and 1690 the church averaged fifty-four baptisms annually). Through a series of innovations Salem had made church membership and participation in the sacraments available to almost the entire community.

Marblehead followed the example of the mother church in Salem. After adopting the half-way covenant, the members directed Samuel Cheever to admit half-way members to full communion "without any publick declaration of the worke of grace" if they proved qualified in private examination. The church left it to Cheever to exercise this responsibility with "prudence and faithfulness." The congregation frankly admitted the source of this idea: "as it hath bin practiced of late years in the Church of Salem out of which we issued. . . ." The members wanted to insure

[11] Salem Church Records, *1*, p. 275.

"that themselves & their children might have as full & large priviledges here as they had in that church & that there might be no abridgement."[12] In 1686 the members requested a further innovation used in Salem. Some inhabitants of Marblehead asked Cheever to baptize them "though they dare not as yet adventure to the Lde table." The congregation resolved "such might be baptized themselves, to have the seal also applyed to their children," if they fulfilled the other qualifications of the synod's fifth proposition.[13] The Marblehead church, apparently completely satisfied with the liberal practices of Salem, demanded that their new church conform.

In Reading the extension of the half-way covenant to the unchurched inhabitants came immediately after the death of John Brock and the election of Jonathan Pierpont as his successor. Pierpont reopened the whole question of who qualified for baptism. The congregation voted that any civil man who publicly professing his faith "& solemnly taking the covenant according to the 5th proposition . . . may indorce His Right & fittness to be baptised himself & His children."[14] In 1689 Pierpont baptized nine of the twenty-four persons he admitted to half-way membership, an almost certain indication that they had no prior church connection.

Cotton Mather had made virtually the same concession in Second Church. In his letter to Richards, Mather lamented the number of persons in Boston

[12] Marblehead Church Records, p. 3.

[13] *ibid.*, p. 5.

[14] Reading Church Records, p. 20.

who had never received baptism; yet they regularly came to hear the Mathers preach and had expressed a desire to join the church. Many of them had told Mather, "It is true, wee should come to the Lords Table; but such is our Weakness, wee dare not." Baptize us, they asked, that we may have some measure of church membership and continue to enjoy your preaching. If Second Church could not accommodate them, they lamented, they would be forced to leave his ministry and seek baptism in another church (most likely Samuel Willard's Third Church). In the past, Mather told Richards, he had turned these people away by the score. After 1693 the doors of Second Church opened wide to receive all men of "Vertuous Conversation" regardless of their prior church relation.[15]

In many of the churches that opened half-way membership to the formerly unchurched portion of the parish, the number of persons that responded was insignificant. Roxbury extended the privilege to only four women in three decades; in Dorchester the total was two before 1690; Charlestown followed the practice for six years and took in only seven inhabitants as half-way members. In Reading, Salem, and Second Church Boston the records suggest a larger initial response. But prior to 1690 this innovation had little effect on church membership in the colony; however, it marked one further erosion of the earlier concept of the church covenant. Though cautiously employed in the early years, by accepting the principle

[15] *Mather Papers*, p. 400.

that individuals could share in the church covenant without evidence of regeneration or descent from a regenerate member, the churches prepared the way for a more liberal application of this practice in the next century. Mass covenant renewals that included everyone in the parish, and half-way membership extended to all persons that desired it are partly the results of this innovation.

When the churches combined the extension of baptism to unchurched inhabitants with easier admission to the Lord's Supper—as occurred in Salem and Marblehead—the danger of admitting unregenerate members to full communion obviously increased, and the connection between visible sainthood and church membership became very tenuous. Although these churches stretched the basic Congregational concept of a pure church almost to the breaking point, they still paid lip service to the form and the idea. They required persons desiring half-way membership to meet the qualifications imposed by the Half-Way Synod with respect to personal conduct and Christian knowledge. Even when churches eased admission to full communion, they demanded that the candidate satisfy the pastor as to his faith and knowledge. Thus, the churches continued to restrict membership to persons who had visible qualifications. They honored the tradition of New England Congregationalism, but they gave up the rigor that that tradition required.

One Massachusetts minister rebelled against the tradition. In Northampton Solomon Stoddard broke the bonds of the New England Way and articulated another set of principles. For a short time Stoddard followed the lead of the revisionist clergy in his Northampton parish. Ordained in September 1672 Stoddard began using the half-way covenant within months. In November the congregation reaffirmed the decision reached just prior to Eleazar Mather's death to open baptism to all godly inhabitants of the town. The church required the children of the church, when they came of age, to present themselves to the elders and, if found acceptable, "publickly own the covenant." The members prepared a standard statement for use in owning the covenant wherein the individual acknowledged the teaching and government of the church in return for its instruction, discipline, and privileges.[16] In the next three months 105 persons owned the covenant: fifty on January 10 and the balance one month later. This total must have included almost every one of the eligible children of the church.[17]

In his first five years Stoddard made the half-way covenant an integral part of the church's polity. However, the experience of saving grace, which alone could qualify persons for full communion, came infrequently to Stoddard's congregation; in these years he admitted only nineteen new communicants. In 1677 the communicants numbered only a few more than at Mather's death. Half-way membership, intended as "a state of Education in Christs house," had failed to fulfill its function. The half-way covenant could prepare the children to receive grace, but it could not provide it. By the end of the decade

[16] Northampton Church Records, p. 23.
[17] *ibid.*, pp. 6-35.

Northampton had admitted to the Lord's Supper only one in eight of those who had owned the covenant.[18]

The difficulty he encountered in bringing men to Christ so profoundly disturbed Stoddard that in 1677 he discarded the half-way covenant and renounced the whole concept of church covenant. He announced to the congregation that he intended to baptize every adult or child that accepted the creed and to admit all godly persons to full communion without the relation of a saving experience. Although Stoddard stopped admitting persons to half-way membership in 1677, he waited until 1679 to implement his radical view of the Lord's Supper because of opposition from some members of his congregation. At the end of that year he terminated his complex bookkeeping system consisting of fourteen columns and turned Northampton in a new direction. Behind this change lay a shift in Stoddard's theology. He conceived of the sacraments not as seals of prevenient grace, but as the means of conversion.[19] Although he did not fully develop his conception of the sacraments until the first decade of the eighteenth century, Stoddard had already undermined two generations of New England theology: regeneration could not be demonstrated; testified regenerate membership was a fraud that kept men from Christ; and, no individual covenants existed for each church.[20]

[18] *loc.cit.*; John Todd, "Statistics of the First Church," *A Sermon*, Northampton, 1834, p. 61.

[19] Solomon Stoddard, *An Appeal to the Learned*, Boston, 1709, pp. 2, 6, 8.

[20] Miller, "Stoddard," pp. 298, 305.

News of Stoddard's innovations traveled quickly, and as early as 1677 Increase Mather attacked them in principle in his election sermon. Mather warned the churches to take care in their admissions to communion lest they betray "what our Fathers have Taught concerning that matter, viz. . . . Faith and Repentance." Already some ministers were "designing to bring all Persons to the Lords Supper, who have an historicall Faith . . . altho' they never had Experience of a work of Regeneration. . . ." The dangers were obvious to Mather: "this would corrupt Churches and ruin all in a little time . . . [and] lay a Foundation to great Apostasie. . . ."[21] Mather and Stoddard confronted each other in the Reforming Synod of 1679. The first draft of *Necessity for Reformation* required "that persons should make a Relation of the work of Gods spirit" to qualify for communion. Mather and Stoddard debated the point, and the final draft called for candidates to make "a Profession of their Faith and Repentance."[22] Each man interpreted this statement according to his predisposition and defended his practice with appeals to the synod's decision.

At the same time Stoddard's views came under attack closer to home. Edward Taylor, preaching his own ordination sermon in Westfield, made an impassioned defense of the principle of particular church covenants and condemned Stoddard's notion of na-

[21] Increase Mather, "A Discourse Concerning the Danger of Apostasy," bound in *A Call from Heaven*, Boston, 1679, pp. 116-117; election sermon, May 23, 1677.

[22] Stoddard, *An Appeal to the Learned*, pp. 93-94.

tional covenant. For more than three decades Taylor maintained his attack on Stoddard's theology. But slowly he became an island of orthodoxy as church after church in the Connecticut Valley succumbed to "Stoddardeanism."[23]

Stoddard has achieved a measure of enduring fame for the innovations that still bear his name. Historians have credited him with shaking the foundations of the New England Way and developing a radical conception of membership and the sacraments.[24] The significance of Stoddardeanism and the accuracy of these claims need to be reconsidered in the light of the practices of other churches. Stoddard's ideas were neither original nor radical. Scattered outposts of presbyterial polity had existed in New England since the 1630's, despite the hostility of Congregationalists. The Hingham and Newbury churches both bid defiance to the prevailing principle of restricted membership and opened participation in the sacraments to the entire community. Historians recognize these early deviations, but they assign to Stoddard a central place because his innovations came from within Congregationalism and instilled a new dynamism into a declining religious system.

Viewed solely from the perspective of the Massachusetts churches this argument has some validity.

[23] Norman S. Grabo, *Edward Taylor*, New York, 1961, pp. 32-39; Miller, *Colony to Province*, p. 284.

[24] Miller, "Stoddard," passim; Thomas A. Schafer, "Solomon Stoddard and the Theology of the Revival," *A Miscellany of American Christianity*, Stuart Henry, ed., Durham, 1963, pp. 331-332; Walker, *Creeds and Platforms*, pp. 280-283.

However, a decade before Stoddard announced his departure from Congregational orthodoxy, several Connecticut churches inaugurated practices that closely approximated Stoddardeanism. John Woodbridge, Jr., in Killingworth, Gershom Bulkeley in Wethersfield, and Benjamin Woodbridge in Second Church Windsor developed comprehensive parishes between 1667 and 1671. All of them reshaped existing Congregational churches to include all godly inhabitants without regard to testimony of regeneration.[25] The larger and more vocal presbyterial faction anticipated Stoddard's innovation, and since the channels of communication and culture tended to follow the Connecticut River in the seventeenth century, the Connecticut churches may well have influenced the Northampton minister in his decision. The orthodox Congregational clergy who condemned the admission of the unregenerate to communion quite probably had in mind a number of Connecticut parishes as well as Northampton.

The claim that Stoddard injected new dynamism into Congregationalism also requires reexamination. Although Mather and Russell complained that Stoddard polluted his church with the unworthy, the records do not support their charge. Stoddard's innovation had little effect on Northampton's church membership. In 1677 seventy-six persons qualified for communion in Northampton. Despite three "harvests" and a supposedly easier admissions policy, three decades later the total of communicants had risen to only ninety-six, a figure which represents approxi-

[25] See Chap. IV.

mately 43 percent of the adult inhabitants.[26] Northampton remained a far cry from the parish church where all except notorious sinners participated in the sacraments. Stoddardeanism was ineffective in Stoddard's own church; or else, Stoddard interpreted "faith and repentance" more rigorously than historians have generally assumed. In the seventeenth century Stoddard never matched the success achieved by several presbyterial parishes in Connecticut in attracting new communicants.

Stoddard's preeminence in the movement to extend church membership stems from his role as propagandist. His debate with Increase Mather in the Reforming Synod made Stoddard the leading spokesman for the presbyterialists. In a series of tracts published between 1699 and 1709 Stoddard elaborated his position and defended himself from Mather's charge that he was subverting Congregationalism. These tracts, which culminated in *An Appeal to the Learned*, demanded carefully wrought arguments and focused attention on Stoddard.[27] Because Connecticut's presbyterialists never engaged in the debate, they left behind no corpus of writings that spelled out their ideas and practices; as a result they have faded into obscurity and left Stoddard occupying stage center like a giant.

In the last quarter of the seventeenth century Stoddardeanism had more psychological than practical impact on western Massachusetts. In the next

[26] Todd, "Statistics of First Church Northampton," p. 61.

[27] For a complete bibliography of the Stoddard-Mather tracts see Miller, "Stoddard," pp. 303-304.

century the polity attributed to him ruled most of the churches in the Valley, and "Pope" Stoddard became the most important figure in the region. In the years prior to 1690 Stoddard's practice simply made more obvious the disintegration of even theoretical unity. The broad spectrum of Massachusetts polity, ranging from that of First Church Boston to First Church Northampton, made it impossible to speak any longer of a New England Way.

John Russell of Hadley blamed the half-way covenant for rending the seamless garment, but this represents a crude oversimplification. The propositions of the Half-Way Synod are only several of a number of attempts to confront a rapidly changing society and an altered religious environment. The lamentations of the jeremiads, the filial pietism, the remembrance of things past—all these mark the response of the later generations to changes they did not understand. The clergy were groping to adjust their institutions to a process they only dimly perceived. By the early 1690's the half-way covenant had become one of the standard adjustments, and it rarely excited vehement opposition. External threats drove Congregationalists into a common front where essentially minor differences in polity had no importance.

The rapprochement between First and Third Churches in Boston is a case in point. After thirteen years of bitterness and recrimination the two churches made peace in 1682. Edward Randolph, New England's indefatigable royal snoop, took credit for inadvertently healing the breach: "heereing of my proposals for [Anglican] ministers to be sent over . . . they are now joyned together, about a fortnight ago, and pray to God to confound the devices of all who disturb their peace and liberties."[28]

Even the Reforming Synod played down the half-way covenant, although less than a decade earlier the issue had divided the entire colony and forced the clergy to become directly involved in politics. The synod concentrated on the evils of the times and tried to eliminate the half-way covenant as a source of controversy. *The Necessity of Reformation* assumed the declension of the "Rising Generation" and called on the churches to remedy this through discipline "according to the Rules of Christ." But it did not spell out the "Rules of Christ" regarding baptism; it gave neither side its sanction. The synod alluded to the half-way covenant only once: "if all the Church duty . . . were faithfully and diligently attended . . . toward the children of the Church . . . Disputes respecting the Subject of Baptism, would be comfortably issued." If churches did what they should, the children would return to experiential religion and make the half-way covenant unnecessary.[29] The results of the synod amounted to little more than a group jeremiad, what Perry Miller called "purgation by incantation," but they gave the churches new demons to exorcise. The half-way covenant paled into insignificance beside the new challenge.

[28] Edward Randolph to the Bishop of London, May 29, 1682, *Hutchinson Papers*, Boston, 2, p. 272; *Boston First Church Records*, 1, pp. 78-80.

[29] *Necessity of Reformation*, Walker, *Creeds and Platforms*, pp. 423-437; see particularly Answers III, IV, and VIII, pp. 433-435.

By 1690 the half-way covenant was an effective part of the new orthodoxy, but this was an orthodoxy without compulsion. Churches applied the principle as they saw fit; they used what they wanted and rejected what they found inapplicable. In the rapidly changing society of seventeenth-century Massachusetts, the autonomy of the individual congregation proved to be the undoing of religious uniformity. Independence provided the flexibility and adaptability that circumstances demanded, but this localism carried within it the forces that eventually toppled the establishment.

TEN

New England Churches and the Half-Way Covenant

IN THE half-way covenant lies a key to understanding the transformation of New England Puritanism in the seventeenth century. Perhaps better than any other single factor it symbolizes the conflicting ideals of Puritanism. The half-way covenant does not signal the failure of the city on a hill as so many historians have assumed, but rather marks a reaffirmation of the Puritan mission.

The Puritan vision of a holy commonwealth contained a dual mission: the creation in the new Israel of a moral, covenanted society where men abide by God's laws; and the establishment within the holy community of truly reformed churches. As New England Congregationalism attempted to fulfill both these functions, the conflict of ideals became more apparent: the broad array of social functions met by the established churches drew them into the community, but the restriction of membership to visible saints tended to separate the churches from the community. This incongruity created a tension, a conflict in values between what Ernst Troeltsch has called church and sect.[1] In Troeltsch's typology the church is closely identified with society, is deeply involved in secular affairs, and demands only general doctrinal adherance. The sect, on the other hand, represents a select group of visible believers set apart from the rest of the community by a distinct value system of its own that emphasizes the in-group relation.

Although the Puritans preserved a balance between church and sect for the first few years, the primacy they gave to conversion as the basis for church membership ultimately destroyed the equilibrium. The imposition of regenerate membership on the structure of the established churches tipped the scales of the New England Way toward sectarianism, but in the process the clergy created a very unstable polity. They retained infant baptism when the logic of their arguments for a pure church called for baptism of believers, as practiced by the Baptists. The half-way covenant was devised to restore some balance between purity and community and to solve the problem of baptized but unregenerate members within pure churches.

From the outset some Congregational ministers recognized the dilemmas inherent in testified regenerate membership and pressed for the recognition of two kinds of membership: the first, for baptized believers who would be subject to the watch and care of the church; and the second, for the core of regenerate communicants. The majority of ministers at the Cambridge Synod endorsed the Mather-Partridge

[1] Ernst Troeltsch, *Social Teachings of the Christian Churches*, Olive Wyon, trans., New York, 1931, *I*, pp. 331-349.

proposals for the extension of baptism as a reasonable counterbalance to the prevailing sectarian practice for the admission of communicants, but in the face of outspoken opposition they backed down. They feared that a debate among the clergy endangered the community more than narrow conceptions of church membership. The chief opponents of the half-way covenant, Davenport and Chauncy, did not lack theological sophistication, nor were they shortsighted purists. They understood the issues clearly, but they were willing to sacrifice the original vision of a holy commonwealth to preserve the purity of the churches.

Opponents of extended baptism successfully imposed their view on the rest of the ministers until it proved detrimental to the churches. When church membership started declining in the decade after the Cambridge Synod, the opponents lost their influence, and revisionist ministers gained the upper hand. This shift became apparent at the Ministerial Assembly of 1657. Twenty-one ministers representing Connecticut and Massachusetts overwhelmingly endorsed the revisionist program. They affirmed the principle of restricting the Lord's Supper to the visibly elect, but they broadened church membership by giving unregenerate children of the church, once they had owned the covenant, the right to present their children for baptism.

Despite the assembly's endorsement, in the following months only four churches implemented the half-way covenant. A number of parishes raised the issue and debated its merits, but postponed a final decision. The situation was untenable: the *Cambridge Platform* gave one answer, the Ministerial Assembly gave another; the ministers were agitating for change, the congregations showed great reluctance; and, the wide variations in the baptismal practices of the churches made a mockery of uniformity. In 1662 the Massachusetts General Court finally intervened by calling a synod to resolve the question and bring order out of the chaos. The seven propositions adopted by the Half-Way Synod reaffirmed the decision of the Ministerial Assembly and incorporated the half-way covenant into the orthodox New England Way.

Although a few ministers had resisted the innovation since 1646, primary opposition to the synod's decision came from the laymen. The synod might have overcome the laity's initial hostility had not the outraged cries of strict Congregationalist ministers encouraged the laymen and given them sound theological arguments. The anti-synodical propaganda of Chauncy, Davenport, and the younger Mathers made it doubly difficult to implement the half-way covenant. Although the Half-Way Synod established a new orthodoxy, most churches refused to accept it.

In each of the four holy commonwealths of New England the attitudes toward the half-way covenant varied considerably. Although by 1660 each colony adhered to basic Congregational polity, each also had a local variation which helped determine its response to the half-way covenant. New Haven and Plymouth, the two smallest colonies, showed the least enthusiasm for the innovation. Both had refused to participate in either the Ministerial Assembly or the Half-Way Synod. Although the churches in New Haven and Plymouth proved equally reluctant to adopt the half-way covenant, the bases of their opposition differed quite radically. John Davenport ran New Haven Colony's ecclesiastical affairs as though the churches were his personal fiefs; and his opposition to the half-way covenant precluded any serious consideration of the issue as long as he remained in control, although ministers discussed the idea covertly. The absorption of New Haven into Connecticut and Davenport's decision to settle in Boston weakened his influence. But he left behind a legacy of strict Congregationalism that took almost a generation to overcome.

Qualms about the half-way covenant in Plymouth Colony stemmed primarily from the liberal admissions policies of the churches. In Plymouth church doors had already opened wider than those in Massachusetts. Although they used testified regenerate membership, the churches generally interpreted conversion so broadly that few people, if any, were turned away.[2] For Plymouth churches to accept the half-way covenant would have meant admitting persons with the weakest signs of faith. Individuals who could not qualify for full communion in Plymouth churches rarely deserved the partial membership created by the half-way covenant. The children of the church the Half-Way Synod had in mind were already within the Plymouth churches. Thus the reaction of Plymouth churches to the extension of baptism resulted from the colony's heritage of Separatism, which made church membership more readily attainable and the need for innovation less compelling.

The major controversies over the half-way cove-

[2] Langdon, *Pilgrim Colony*, pp. 129-133.

nant occurred in Connecticut and Massachusetts. Prior to 1662 both colonies had responded very similarly to the enlargement of baptism. The Connecticut Gen- eneral Court had provided the initiative for the Ministerial Assembly; the Massachusetts Court had called the meeting; both courts had recommended that the churches adopt the assembly's conclusions. Only a few churches in each colony followed this advice and began to practice extended baptism. After 1662 the course of the half-way covenant in these two colonies diverged noticeably.

Since Connecticut had not participated in the Half-Way Synod, the "official" solution to the question of baptism promulgated by the synod did not directly affect the colony. Connecticut found its answer independently. The existence of three clerical factions, each with its own solution to baptism and its own lay following, compounded the problem in Connecticut and ultimately determined the resolution. To strict Congregationalists and revisionist Congregationalists, Connecticut added a third party, presbyterialists, that hoped to make the half-way covenant superfluous by establishing comprehensive parishes. To resolve the issue of baptism through a synod required that one faction have sufficient strength to dominate the council and force through its own program. But unlike Massachusetts, no faction in Connecticut controlled a majority, and this confounded the General Court's efforts to find an answer.

In the absence of a majority the Connecticut General Court entered more decisively into the question of church membership than the Massachusetts Court.

In the Bay Colony the Court's role consisted entirely of calling synods and commending the results to the churches (except for the aberration of 1670). In its first proposal regarding church membership the Connecticut Court endorsed presbyterial petitions that would have opened the churches to all godly, civil men. When conservatives condemned this policy, the Court threw the question back to the ministers; and after three years of fruitless skirmishing the clergymen were forced to admit they could not reach an agreement. Connecticut's official solution to the divisive issues was not to have a solution. The Court announced in 1669 that until further light appeared on the subject of baptism the colony would tolerate the diverse practices that had grown up. Within a limited range this decision left each church free to follow its own course without fear of subverting an orthodoxy or suffering reprisals from the civil authorities.

One by-product of this policy of toleration was a series of church schisms. After 1662 debates over the half-way covenant had divided several Connecticut congregations, but in most cases the majority successfully imposed its polity on the rest of the members. Until 1669 the dissenting minorities had little recourse from this coercion. By endorsing toleration the Court freed these minorities and sanctioned the erection of new churches within the old parishes.

The source of schisms lay deeper than the half-way covenant; the controversy over baptism only hid the fundamental disagreement over membership and structure. The superficiality of the half-way covenant as an issue was apparent in several churches; when schism finally occurred, both factions adopted extended baptism. The basic cleavage was presbyterial versus Congregational polity. As the presbyterial ministers in Connecticut gained strength and prestige in the decades after 1660, they successfully converted churches to their polity. Confronted by this threat, Congregationalists drew together and forgot their differences over baptism. Several ministers who had previously denounced revisionism started using the half-way covenant themselves to undercut the appeal of the presbyterialists. By the mid-1670's debates over the half-way covenant had virtually ceased in Connecticut, and most churches either had adopted the innovation or had moved toward the comprehensive parish. By 1690 extended baptism in one form or another completely dominated Connecticut parishes.

Connecticut's role in the evolution of Congregationalism has received almost no recognition. Historians have concentrated on Massachusetts, virtually ignoring the rest of New England. Because Connecticut was the "land of steady habits" and a center of orthodoxy in the eighteenth and early nineteenth centuries, historians have assumed that the same conditions prevailed in the seventeenth century. As a result there is a hiatus in the written history of Connecticut between Thomas Hooker and the Saybrook Platform. However, Connecticut in fact innovated and experimented as much in that first century as the Bay Colony. For example, Solomon Stoddard had received credit for revitalizing Congregationalism with a daring innovation that discarded testified regenerate membership and opened the churches to all godly inhabitants. But Connecticut's presbyterialists anticipated "Stoddardeanism" by at least a decade and had far more success in applying the principle. A generation before Solomon Stoddard and Increase Mather filled the Boston pressess with their tracts on church membership and split Massachusetts into two distinct polities, the Connecticut churches faced and resolved the same issue. Connecticut has been relegated to a historical limbo because of its lack of theological literature. The literature of Puritanism has provided the primary source for interpreting the seventeenth century, and since Connecticut's ministers turned to the presses less frequently, historians have ignored the colony. So long as historians of Puritanism extrapolate church and social history from the published products of the New England mind, they will continue to distort the Puritan experience and ignore Connecticut.

In Massachusetts the focus of the controversy over the half-way covenant shifted after 1662. Prior to the Half-Way Synod the issue of extended baptism had, for the most part, engaged the attention of the ministers rather than the laymen. Although members of a few churches had become involved as a result of attempts to implement the half-way covenant, generally the laity had not participated in the debate. In the eighteen months following the synod dissension among the clergy reached new heights of acrimony, but when this phase passed, serious division of the ministers ended. A few recalcitrants, such as Davenport, remained, but the majority of the ministers now supported the synod's propositions and attempted to implement them in their churches. After this, opposition to the half-way covenant came almost entirely from the laity. Laymen distrusted any change in the New England Way, and few of them understood the need for change fully. They may have grasped the ministers' arguments that admission to full communion had declined and that the churches had a responsibility to the children of the church, but they failed to comprehend that altered circumstances in New England required institutional adaptations. For at least a decade the laity continued to measure true religious behavior by a standard that was out of touch with new circumstances.

When Massachusetts ministers carried the synod's propositions back to their churches, they encountered far more opposition than they had anticipated. Despite the endorsement of synod and General Court, congregations remained hostile to the half-way covenant. If the lay opposition perplexed the clergy, the average layman probably found his own position equally uncomfortable. He had learned since childhood to respect the ministers and defer to their learned judgment in ecclesiastical matters. Now the ministers had endorsed an innovation in polity that seemed to violate the entire religious tradition. This ambivalence toward the clergy may partially explain the political crisis of 1670-1671. Davenport spurred the laity's resentment into an open condemnation of the clergy and the half-way covenant. The next year the laity recoiled from this act like a child who has struck his parent and elected a slate of deputies pledged to redeeming the clergy's honor.

In the decade after the synod the general reluctance of congregations to accept the half-way covenant was apparent. Although about two-fifths of the Massachusetts churches had adopted the principle of extended baptism by 1672, only a few used the half-way covenant extensively or made it an effective part of the church's polity. In churches such as Roxbury and Charlestown members deferred to the minister and accepted his judgment that the half-way covenant was necessary, but they refused to use it themselves and thereby rendered the innovation meaningless. Most churches refused even to accept the principle. Ministers pled with them in vain. The majority of members, or at least an extensive minority, remained intransigent. After ten years as official orthodoxy the propositions of the Half-Way Synod had had almost no effect on church membership.

Within the churches the half-way covenant became an integral part of the New England Way only after 1675. The disasters that began with King Philip's War and culminated with the Andros regime upset the stability of Massachusetts and fundamentally changed the religious needs of its citizens. One way in which the churches of the colony responded to the crises was through implementation of the half-way covenant. Insecurity and anxiety convinced church members, as the ministers had never been able to, that they must extend church membership.

After 1675 many of the churches that had adopted the half-way covenant a decade or more earlier, but had never made any serious attempt to implement the decision, urged children of the church for the first time to own the covenant. The scruples which had held members back in the past disappeared. This change of attitude transformed the half-way covenant from an occasional event into a regular and acceptable part of the polity. A similar result was achieved in churches that had resisted any encroachments on traditional polity prior to 1675 and had defeated every attempt by the clergy to introduce the half-way covenant. Church members saw the hand of God in the disasters, and they found one source of His displeasure in their neglect of the children of the church. The remedy was obvious, and several churches adopted the half-way covenant as part of their covenant of reformation.

Extended baptism had become such a standard part of the New England Way after 1675 that almost every Massachusetts church founded after that date adopted the principle at its inception. Strict congregationalist churches remained, and some churches that had adopted the half-way covenant after 1675 reverted to strict Congregationalism or allowed the practice to lapse into infrequent use. But by 1690 these exceptions represented less than one-fourth of the total churches in the colony. Despite the differences in practice that still existed, the half-way covenant no longer generated controversy. Congregational ministers and laymen accepted latitude in baptism and then joined together to fight common enemies.

If the half-way covenant can be interpreted as part of a general religious awakening caused by fifteen years of crisis (1675-1690), then the concept of declension, which has often been used to explain religious behavior at that time, must be seriously questioned. Church membership statistics for this decade and a half disprove most of the assumptions about declension. In these years, when the decline of religiosity was supposed to have been most precipitous, there was, in fact, a remarkable revival of religion and an increase in church membership. Admissions to full communion reached their lowest ebb, not in 1690, but in the middle of the century, when Congregationalism was most secure. Personal piety and the need for religious ties increased as Massachusetts society became less secure. The increase in full communicants, the implementation of the half-way covenant, the mass covenant renewals, and the inclusion of formerly unchurched inhabitants in the church covenant are signs of an awakening, not a decline.

If the period from 1675 to 1690 did not signal the decline of Puritanism, the response to the crises of these years permanently altered Congregationalism and modified its institutions in such a way that New England could never retrace its steps. These modifications came in two stages. The first period of calamities, such as King Philip's War, the epidemics, and the fires, changed the churches internally. Covenants of reformation and utilization of the half-way covenant represent adjustments of polity and new attempts to fulfill the increased religious needs of church members and their children; they had little effect on the community as a whole, and they did not alter the churches' traditional relation to society.

The greatest catastrophe of the period, however, from the standpoint of the colony's religious mission, was the revocation of the charter. For a half-century the charter had insured Puritan control of the civil government, and the government had helped bind the whole community in covenant with God. When Massachusetts lost its charter, and with it the "due forme of government" that Winthrop and his friends had established, only the churches remained to fulfill the mission. Revocation of the charter could not destroy the churches, but it threatened their privileged status; this had two effects. First, New Englanders who had hitherto hung back from church membership because of religious scruples, now came forward to strengthen by their membership the principal institution that remained for expression of the Puritan way. Congregationalists in Massachusetts discovered, as would Lyman Beecher a century and a half later in Connecticut, that separation of church and state could revitalize the faith. Although Congregationalism remained the established religion of Massachusetts, loss of the charter cut the bond that had created the New England Way. Thus revocation of the charter may partially explain the increase in church membership that occurred in the 1680's.

A second result of the loss of the charter, one that had a more permanent impact, was the development of a new relation between the churches and the rest of society. The Congregational churches were brought further into the world. Without the support of the civil government to hold the community to the covenant, the churches were forced to throw off some of their sectarian practices and assume the burden of the entire community's religious life.[3] After revocation of the charter, the churches had to reach out into the community for new members and change their attitude toward the unchurched. The old "tribalism" no longer sufficed; the churches became evangelical. In part, this transformation of Congregationalism is what historians have labelled declension. New England Congregationalism was turning toward Troeltsch's "church" and casting off its narrow sectarianism. Puritanism changed as economic, social, and political realities changed. The churches developed new functions that fulfilled the new needs of the community.

In this transformation of Congregationalism the half-way covenant played a major role. It was an institutional adaptation whose function varied as the needs of the churches and society changed. Originally revisionist ministers had envisioned the half-way covenant as a counterbalance to the sectarianism of testified regenerate membership, a restoration of the dual mission of the "errand into the wilderness." Next it became a means of religious expression for children of the church who doubted their qualifications for communion but wanted closer ties to the church in a period of stress. Ultimately the half-way covenant served to draw in the unchurched inhabitants, to

[3] This effect is the opposite of what one would expect from reading Troeltsch. The established, protected religious group should come closest to "church," and disestablishment should foster sectarianism. Massachusetts' experience suggests that the sociology of religion must always be tempered by the prevailing intellectual and social systems.

bring new adults and children under the parochial wing of the churches. By the turn of the century purity had been largely sacrificed to community. Most New England parishes had settled down into three basic divisions: the communicants, the half-way members, and the inhabitants who either could not or would not join the covenanted community. The quiet that settled over the ecclesiastical life of Massachusetts after 1700 is perfectly exemplified by the demise of the jeremiads and the emergence of Cotton Mather's "do-good" piety.[4]

Although dormant as an issue for nearly fifty years, New England had not yet written the last chapter on the half-way covenant. Religion of the heart has its seasons, its times of heat and of cold and of rebirth. The internal fires of experiential religion burst forth again in the Great Awakening and thrust the half-way covenant into the forefront. The new despisers of formality and deadness condemned the old innovation and made it once again a focal point of controversy. Even in the heat of the revival many, if not most, of the new members joined the churches as half-way members, a practice that appalled the New Lights. In a passage that might have been written by John Davenport a century earlier, Ebenezer Devotion of Windham wrote: "We dissent from them, because they Admit of Half-membership. . . . [We dissent] Because they receive Members into the Church, without giving Personal Satisfaction to the Church, that they are true Members of CHRIST,

[4] Miller, *From Colony to Province*, pp. 395-416.

by declaring what GOD hath done for their Souls."[5]

The extreme New Lights, like Isaac Backus, who separated from their old Congregational churches and created new pure churches of visible saints, struggled to rid themselves of the old corruptions. In fact, as many of these became Separate Baptists, they finally solved the dilemma that had plagued New England since the 1630's. The Baptists eliminated the contradiction of the practice of infant baptism in churches of visible saints by restricting baptism to believers. The half-way covenant had no place in a church of saints.

Most New Light ministers rejected both the half-way covenant and the Baptist impulse. Where they were successful, they recreated the unstable "half-way house," which regenerate membership had first introduced to New England. When the religious enthusiasm passed, these churches faced all over again the problem that revisionist ministers like Richard Mather had strived to solve in the 1640's. Many, like Ebenezer Devotion, who were unwilling to eliminate infant baptism, reluctantly returned to the half-way system they found so distasteful. Not all the New Lights were even temporarily successful, however. Northampton dispatched its eminent pastor Jonathan Edwards to the Indian wilderness of Stockbridge when he explicitly denounced the half-way covenant. Others, while they strived for circumcision of the heart, were forced by their determined con-

[5] Ebenezer Devotion, *An Answer of the Pastor and Brethren of the Third Church in Windham*, quoted in C. C. Goen, *Revivalism and Separatism in New England; 1740-1800*, p. 38.

gregations to retain the half-way covenant.[6] Edwards' disciples, particularly Joseph Bellamy, continued to inveigh against the practice for the next three decades. In quantity and venom their tracts exceeded the spirited dispute of 1662-1664.[7]

That the half-way covenant reappeared as a source of controversy should surprise no one. In one way or another the basic issues that underlay the strife are as old as Christianity and as modern as twentieth-century fundamentalism. The visibly holy, drawn by the moving of the Spirit to erect pure churches gathered out of the world, rarely sustain their fervor in the succeeding generations. Spontaneity is lost, and experiential piety becomes routinized. Children cherish the past, imitate it, but cannot recapture it. Slowly the churches accommodate their purity to the world and redefine their mission or goal to fit the new standards. When the Spirit moves anew, the saints gather at the river once again. As the Puritans were called out of Anglicanism, so the New Lights were called out of the remnants of Puritanism. Every generation has its half-way covenant.

[6] This brief survey of the relationship of the half-way covenant to the New Lights in the period following the Great Awakening is deeply dependent on Goen's, *Revivalism and Separatism.* That volume carries through the second half of the eighteenth century many of the points developed in this study.

[7] See the excellent bibliography of these latter-day tracts in Walker, *Creeds and Platforms*, pp. 241-244.

APPENDIX

GRAPH 5. ROXBURY

Entered Full Communion 1665-1690

- - - - - - - MEN ———— WOMEN

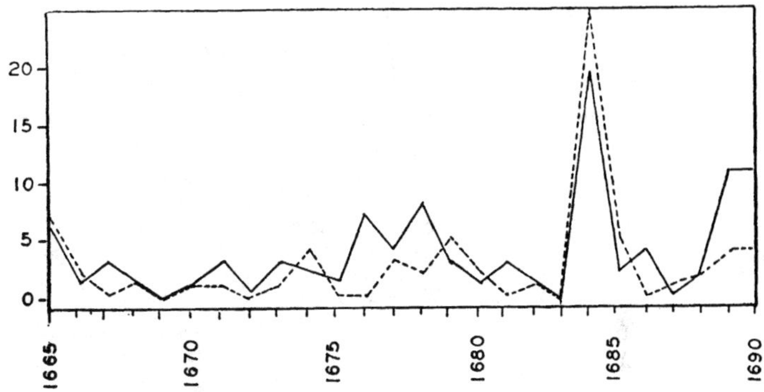

GRAPH 6. ROXBURY

Owned the Covenant 1665-1690

- - - - - - - MEN ———— WOMEN

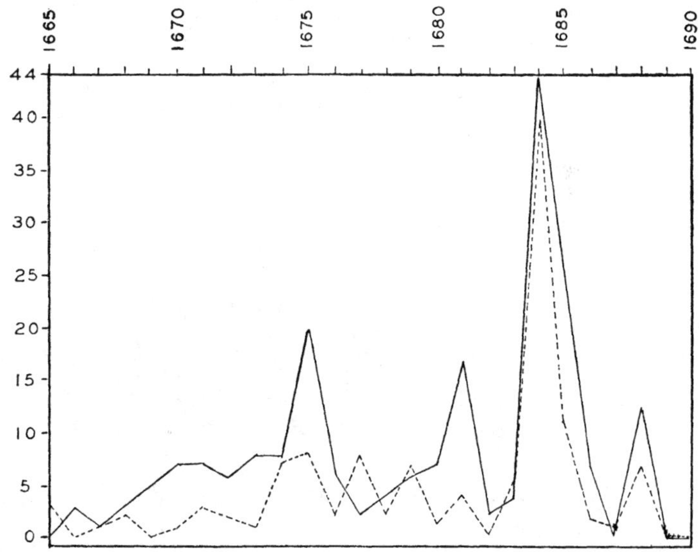

TABLE 1. ROXBURY	*Men*	*Women*
1. entered communion—1660-69	16	28
2. entered communion—1670-79	17	34
3. entered communion—1680-89	42	49
4. total entered communion—1660-89	75	111
5. owned covenant—1660-69	6	14
6. owned covenant—1670-79	41	73
7. owned covenant—1680-89	73	118
8. total owned covenant—1660-89	120	205
9. new communicants—median age—1660-69	ID	ID
10. new communicants—median age—1670-79	ID	ID
11. new communicants—median age—1680-89	29.2	23.5
12. owned covenant—median age—1660-69	27.5	21.0
13. owned covenant—median age—1670-79	22.8	18.6
14. owned covenant—median age—1680-89	20.5	16.4
15. covenant to communion—1660-69	5	6
16. covenant to communion—1670-79	22	30
17. covenant to communion—1680-89	16	31
18. covenant to communion—total—1660-89	53	67
19. covenant to communion—median years elapsed—1660-69	13.0	8.4
20. covenant to communion—median years elapsed—1670-79	10.1	7.7
21. covenant to communion—median years elapsed—1680-89	3.9	6.5
22. communion w/o covenant—1660-69	15	25
23. communion w/o covenant—1670-79	9	16
24. communion w/o covenant—1680-89	16	18
25. total communion w/o covenant—1660-89	40	59

ID = Insufficient data

TABLE 2. CHARLESTOWN	*Men*	*Women*
1. entered communion—1660-69	16	31
2. entered communion—1670-79	29	68
3. entered communion—1680-89	32	58
4. total entered communion—1660-89	77	157
5. owned covenant—1660-69	3	3
6. owned covenant—1670-79	4	13
7. owned covenant—1680-89	21	53
8. total owned covenant—1660-89	28	69
9. new communicants—median age—1660-69	30.9	28.0
10. new communicants—median age—1670-79	30.2	27.6
11. new communicants—median age—1680-89	32.7	28.3
12. owned covenant—median age—1660-69	30.6	22.5
13. owned covenant—median age—1670-79	19.8	23.2
14 owned covenant—median age—1680-89	29.1	22.9
15. covenant to communion—1660-69	3	2
16. covenant to communion—1670-79	2	5
17. covenant to communion—1680-89	6	16
18. total covenant to communion—1660-89	12	23
19. covenant to communion—median years elapsed—1660-69	4.2	2.4
20. covenant to communion—median years elapsed—1670-79	12.8	5.2
21. covenant to communion—median years elapsed—1680-89	17.8	16.7
22. communion w/o covenant—1660-69	15	28
23. communion w/o covenant—1670-79	27	66
24. communion w/o covenant—1680-89	25	55
25. total communion w/o covenant—1660-69	67	149

TABLE 3. BOSTON THIRD CHURCH	*Men*	*Women*
1. entered communion—1669	28	0
2. entered communion—1670-79	41	150
3. entered communion—1680-89	45	76
4. total entered communion—1669-89	114	226
5. owned covenant—1669	1	4
6. owned covenant—1670-79	24	22
7. owned covenant—1680-89	106	200
8. total owned covenant—1669-89	131	226
9. new communicants—median age—1669	ID	NA
10. new communicants—median age—1670-79	ID	ID
11. new communicants—median age—1680-89	32.6	25.1
12. owned covenant—median age—1669	ID	ID
13. owned covenant—median age—1670-79	26.0	13.0
14. owned covenant—median age—1680-89	26.0	19.3
15. covenant to communion—1669	0	3
16. covenant to communion—1670-79	6	8
17. covenant to communion—1680-89	23	55
18. total covenant to communion—1669-89	29	66
19. covenant to communion—median years lapsed—1669	ID	15.8
20. covenant to communion—median years elapsed—1670-79	9.8	14.3
21. covenant to communion—median years elapsed—1680-89	8.1	8.3
22. communion w/o covenant—1669	28	0
23. communion w/o covenant—1670-79	39	150
24. communion w/o covenant—1680-89	29	53
25. total communion w/o covenant—1669-89	96	203

NA = Not applicable to this church   ID = Insufficient data

GRAPH 7. CHARLESTOWN
Entered Full Communion 1665-1690
------- MEN ———— WOMEN

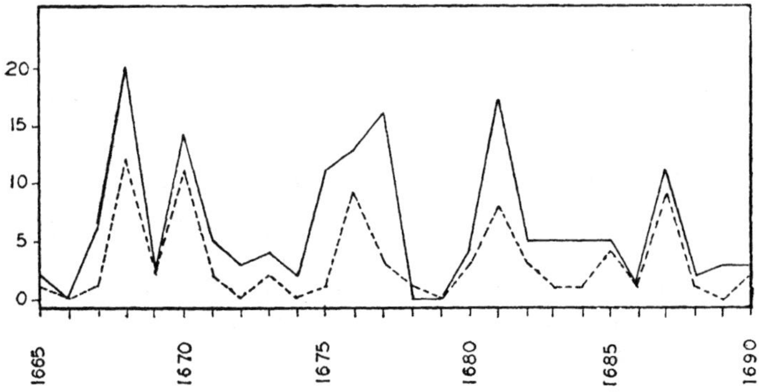

GRAPH 8. CHARLESTOWN
Owned the Covenant 1665-1690
------- MEN ———— WOMEN

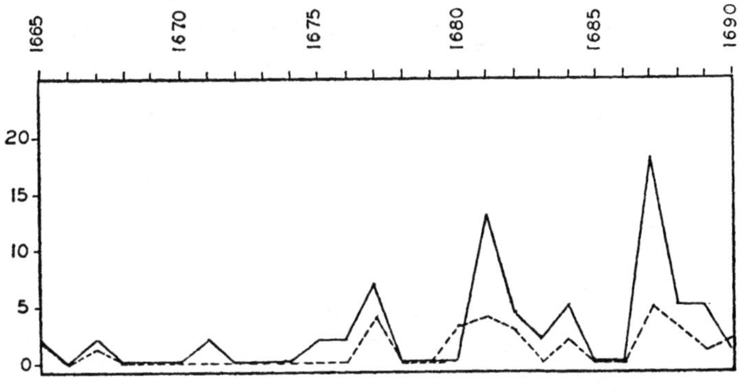

GRAPH 9. BOSTON THIRD CHURCH

Entered Full Communion 1669-1690

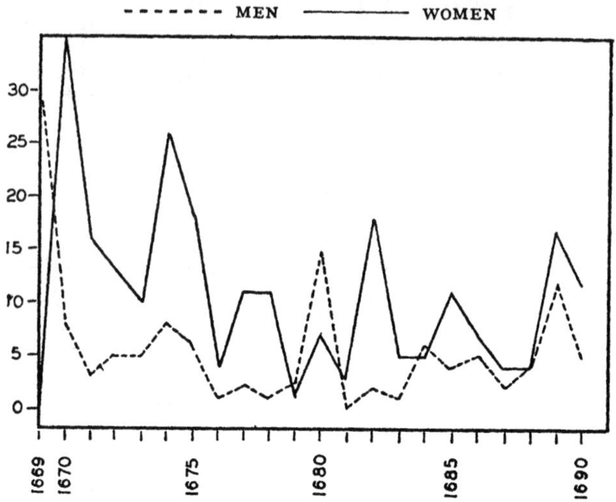

GRAPH 10. BOSTON THIRD CHURCH

Owned the Covenant 1669-1690

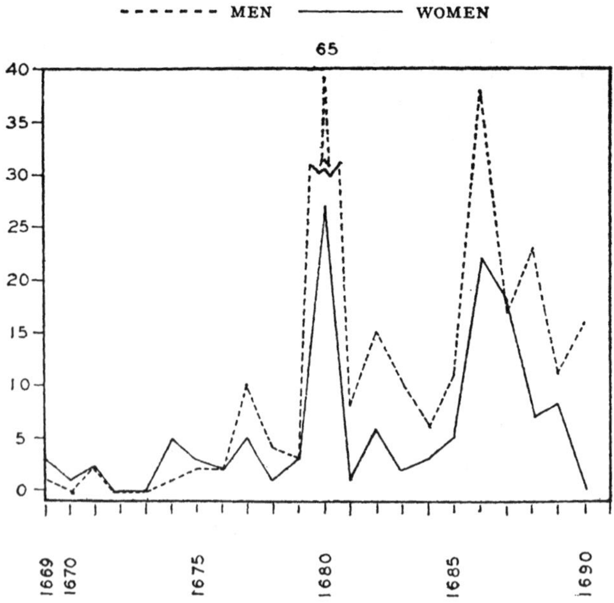

TABLE 4. DORCHESTER	*Men*	*Women*
1. entered communion—1660-69	14	23
2. entered communion—1670-79	31	38
3. entered communion—1680-89	28	29
4. total entered communion—1660-89	73	90
5. owned the covenant—1660-69	NA	NA
6. owned covenant—1677-79	70	44
7. owned covenant—1680-89	6	15
8. total owned covenant—1677-89	76	59
9. new communicants—median age—1660-69	25.6	23.7
10. new communicants—median age—1670-79	27.8	33.3
11. new communicants—median age—1680-89	20.8	23.9
12. owned covenant—median age—1660-77	NA	NA
13. owned covenant—median age—1677-79	24.7	21.5
14. owned covenant—median age—1680-89	24.5	24.1
15. covenant to communion—1660-76	NA	NA
16. covenant to communion—1677-79	24	21
17. covenant to communion—1680-89	4	1
18. total covenant to communion	28	22
19. covenant to communion—median years elapsed—1660-76	NA	NA
20. covenant to communion—median years elapsed—1677-79	10.0	9.6
21. covenant to communion—median years elapsed—1680-89	11.5	5.3
22. communion w/o covenant—1660-76	NA	NA
23. communion w/o covenant—1677-79	13	18
24. communion w/o covenant—1680-89	15	21
25. communion w/o covenant—1677-89	28	39

NA = Not applicable to this church

GRAPH 11. DORCHESTER

Entered Full Communion 1665-1690

- - - - - - - MEN ——————— WOMEN

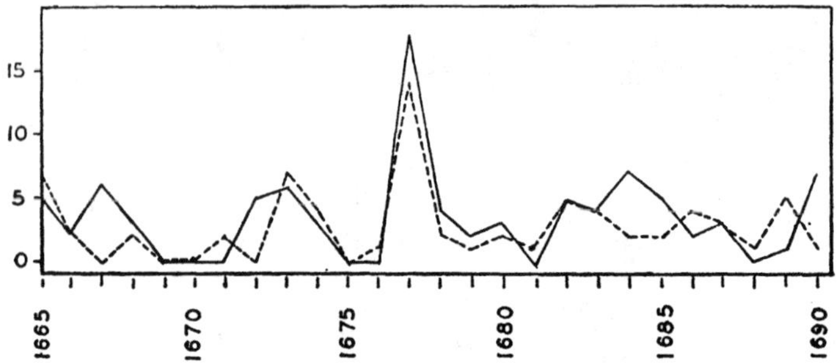

GRAPH 12. DORCHESTER

Owned the Covenant 1677-1690

- - - - - - - MEN ——————— WOMEN

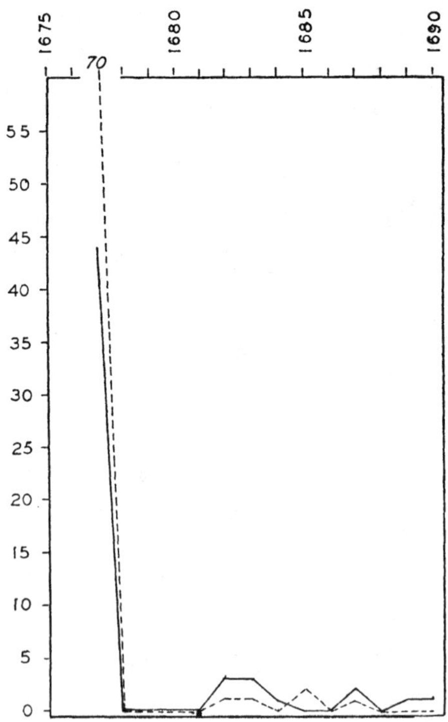

SELECT BIBLIOGRAPHY

PRIMARY WORKS

Church Records: *Massachusetts*

Time, fire, and man have taken their toll of seventeenth-century church records in New England. Although in the last century historical societies and state archives have attempted to preserve the extant materials, most churches have no records of the years prior to 1700. For other churches often only fragments of the original records remain. However, the exceptions to this rule provide a rich source for the study of seventeenth-century Congregationalism. At their best, church records included complete entries for baptisms, admissions to communion, and persons who accepted the half-way covenant, as well as records of church meetings and votes, disciplinary actions, and dismissals from the church.

Several Massachusetts churches have excellent unpublished records, which date back to the formation of the church. Among the best of these are the Salem Church Records. The three typed, bound volumes of records, which are in the possession of First Church of Christ in Salem, contain a vast array of material relating to the oldest church in the Bay Colony. The Northampton First Church of Christ Records, 1661-1924 (available on microfilm at the Forbes Library in Northampton), include the tenure of Solomon Stoddard, although the records are less than satisfactory after 1677. Records of the First Parish of Reading, 1648 to 1846, start effectively with the tenure of John Brock in 1666; a typed transcription of these records, made by the Works Progress Administration in 1934, is in the Reading Town Library. The manuscript of the Publick Records of the Church of Christ at Westfield is in the Westfield Atheneum, but it was not made available to me. A typed record of baptisms, copied from the records, may be used at the library, but for my purposes it proved less than adequate. The Milton Public Library has a photostatic copy of the Milton Church Records, 1681-1918, which provides a bare sketch of the church's first two decades. The first volume of the Records of the First Congregational Church in Marblehead; 1684-1732, is an excellent source for that church; the manuscript, in an unusually legible script, is in the possession of First Church Marblehead. Several other fragmentary church records that proved useful were: Boston Second Church Records, three volumes in the Massachusetts Historical Society, which may be consulted only with written permission from Second Church; and Records of the West Parish of Barnstable, 1668-1807, a photostatic copy made by the Massachusetts Historical Society (1924), available in several libraries, including Yale University.

With the few exceptions noted above, most of the complete church records from seventeenth-century Massachusetts have been published. All of the following proved invaluable in this research: *Records of the First Church in Boston; 1630-1868*, edited by Richard D. Pierce, *Publications* of the Colonial Society of Massachusetts (5 vols., Boston, 1961), XXXV-XXXIX; *Records of the First Church in Charlestown, Massachusetts; 1632-1789*, edited by James F. Hunnewell (Boston, 1880); *Records of the First Church at Dorchester; 1636-1734*, edited by Charles Pope (Boston, 1891); *Plymouth Church Records; 1620-1859, Publications* of the Colonial Society of Massachusetts (2 vols., Boston, 1920), XXII-XXIII; and, *Roxbury Land and Church Records, Reports* of the

Record Commissioners (Boston, 1884), VI. The records for Third Church Boston are no longer extant, but the combination of two volumes makes it possible to reconstruct events in that church prior to 1690; *An Historical Catalogue of the Old South Church* (Boston, 1883), contains a list of all admissions to the church and the "Third Church Narrative," reproduced in Hamilton A. Hill, *History of the Old South Church Boston; 1669-1884* (2 vols. Cambridge, 1890), provides an account of the church up to 1691. Also useful, although less complete, is *A Memorial Volume: The Record of Baptisms, Marriages, and Deaths . . . in the Town of Dedham, Massachusetts; 1638-1845*, edited by Don Gleason Hill, Dedham, 1888), which reproduces the early Dedham Church Records; they contain an excellent account of the church's formation but stop just prior to John Allen's death in 1669.

In addition, several fragmentary church records gave some indication of church practices late in the century: "Records of the Topsfield Church," *Historical Collections* of the Topsfield Historical Society (Topsfield, 1909), XIV; *Records of the First Church in Beverly, Massachusetts; 1667-1772* (Salem, 1905); *Articles of Faith and Covenant Adopted by the First Church of Christ in Bradford, Massachusetts; 1682-1885* (Haverhill, 1886); *Early Records of Rowley, Massachusetts, First Record of the First Church* (Salem, 1898); and "Records of the First Church at Salisbury, Massachusetts," *Historical Collections* of the Essex Institute, (Salem, 1879), XVI.

CHURCH RECORDS: *Connecticut*

Although the Connecticut State Library has collected church records from every parish in the state, the extant records for the period prior to 1690 are very fragmentary. Published records of Connecticut churches are nonexistent. The best of the records, all in the Connecticut State Library on microfilm, include: Middletown First Congregational Church Records, 1668-1762, beginning with the ordination of Nathaniel Collins in 1668 and containing basic parish records through 1690; New London First Congregational Church Records, 1670-1757, including a complete list of baptisms; Stonington First Congregational Church and Ecclesiastical Society Records, 1674-1744, containing a clear list of all church admissions and baptisms, but less satisfactory for church affairs; and, Records of the First Congregational Church in Woodbury, 1670-1829.

The following records, also at the State Library, are even less inclusive, but they provide some idea of church polity: Branford First Congregational Church Records, 1687-1866; Farmington First Church of Christ (Congregational) Records, 1652-1938; Hartford First Church Records, 1684-1930; Milford First Congregational Church Records, 1639-1926; New Haven First Church of Christ and Ecclesiastical Society Records, 1639-1926; Stratford First Congregational Church Records, 1688-1812; and Windsor First Congregational Church Records, 1636-1932. The dates given with these records are invariably misleading; the records, except for fragments, usually begin in the following century.

Public Records

The published colonial records of each of the holy commonwealths contain a treasury of information relating to religious and domestic affairs in seventeenth-century New England. The best are *Records of the*

Governor and Company of the Massachusetts Bay on New England, edited by Nathaniel B. Shurtleff (5 vols. in 6, Boston, 1853-54). The Massachusetts records include each session of the General Court, the names of all the members of the Court, and, because of the intimate connection between churches and state, reveal a great deal about religious issues and the involvement of the General Court in them. Shurtleff also edited the *Records of the Colony of New Plymouth in New England* (12 vols., Boston, 1857), but these documents were less valuable because the General Court of Plymouth was less involved in the activities of Plymouth churches. J. Hammond Trumbull edited three volumes of Connecticut records, which contribute significantly to understanding that colony's ecclesiastical problems, particularly between 1656 and 1669: *Public Records of the Colony of Connecticut Prior to the Union with New Haven Colony* (Hartford, 1850); *Public Records of the Colony of Connecticut; 1665-1689* (2 vols., Hartford, 1852-59). Less valuable are *Records of the Colony and Plantation of New Haven; 1638-1664*, edited by Charles J. Hoadly (2 vols., Hartford, 1857-58), since the early demise of New Haven antedates the focus of this research.

The state achives provide a valuable supplement to the colonial records. The archives, located at the State Library in Hartford and the State House in Boston, comprise a variety of material relating to the Congregational churches, and they are an excellent example of careful preservation of rare manuscripts. Particularly useful were the Massachusetts Archives; Ecclesiastical, 1637-1679, which include more than three hundred papers involving the relationship between the civil government and the Massachusetts churches. These papers include church and individual petitions, as well as decisions of the magistrates and deputies regarding church affairs. The Connecticut Archives; Ecclesiastical Affairs, 1658-1789, are less inclusive, but contain a number of petitions to the General Court involving church affairs. The Massachusetts Archives; Legislature, 1643-1732, contain a limited amount of material relating to religious questions.

Quantitative analysis of religious behavior requires a vast amount of information regarding vital statistics, and New England's genealogists have accumulated a mass of data for the seventeenth century. Although no quantification was attempted for Connecticut churches in this research project, the State Library has a mammoth card catalogue of vital statistics, indexed by surnames, for colonial Connecticut. In Massachusetts there are published vital statistics for almost every town. Although the compilers of these volumes were handicapped by the destruction of many early records, they gleaned from church, town, and personal records the most complete list of vital statistics possible, and every volume has an admirable index. The most useful of these was *Vital Records of Roxbury, Massachusetts to 1849* (2 vols., Salem, 1925). The vital statistics for Boston were not included in this series, but most of them are included in the *Reports* of the Record Commissioners: *Boston Births, Baptisms, Marriages, and Deaths; 1630-1699* (Boston, 1883), IX; and *Dorchester Births, Marriages, and Deaths to 1825* (Boston, 1890), XXI. In all of the vital statistics the records of births are the most complete; deaths are usually only 50 percent complete; and, marriage records represent only a small fraction of the total.

The *Reports* of the Record Commissioners also contain several volumes of town records that include some material relating to the churches, but are more important for their information on individual land holdings and town offices. Those that proved most fruitful include: *Boston Town Records; 1660-1701* (Boston, 1881), VII; *Dorchester Town Records* (Boston, 1883), IV; and, *Roxbury Land Records* (Boston, 1884), VI.

DIARIES

A large number of the journals and diaries kept by seventeenth-century Puritans have been preserved and are readily available in published editions. Although the diaries vary widely in their quality and focus, they offer an excellent insight into Puritan society and are a rich source of political and ecclesiastical data. The most useful journals were those of ministers. Of particular value and interest was the Notebook of the Reverend John Fiske (MS., Essex Institute, Salem) which covers the period from 1644 to 1675, when Massachusetts underwent major transformation. It is not as introspective as many of the diaries, dealing more with the affairs of Fiske's parishes in Winham and Chelmsford, including discipline, relations of regenerative experiences, and the earliest example of owning the covenant. It is an invaluable source of information dealing with Congregational polity in the middle third of the century. "Bradstreet's Journal, 1664-1683," New England Historic and Genealogical *Register* (Boston, 1855), IX, although it is quite short, helps illuminate many of the factions in Connecticut in a crucial period. The "Diary of Cotton Mather; 1681-1708," *Collections* of the Massachusetts Historical Society (Boston, 1911), seventh series, VII, gives valuable information on Second Church Boston and suggests some of the problems the Bay Colony faced after the revocation of the charter. "Peter Thacher's Journal," *History of Milton*, edited by Albert K. Teele (Boston, 1888), is an excellent supplement to the Milton Church Records for the first fifteen years (1681-1696).

Laymen kept several of the best diaries, but they focus less on church affairs than on politics and society. The journal of Governor John Winthrop is an incomparable source for the years prior to 1650. *Winthrop's Journal; 1630-1649*, edited by James K. Hosmer (2 vols., New York, 1908). *The Diary of Samuel Sewall; 1674-1729*, *Collections* of the Massachusetts Historical Society (3 vols., Boston, 1878-82), fifth series, V-VII, is the best for the last quarter of the century. Sewall, an American Pepys, left a memorable record of Massachusetts society and daily life. The years between Winthrop and Sewall are covered by Sewall's father-in-law in "The Diaries of John Hull," *Transactions* of the American Antiquarian Society (Boston, 1857), III. Although not as extensive as the others, Hull's diary does give some valuable information on First Church Boston and the half-way covenant.

Other diaries that had some value include: "The Reverend Seaborn Cotton's Commonplace Book," edited by Samuel E. Morison, *Publications* of the Colonial Society of Massachusetts (Boston, 1931), XXXII; "Manuscript of the Rev. Josiah Flynt, of Braintree and Dorchester," Dedham Historical *Register* (Dedham, 1899), IX; *Lawrence Hammond: Diary; 1677-1694*, edited by Samuel Green (Cambridge, 1892); Diary of Rev. John Lathrop from 1634 to 1653 (MS., New England Historic and Genealogical Society, Boston); *Diary of Thomas Minor, Stonington, Connecticut; 1653-1684*, edited by Sidney H. Miner and George D. Stanton (New London, 1899); "Diary of Rev. Jonathan Pierpont," New England Historic and Genealogical *Register* (Boston, 1859), XIII, and, "Diary of Michael Wigglesworth," edited by Edmund S. Morgan, *Publications* of the Colonial Society, of Massachusetts (Boston, 1951), xxxv.

One eighteenth-century record deserves inclusion here. The Itineraries of Ezra Stiles, 1760-1794 (MS., 6 vols., Yale University Library) provide a mine of information relating to the churches of New England. In addition to his own observations, Stiles incorporated a number of transcripts from original letters and records that have since been lost. These bound and very legible manuscripts deserve careful reading by students of Congregationalism.

Ecclesiastical and Theological Sources

New England Puritans created a vast literature expounding and defending Congregationalism and the New England Way in particular. Most of this was written before 1660 and provided the basis for Congregational theology until the next century. The most indispensable and comprehensive explication of New England Puritanism is Thomas Hooker, *A Survey of the Summe of Church-Discipline* (London, 1648); Hooker's own emphasis on salvation may have been seen best in *The Covenant of Grace Opened* (London, 1649). The most prolific advocate of Congregationalism was John Cotton. His *Way of the Congregational Churches Cleared* (London, 1648) is one of the best statements of the development of New England polity, and it amplifies much of the material in Questions and Answers Upon Church Government (1635, transcribed by Henry M. Dexter, Yale University). Two Cotton tracts of particular value for this research were: *The Grounds and Ends of the Baptisme of the Children of the Faithful* (London, 1647), and *Of the Holinesse of Church-Members* (London, 1650). The same subject is treated in Thomas Shepard's *The Church Membership of Children and*

Their Right to Baptisme (Cambridge, 1663), which was published by his son at the height of the debate over the half-way covenant. Another excellent statement of the New England Way is John Norton, *The Answer to a Whole Set of Questions of the Celebrated Mr. William Apollonius*, translated from the original Latin edition of 1645 by Douglas Horton (Cambridge, 1958). A somewhat more liberal conception of the covenant may be found in Peter Bulkeley, *The Gospel-Covenant, or the Covenant of Grace Opened* (London, 1846). *A Platform of Church Discipline* (Cambridge, 1649), the work of the Cambridge Synod of 1648, is the fundamental statement of New England polity, and it was written as the Congregational counterpart to the Westminster Confession. This statement was modified by the Half-Way Synod in *Propositions Concerning the Subject of Baptism* (Cambridge, 1662), and slightly altered by the Reforming Synod's *The Necessity of Reformation* (Boston, 1679). All three are included in their entirety in Williston Walker, *Creeds and Platforms of Congregationalism* (Boston, 1960).

Although the most articulate criticism of Congregationalism came from England, several temporary or permanent residents of New England added their dissent. James Noyes, *The Temple Measured: or a Brief Survey of the Temple Mystical, which is the Instituted Church of Christ* (London, 1647) defends the Presbyterian polity and advocates more open membership. Major John Child defended his brother, Robert Child, from the criticism of 1647 in *New Englands Jonas Cast Up at London* (1647), reprinted in *Collections* of the Massachusetts Historical Society (Boston, 1846), second series, IV. Thomas Lechford, after a brief and unhappy stay in Massachusetts, condemned the colony and its churches in *Plaine Dealing; or Newes from New England* (London, 1642), reprinted in *Collections* of the Massachusetts Historical Society (Boston, 1833), third series, III.

The Half-Way Synod called forth several major tracts that illuminate the issues involved in the extension of baptism. An excellent collection of anti-synodical literature written during and immediately after the synod may be found in Papers Relating to the Synod of 1662, transcribed by David Pulsifer (MS., Yale University). The original manuscripts have since disappeared, although many of them were later published with alterations and under different titles. The Pulsifer volume includes: Charles Chauncy, Eleazer Mather, Increase Mather, and John Mayo, "The Judgement of the Dissenting Brethren of the Synod" and "A Plain Proposall of the Dissenting Messengers"; John Davenport, "A Reply to the 7 Propositions Concluded by the Synod Setting at Boston June the 10th. 1662"; Nicholas Street, "Considerations upon the 7 Propositions Concluded . . . June 10: 1962"; and, "Mr. Davenport's and Mr. Street's Papers Contra the Result of the late Synod." The published versions were: Chauncy, *Anti-Synodalia Scripta Americana* (London, 1662); Davenport, *Another Essay for the Investigation of the Truth, In Answer to Two Questions* (Cambridge, 1663), which includes "An Apolegeticall Preface" by Increase Mather and Street's "Considerations Upon 7 Propositions." Davenport's last essay on the synod, A Vindication of the Treatise, entitled Another Essay (MS., American Antiquarian Society, Worcester), was never published.

The defense of the synod was undertaken by John Allen, *Animadversions Upon the Antisynodalia Americana* (Cambridge, 1664), and Richard Mather, *A Defence of the Answer and Arguments of the Synod*

Met at Boston (Cambridge, 1664). The latter also includes Jonathan Mitchel's "An Answer to the Apologetical Preface." The final defense of the synod's orthodoxy was Increase Mather, *The First Principles of New England, Concerning the Subject of Baptism and Communion of Churches* (Cambridge, 1675).

Massachusetts election sermons, since they combined religion and politics, often reveal the problems confronting the churches and are useful on the half-way covenant as a political issue. See particularly: John Higginson, *The Cause of God, and His People in New-England* (Cambridge, 1663); Jonathan Mitchel, *Nehemiah on the Wall in Troublesom Times* (Cambridge, 1671); William Stoughton, *New Englands True Interest, Not to Lie* (Cambridge, 1670); John Davenport, *A Sermon Preached at the Election of the Governour* (1670); Samuel Danforth, *A Brief Recognition of New Englands Errand into the Wilderness* (Cambridge, 1671); John Oxenbridge, *New-Englands Freemen Warned and Warned to be Free Indeed, having an Eye to God in their Elections* (Cambridge, 1673), Thomas Shepard, Jr., *Eye Salve, or a Watchword From Our Lord Jesus Christ to His Church* (Cambridge, 1673); Urian Oakes, *New England Pleaded With and Pressed to Consider the Things which Concern Her Peace* (Cambridge, 1673); William Hubbard, *The Happiness of the People in the Wisdome of Their Rulers Directing* (Boston, 1676); and Samuel Torrey, *A Plea for the Life of Dying Religion* (Boston, 1683). With the exception of Stoughton, Davenport, and Oxenbridge, all these sermons defended the propositions of the Half-Way Synod.

Many letters relating to seventeenth-century New England are reprinted in the *Collections* of the Massachusetts Historical Society and *Publications* of the Colonial

Society of Massachusetts. Two collections of letters were particularly valuable for their material relating to Congregational polity. *The Letters of John Davenport: Puritan Divine*, edited by Isabel MacBeath Calder (New Haven, 1937), help clarify Davenport's decision to settle in Boston and his attitude toward the half-way covenant. "The Correspondence of John Woodbridge, Jr., and Richard Baxter," edited by Raymond P. Stearns, *New England Quarterly* (1937), x, makes the conflict between Congregationalists and presbyterialists in Connecticut more intelligible.

Several collections of seventeenth-century papers also provide an excellent source for ecclesiastical affairs. *Hoadly Memorial; Early Letters and Documents Relating to Connecticut, 1643-1709*, *Collections* of the Connecticut Historical Society (Hartford, 1924), XXI, contain considerable data for Connecticut. *The Winthrop Papers* (5 vols., Boston, 1929-44) include only family papers up to the death of John Winthrop in 1649, but they are a useful supplement to *Winthrop's Journal*. *The Hutchinson Papers*, *Publications* of the Prince Society (3 vols., Boston, 1865), include many of the documents collected by Massachusetts' later governor. Several contemporary histories of New England also include valuable information: Nathaniel Morton, *New England's Memorial* (Boston, 1855 [original edition, 1654]); Edward Johnson, *Wonder-Working Providence of Sions Saviour in New England*, edited by William Poole (Andover, 1867 [original edition, 1654]); and, William Hubbard, *A General History of New England From the Discovery to 1680* (Boston, 1848 [written in 1680]). The best source, if not the best history, is Cotton Mather, *Magnalia Christi Americana* (2 vols., Hartford, 1820 [original edition 1702]), which presents a sustained historical defense of testified regenerate membership and includes short biographies of most New England ministers of the first three generations. It is an extraordinary example of Mather's florid style and is an impressive achievement.

SECONDARY

General Historical Background

The general literature of New England Puritanism is extensive, and the following volumes represent only those that proved to be most valuable. Brooks Adams, *The Emancipation of Massachusetts: The Dream and the Reality* (Cambridge, 1919) and James T. Adams, *The Founding of New England* (Boston, 1921) are both hostile to Puritanism and attack the Massachusetts clergy. They mistakenly tend to identify the laity with liberalism throughout. Leonard Bacon, *Thirteen Historical Discourses* (New Haven, 1839) defends the orthodox Congregationalism of the first generation and sees in all religious change evidence of declension. Isabel MacBeath Calder, *The New Haven Colony* (New Haven, 1934) is the definitive study of Davenport's Colony. George E. Ellis, *The Puritan Age and Rule in the Colony of the Massachusetts Bay, 1629-1685* (Cambridge, 1898) is adequate, but outdated. George L. Haskins, *Law and Authority in Early Massachusetts: A Study in Tradition and Design* (New York, 1960) deals with the evolution of Massachusetts law and courts and is particularly good on the late 1640's. Although Joseph B. Felt, *Ecclesiastical History of New England* (2 vols., Boston, 1862) is written as chronological annals, it still serves well and contains some otherwise unobtainable documents. Thomas Hutchinson, *The History of the Colony and Province of Massachusetts Bay* (3 vols., Cambridge, 1936) is also both a history and a source. George D. Langdon, Jr., *Pilgrim Colony; A History of New Plymouth, 1620-1691* (New Haven, 1966) is the first adequate history of that colony, and it should remain the standard for some time. Samuel Eliot Morison has mastered the sea, history, and graceful style. He exhibits the latter two in *Builders of Bay Colony* (Boston, 1930), a fine study of Puritanism through eleven sympathetic biographies. Morison's *Harvard College in the Seventeenth Century* (2 vols., Cambridge, 1936) is a model for educational studies. Benjamin Trumbull, *A Complete History of Connecticut, Civil and Ecclesiastical* (2 vols., New London, 1898) remains the best history of Connecticut and, in addition, contains valuable documents. Williston Walker's two volumes on Congregationalism, *A History of the Congregational Churches in the United States* (New York, 1894) and *Creeds and Platforms of Congregationalism* are excellent; the latter is particularly valuable as a source.

Church and Town Histories

The histories of New England towns and churches are like gifts; one rarely knows what is inside. Written by scholars, genealogists, antiquarians, and ministers, they range from extraordinarily good to extremely poor. Yet, the custom of including extensive documentary material, quite common in the last century, means that even the poorest volumes sometimes provide pleasant surprises. There is hardly a town in Massachusetts that does not have at least one history and many have two or more. Connecticut towns do not have as extensive a literature, but the histories are still common. Church histories are rarer, although bicentennial and tricentennial celebrations often result in the preparation of historical essays that seldom bear reading. The volumes listed below include only those histories which contributed significantly to this research or are outstanding examples of the genre.

Joshua Coffin, *A Sketch of the History of Newbury, Newburyport, and West Newbury from 1635 to 1845* (Boston, 1845) is a good early example and includes information on Massachusetts' most successful Presbyterian church. Similar nineteenth-century histories, which contain useful material relating to Massachusetts towns and churches include: Charles M. Ellis, *The History of Roxbury Town* (Boston, 1847); Joseph B. Felt, *Annals of Salem from Its First Settlement* (Salem, 1827); Richard Frothingham, Jr., *History of Charlestown, Massachusetts* (Boston, 1845); and, Sylvester Judd, *History of Hadley* (Northampton, 1863). James R. Trumbull, *History of Northampton, Massachusetts from its Settlement in 1654* (2 vols., Northampton, 1898) is particularly good on the early period, but may be supplemented by the Judd MS. at Forbes Library, Northampton. Although this collection is completely disorganized, it contains extensive materials on seventeenth-century Northampton. James D. Phillips, *Salem in the Seventeenth Century* (Cambridge, 1933) provides valuable information on Salem residents and the growth of the town. One of the best of recent works is Darrett Rutman, *Winthrop's Boston; Portrait of a Puritan Town* (Chapel Hill, 1965). This is not a full town history, but a provocative study of Boston between 1629 and 1650 and the emergence of a new, compromised Puritan ethic.

Some of the better Connecticut town histories include: William Cothren, *History of Ancient Woodbury, Connecticut; 1659-1854* (Waterbury, 1854); Samuel Orcutt, *A History of the Old Town of Stratford and the City of Bridgeport, Connecticut* (New Haven, 1886); and, Richard A. Wheeler, *History of the Town of Stonington, Connecticut from its First Settlement in 1649 to 1900* (New London, 1900). Connecticut had two exceptional town historians whose works are invaluable. Frances M. Caulkins, *History of New London, Connecticut; 1620-1860* (New London, 1895) and *History of Norwich, Connecticut* (Hartford, 1866), although the quintessence of filial pietism, present excellent documents and sound history. Henry M. Stiles in both *The History of Ancient Wethersfield, Connecticut* (New York, 1904) and *The History and Genealogies of Ancient Windsor, Connecticut; 1635-1891* (Hartford, 1891) gives substantial and well-documented histories of important towns. William H. Wilcoxson, *History of Stratford, Connecticut, 1639-1939* (Stratford, 1939) is a good recent history of that town.

Church histories tend to be more satisfactory than town histories because the topic is limited and the reliance on church records is direct; they may be duller, but they are more useful. For Massachusetts churches, a good brief survey is Joseph S. Clark, *A Historical Sketch of the Congregational Churches in Massachusetts from 1620 to 1858* (Boston, 1858). Clark's volume may soon be supplanted by the work of Harold Field Worthley, who has prepared a two volume compilation of all ministers and church-officers, and a brief history of every Congregational church in Massachusetts from 1620 to 1806. The better church histories include: William I. Budington, *History of the First Church, Charlestown* (Boston, 1845); Arthur B. Ellis, *History of the First Church in Boston, 1630-1880* (Boston, 1881); William Emerson, *An Historical Sketch of the First Church in Boston* (Boston, 1812) although the publication of the church records has undercut its chief value; Chandler Robbins, *History of the Second Church, or Old North* (Boston, 1852);

and, Walter E. Thwing, *History of the First Church in Roxbury, Massachusetts; 1630-1904* (Boston, 1908). The outstanding church history is Hamilton A. Hill, *History of the Old South Church Boston; 1669-1884* (2 vols., Cambridge, 1890) which combines exhaustive research with the publication of every relevant document.

Connecticut church histories are generally less satisfactory. George L. Walker, *History of the First Church in Hartford; 1633-1883* (Hartford, 1884) is an exception. Walker's treatment of the seventeenth century is superior. Another useful volume, although not as well written is Richard A. Wheeler, *History of the First Congregational Church, Stonington, Connecticut; 1674-1874* (Norwich, 1875). Wheeler's appendices include all baptisms and admissions to the Stonington Church. See also: S. Leroy Blake, *Early History of the First Church of Christ in New London, Connecticut* (New London, 1897); Oscar Maurer, *A Puritan Church and its Relation to Community, State, and Nation* (New Haven, 1938); and Edwin P. Parker, *History of the Second Church of Christ in Hartford* (Hartford, 1892).

Theological and Social Thought

The contribution of Perry Miller to our knowledge of Puritan theology and society is so immense that every student of the seventeenth century has incurred an unpayable debt to him. Miller's *The New England Mind: The Seventeenth Century* (Cambridge, 1939) brilliantly penetrates the labyrinth of Puritan theology, and is an extraordinary achievement in intellectual history. He synthesized the heart of this volume in "The Marrow of Puritan Divinity," *Errand Into the Wilderness* (Cambridge, 1956), which focuses on the federal theology, and is the best short study of Puritan theology. In

Orthodoxy in Massachusetts; 1630-1650 (Cambridge, 1933) Miller studied the roots of Separating and Non-Separating Congregationalism and the organization of the New England churches. *The New England Mind: From Colony to Province* (Cambridge, 1953) portrays the transformation which occurred in Massachusetts between 1648 and 1725. It is the chronological sequel to *Orthodoxy in Massachusetts* and both volumes occur within the intellectual framework established in *The Seventeenth Century*. Miller's essay "Errand Into the Wilderness" in *Errand Into the Wilderness* is a sensitive study of the original mission. "The Half-Way Covenant," *New England Quarterly* (1933), VI, is concerned primarily with the theology of extended baptism and the Puritans' changing sense of the qualifications for church membership. Miller also has made the best study of Stoddard in "Solomon Stoddard, 1643-1729," *Harvard Theological Review* (Cambridge, 1941), XXXIV. Stoddard needs a biography and Miller's essay may be supplemented by: Thomas A. Schafer, "Solomon Stoddard and the Theology of the Revival," *A Miscellany of American Christianity*, edited by Stuart C. Henry (Durham, 1963), and "Stoddardianism," *The New Englander* (New Haven, 1846), IV.

Bernard Bailyn, *The New England Merchants in the Seventeenth Century* (Cambridge, 1955) attributes the transformation of Massachusetts to the pressure of the developing mercantile class. Frank H. Foster, *A Genetic History of the New England Theology* (Chicago, 1907) is an excellent but brief examination of covenant theology. Sanford Fleming, *Children and Puritanism: The Place of Children in the Life and Thought of the New England Churches; 1620-1847* (New Haven, 1933) is a good broad study of Puritan children. A valuable source for

Reformed theology and a yardstick for New England theology is Hernrich Heppe, *Reformed Dogmatics*, translated by G. T. Thomson (London, 1950). Babette M. Levy, *Preaching in the First Half Century of New England History* (Hartford, 1945) is an excellent explication of the Puritan "plaine style."

Edmund S. Morgan, *The Puritan Dilemma; The Story of John Winthrop* (Boston, 1958) is an outstanding biography and reveals the tension inherent in Puritanism. Morgan's *The Puritan Family; Essays on Religion and Domestic Relations in Seventeenth-Century New England* (Boston, 1944) develops the idea of tribalism and the family unit. In *Visible Saints: The History of a Puritan Idea* (New York, 1963) Morgan develops the origins of testified regenerate membership in Non-Separating Congregationalism; it is a brilliant book and has shaped my own research in a significant way. Morgan's "New England Puritanism: Another Approach," *William and Mary Quarterly* (Williamsburg, 1961), third series, XVIII, offers a speculative reinterpretation of late seventeenth-century Puritanism. Darrett Rutman, "God's Bridge Falling Down 'Another approach' to New England Puritanism Assayed," *William and Mary Quarterly* (Williamsburg, 1962), third series, XIX, presents a rebuttal to Morgan which is not completely satisfactory. Another good biography of a major Puritan is Kenneth B. Murdock, *Increase Mather: The Foremost American Puritan* (Cambridge, 1925). Clifford K. Shipton, "The New England Clergy of the 'Glacial Age,' " Publications of the Colonial Society of Massachusetts (Boston, 1937), XXXII, re-interprets the hostile view of the ministers presented by Brooks Adams and James F. Adams. The recent excellent study by Norman Pettit, *The Heart Prepared: Grace and Conversion in Puritan Spiritual Life*

(New Haven, 1966), has revised many of our earlier assumptions about preparation and has added significantly to the understanding of baptism as a Puritan sacrament.

BIBLIOGRAPHICAL

The best bibliographical aid for anyone interested in Puritanism is Henry M. Dexter, *Congregationalism of the Last Three Hundred Years, as Seen in Its Literature* (New York, 1880). This includes an immense bibliography of English and American Puritanism arranged chronologically. The best bibliography of primary and secondary works relating to Puritanism may be found in the revised edition of Perry Miller and Thomas H. Johnson, *The Puritans* (2 vols., New York, 1963). Verne D. Morey, "American Congregationalism: A Critical Bibliography, 1900-1952," *Church History* (1952), XXI, is also useful. Two good specialized bibliographies are: Harriette M. Forbes, *New England Diaries, 1602-1800* (Topsfield, 1923), and Robert W. G. Vail, "Checklist of New England Election Sermons," *Proceedings* of the American Antiquarian Society (Worcester, 1953), XLV.

INDEX

INDEX

INDEX

INDEX